ROUTLEDGE LIBRARY EDITIONS:
HOUSING POLICY AND HOME OWNERSHIP

Volume 2

HOUSING AND LOCAL GOVERNMENT

HOUSING AND LOCAL GOVERNMENT
In England and Wales

J. B. CULLINGWORTH

R Routledge
Taylor & Francis Group

LONDON AND NEW YORK

First published in 1966 by George Allen & Unwin Ltd

This edition first published in 2021
by Routledge
2 Park Square, Milton Park, Abingdon, Oxon OX14 4RN

and by Routledge
52 Vanderbilt Avenue, New York, NY 10017

Routledge is an imprint of the Taylor & Francis Group, an informa business

British Library Cataloguing in Publication Data
A catalogue record for this book is available from the British Library

ISBN: 978-0-367-64519-9 (Set)
ISBN: 978-1-00-313856-3 (Set) (ebk)
ISBN: 978-0-367-67790-9 (Volume 2) (hbk)
ISBN: 978-0-367-67805-0 (pbk)
ISBN: 978-1-00-313291-2 (Volume 2) (ebk)

Publisher's Note
The publisher has gone to great lengths to ensure the quality of this reprint but
points out that some imperfections in the original copies may be apparent.

Disclaimer
The publisher has made every effort to trace copyright holders and would welcome
correspondence from those they have been unable to trace.

HOUSING AND
LOCAL GOVERNMENT

IN ENGLAND AND WALES

BY

J. B.
CULLINGWORTH

London
GEORGE ALLEN & UNWIN LTD
RUSKIN HOUSE · MUSEUM STREET

PRINTED IN GREAT BRITAIN
in 10 on 11 point Times Roman type
BY SIMSON SHAND LTD
LONDON, HERTFORD AND HARLOW

Introduction

THE MAIN OBJECT of this book is to provide an introduction to the work of local authorities in the field of housing. It differs from a straightforward legal text in several ways. First, it is by no means a comprehensive account of housing law: it attempts to provide only the main outlines. Secondly, it goes beyond a statement of the law to an account of some of the problems for which the law is designed to deal. Thirdly, it attempts to provide an outline of the administrative setting within which the law operates. At the same time the book differs from a polemic in that it is more concerned with a description of problems, policies and programmes, than with attempting to show how much better things would be if certain changes were introduced. But given the broad objectives of the book and the limitations of space (not to mention the paucity of research on the actual workings of local government) only a slender account can be given of the ways in which local authorities actually implement housing policy.

The aim has been to provide a readable account of housing policy and its administration by local authorities. It needs to be stressed, however, that 'housing policy' is virtually indefinable. It may be taken to deal with the number of houses that are required, the allocation and price of land, the structure of the building industry and the development of industrialized building, the design and layout of houses, rents and subsidies, redevelopment and replanning of old areas, standards and family aspirations, and so forth. Architects, builders, treasurers, planners, sociologists, economists, politicians, landlords and tenants, all talk of 'housing policy', but all talk about rather different things or, at least, give a different emphasis to the many matters which can be included under the term. At the extreme one school of thought may regard the distribution—and redistribution—of income, or the supply of land, as the most important aspect of housing policy, while another school of thought may think almost entirely in terms of local authority house-building programmes, or rents, subsidies and interest rates. To cover, within the bounds of a modest book, all the matters which are relevant is impossible.

This is stated, not in order to forestall criticism, but to highlight the fact that what is included and what is excluded is partly determined by the writer's own predilections and interests, and partly dictated by the writer's view of who is likely to need a book of this sort. Apart from the intelligent layman (who, on the evidence of publishers' blurbs, appears to have an extremely wide range of interests), this book is directed specifically at those who are looking for a reasonably short introduction to housing policy and administration—mainly students of social policy and local government. It forms a companion volume to the author's *Town and Country Planning in England and Wales*, published earlier in this series. Some topics which would otherwise have been included in the present book have been discussed in the earlier work. This applies particularly to the acquisition of land, compensation for compulsory acquisition and the expanded towns programme.

The first chapter, which is the longest, sketches the historical development of housing policy. Chapter II discusses the role and status of the central government *vis-à-vis* local authorities, and outlines the structure of local government. The third chapter deals with the administrative organization of local housing authorities and administrative aspects of housing management. This is followed by a description of the existing stock of council houses (with some comparisons with owner-occupied and privately-rented houses) and a short discussion of local authority house building. Chapter V provides a picture of the families who live in council houses and the methods adopted by local authorities in selecting tenants. Chapters VI to XI deal with particular aspects of housing policy—standards, finance, slum clearance, the improvement of older houses, overcrowding and multiple occupation, and assistance to owner-occupiers and housing associations. In Chapter XII a few 'social aspects' of housing are selected for discussion—'social balance', community facilities on new estates, 'unsatisfactory' tenants and 'problem families', and the housing and welfare of old people. The final chapter is of a different character: it attempts to provoke thought on questions such as why the State is involved in housing policy, whether we need council housing at all, and whether housing policies are geared to meeting contemporary needs.

It is always difficult to make a book of this type up-to-date. The difficulties have, in this instance, been even greater than usual owing to the major changes in housing and other related policies being introduced by the present Labour Government. The final revision of the text was postponed until the publication of the White Paper on *The Housing Programme 1965 to 1970*. As much as possible of this White Paper and recent legislation has been incorporated in the text, but even so events will undoubtedly make this inadequate. The reader can only be warned that for changes introduced after November 1965 he will have to look elsewhere. (A good source is the spate of circulars emanating from the Ministry of Housing and Local Government.)

Many people have assisted in various ways in the writing of this book. Particular thanks are due to officials of local authorities and the Ministry of Housing and Local Government who have been most helpful in explaining the realities of administrative procedures and in guiding me through the legal labyrinth. My academic colleagues, especially those who have worked on the Rowntree Housing Study, have also contributed in no small way to the improvement of the book's contents. I have no doubt that inadequacies and errors remain, but for these there can be no sharing of responsibility. Finally, I must record my indebtedness to my wife who has not only typed and improved the manuscript, but has also been unfailing in her support, assistance and tolerance.

Contents

List of Tables

CHAPTER I

An Historical Sketch

THE DISTINGUISHING FEATURES of housing as compared with other goods are its high capital cost and its extreme durability. In the absence of a developed system of house purchase by instalments the majority of houses must be provided on a rental basis. This was the position in England before the First World War. The capital cost of a house was far in excess of what an average working class family could afford, and the facilities for house mortgages were very limited. Since local authority housing was even more limited it followed that the majority of families lived in privately rented houses. These were regarded as a good long-term investment: hence the expression (which lives on despite its contemporary absurdity) 'as safe as houses'. The procedure was simple and, as long as the demand for housing (which is very inelastic) was increasing, or remained stable, there was little risk involved: bad payers could always be evicted. For those who wished, management was direct, personal and tangible: it was not necessarily dependent upon the efficiency of some remote third party. Furthermore, 'the man of property' was a man of substance—who thereby acquired some local social standing.

The quality of houses depended on the prevailing standards of the time and on the financial capacity and inclination of consumers. Houses were supplied to meet a demand which was 'effective' and, since the effective demand from working-class families was for accommodation at a low price, the quality was similarly low. However, the growth of population during the nineteenth century (from under 9 million in 1801 to over 32 million in 1901) and, even more important, the tremendous growth of towns, created public health problems which could be coped with only if housing and environmental standards were raised. The industrial towns of the nineteenth century were unknown in history: they gave rise to housing conditions which became intolerable even by the standards of the day. The development of medical knowledge, the realization that overcrowded insanitary urban areas resulted in an economic loss which had to be borne at least in part by local ratepayers, the experience of the class-less visitation by cholera, the fear of social unrest, and a gradual appreciation of the necessity for some interference with market forces and private property rights in the interests of social well-being—all these factors combined to force action in the field of public health and housing. An Act of 1868 (the Artisans and Labourers Dwellings Act, more commonly known as the Torrens Act) made it the duty of owners to keep their houses in good repair, and empowered local authorities to act in default and to close insanitary houses. Ineffective though this proved to be, it established the principle that the State could interfere with property rights in the interests of the public health. Later legislation reinforced this principle and attempted to make its administration more effective. Similarly with the standard of new building, 'by-law' control administered by the growing profession of sanitary inspectors gradually succeeded in controlling the worst forms of slum building.

The effect of these social controls was to widen the gap between the rent-paying capacity of working class families and the economic price at which working class dwellings could be provided. Indeed, with increasingly effective controls preventing new slum building, public health officials became 'the most steadfast opponents of house-building for workers'.[21] A few local authorities attempted to fill the gap by building houses (Liverpool—using local act powers—was the first, in 1869) but generally this remained a policy to be followed only as a last resort.* Powers permitting local authorities to build houses were at first restricted to the rehousing of families displaced by slum clearance, but later legislation established the principle that local authorities could erect workers' dwellings whenever they considered them necessary. However, as in many fields of social policy, it was war which acted as a major catalyst. Lloyd George promised 'homes fit for heroes' and, in the conditions immediately following the First World War, there seemed no way for these to be provided on the scale needed and at rents which the heroes could afford, other than by local authorities with financial assistance from the Exchequer.† The powers of local authorities were now extended, housing subsidies were introduced (both for local authorities and for private builders) and a definite obligation was laid on local authorities to provide for the housing needs of their areas. At the same time powers for the

* Until an adequate general history is written, the reader must refer to local accounts. See, e.g. A. Briggs, *History of Birmingham*, Vol. II, Oxford University Press, 1952; A. Redford, *A History of Local Government in Manchester*, Vols. II and III, Longmans, 1940; B. D. White, *A History of the Corporation of Liverpool 1835-1914*, Liverpool University Press, 1951; and S. Pollard, *A History of Labour in Sheffield*, Liverpool University Press, 1959.

† The following account of housing in the inter-war period leans heavily (as any account must do) on Marian Bowley's indispensable *Housing and the State*, Allen and Unwin, 1944. This is the only adequate history of housing yet produced; but see also J. R. Jarmain, *Housing Subsidies and Rents*, Stevens, 1948.

acquisition of land were widened and the basis of compensation for the compulsory acquisition of land was changed. Up to this time local authorities had to pay a *solatium* of 10 per cent in recognition of the fact that the acquisition was compulsory (though this practice was derived from custom and case law: the only statutory reference to it is its prohibition in the Acquisition of Land (Assessment of Compensation) Act of 1919).[5] The new legislation provided that compensation was to be based on open market value assuming a willing seller and a willing buyer.

The new involvement of local and central government in the direct provision of working-class housing was not meant to imply a permanent commitment. Indeed it was optimistically (and erroneously) thought that the housing problem was a simple question of a physical shortage largely caused by the war. Nevertheless, once responsibility for the provision of houses was accepted it proved difficult to withdraw. Though changing political climates at some times reduced the role of state housing provision and at other times increased it, there was no going back. 'Council housing' had come to stay.

The subsidy arrangements introduced in 1919 were very generous. All losses incurred by a local authority in excess of a penny rate were to be borne by the Exchequer. The object was to enable local authorities to charge rents which working-class families could afford, while at the same time avoiding a heavy rate burden. Unfortunately no steps were taken to ensure that what was now financially possible was also physically possible. As a result, in the scarcity of these early post-war years, costs rose enormously and the scheme was rapidly abandoned in 1921. It was generally held that the subsidized building programme was itself responsible for the rise in building costs and, furthermore, that this was making it all the more difficult for private enterprise to fulfil its traditional role as the main supplier of working-class houses. A reduction in subsidized activity would, therefore (to quote the Third Annual Report of the Ministry of Health), 'in conjunction with the general tendency to deflation in the price of commodities, in due course secure such a reduction in the cost of working-class housing as to pave the way for the resumption of unsubsidized building by private enterprise'. The abandonment of the scheme (under which over 170,000 local authority houses and 40,000 private houses were built) was followed by an interim measure designed to bridge the gap between the existing abnormal post-war conditions and the return of 'normal' conditions. A flat-rate subsidy of £6 a house for twenty years was made available (under the Chamberlain Housing Act of 1923) for all houses conforming to certain space standards whether provided by local authorities or private builders. A 50 per cent grant towards losses incurred on slum clearance was made available to local authorities and they were also

B

given powers to make loans to private builders; to give guarantees to
building societies in respect of advances to house purchasers; and to
make loans to landlords wishing to undertake repairs and conversions.
The object was simply to stimulate activity during a transitional
period until the return of normal economic conditions. The role of
local authorities was thus intended to be a subordinate one, and they
were to operate only in those areas where private builders could not
meet local needs.

The basic assumption was that the housing shortage was only
temporary. Once normal conditions returned, state and municipal
activity could again confine itself to the problem of insanitary housing. The same thinking underlay rent control policy. Rents had been
frozen at pre-war levels by an Act of 1915; a further Act of 1919 had
continued and extended control, though limited increases in rents
were allowed. The legislation was temporary and the official view was
that it should be repealed as soon as the 'emergency' had passed. The
Onslow Committee, reporting in 1923, believed that the unwillingness
of private enterprise to take up its traditional role in supplying
working-class housing was due to rent control. Though new houses
were not subject to control, 'investors feel that they have no security
that future legislation will not bring these new houses under
restrictions': this 'psychological factor' could be removed only by the
acceptance by the Government of a policy of rapid decontrol. But
immediate decontrol would cause hardship. They therefore felt that
they should make recommendations which would 'restore in as large
a degree as possible the freedom of contract between landlord and
tenant, and thus restore confidence to the builder and the investor',
while at the same time minimizing 'the cases of hardship which would
arise were the whole of the present restrictions to be allowed to lapse
simultaneously'. The Government accepted this view and, in effect,
by the 1923 Rent Act, transferred control from houses to tenants:
decontrol in future would be automatic whenever vacant possession
was obtained. (The similarity with the 1957 Rent Act is striking.)

The Housing Act and the Rent Act of 1923 were thus both con-
ceived as transitional measures to deal with a transitional housing
shortage. The election of the Labour Party to office in 1924 brought
about a radical change in policy. The Labour Party placed no reliance
on the ability or willingness of private enterprise to provide low-cost
working-class housing. In their view the housing conditions of the
working classes could be improved only by direct municipal responsibility for house building. The Wheatley Act of 1924 reinstated the
position of local authorities: the requirement that they had first to
show that private enterprise provision could not meet the need for
working-class houses was abolished. At the same time there was the
first legislative acceptance of the view that the housing problem was

not short-lived. It was hoped that in fifteen years some 2½ million houses would be provided by local authorities, public utility societies and housing associations. Subsidies, amounting to £9 a house for forty years, were to be available for all such houses built before October 1939. Furthermore, steps were taken to increase the capacity of the building industry. This was the famous 'gentleman's agreement' between Wheatley (the Minister of Health) and the building trade unions. In essence this was a promise that an increased and steady building programme would be implemented, thus allowing the trade unions to expand the number of apprentices admitted to the trade and to shorten the period of apprenticeship without fear of unemployment.

Rents were to be fixed at the general level of the pre-war rents of working-class houses. To achieve this local authorities were to make a contribution (of up to £4 10s a year) from the rates. Only where subsidies and rate contributions were insufficient (at ruling costs) to bring rents down to this pre-war level were higher rents to be charged.

The Labour Administration was short-lived, but the position of local authorities and the subsidy arrangements remained unchanged when the Conservatives passed a consolidating Housing Act in 1925, though falling costs led to a reduction in subsidies in 1927. Over 500,000 council houses were built under the Wheatley Act before the subsidy was abolished in 1933. The Wheatley Act did not replace its predecessor. The Chamberlain subsidies remained until 1929 and 75,000 council houses benefited from them. But its major significance was in the private sector : some 360,000 privately-built houses received subsidies in the seven years up to 1930. The subsidies were usually in the form of a capitalized sum which up to 1927 amounted to £75 but was then reduced to £50. In the four years 1926 to 1930 the total number of subsidized private houses (262,000) exceeded the number provided without subsidy (255,000). Thereafter the fall in building costs (together with lower interest rates and down-payments) allowed private unsubsidized building to cater for successively lower tiers of the market for houses with rateable values between £15 and £26 —the tiers above the local authority level.

By 1931 the housing situation had considerably improved. Over 1½ million houses had been built since the war—585,000 by local authorities and 1,075,000 by private enterprise. More than £1,000 million had been spent in this production, representing (in the words of the 1931 Marley Report on the Rent Acts) 'a housing effort which (up to this time) has probably never elsewhere been equalled'.[23] Nevertheless the position was by no means nearly as favourable as the house-building figures suggested. The population had increased by over two millions since the war and the increase in households had been proportionately far greater. Virtually all the private houses had been built for sale, and the rented houses (provided by local authorities) had been let at rents beyond the reach of the large number of poor working-class families. It had generally been thought that the provision of relatively high-cost houses would relieve the housing problem of the poor by a filtering-up process: as the better-off moved into new houses the accommodation which they vacated would be occupied by poorer families. In fact this did not happen mainly because of the growth in demand from that section of the population which could afford to pay rents higher than those which the poorer sections of the working class could manage. Though local authorities were supposedly providing directly for working-class families, in fact, with a fixed subsidy, rents within the reach of the poor could be charged only at the expense either of other tenants or of the ratepayers at large—and, of course, the more successful a local authority was in meeting the needs of the poorest families the greater would this burden be. Apart from financial (and political) difficulties, the legal power of local authorities to charge 'differential rents' was far from clear. In the outcome local authority rents were largely determined by costs and, with the existing subsidy provisions, these resulted in rents up to double those of existing (controlled) working-class housing.[51] Nevertheless local authority building resulted in the provision of lower-value houses than were being provided privately. While all the 500,000 houses built for local authorities during this period had rateable values under £14, all but 14,000 of the one million private houses had values higher than this. Unlike the position before the war almost all these houses were sold to owner-occupiers. Indeed, the building societies had almost completely replaced the private investor who used to buy property as a permanent investment. But though owner-occupation had spread with great rapidity among not only the middle-class but also the better-paid working-class families (and was to continue to do so during the 'thirties) the great majority of the working class were not in a position to buy their own houses. Yet the very fact that there was private building at 'an unprecedented rate' for owner-occupiers made it unlikely that private enterprise would 'return to the building and financing of houses to let, at least at rents within the means of working-class tenants'.

The Marley Committee concluded that the housing shortage was now largely confined to the poorer-paid workers. The decontrolling provisions of the 1923 Act (under which houses became decontrolled on vacant possession) had not, in the Committee's opinion, worked smoothly for this type of house. Mobility was hampered by the fact that any empty house to which a working-class family wished to move would have to be a decontrolled one. Thus a move would entail the loss of security of tenure and the payment of a 'considerably higher' rent. Figures supplied by the Ministry of Labour showed that only one-eighth of working-class houses had been vacated (and thus decontrolled) since 1923. On the other hand, between a quarter and a third of the 'more expensive' and virtually all the 'most expensive' houses had been decontrolled in this way.

The solution adopted by the Government (in the 1933 Rent Act) was to completely decontrol the 'more expensive' houses (which were in adequate supply), to continue the decontrolling provisions of the 1923 Act for the 'less expensive middle-class houses' (which were being provided for sale in large numbers), and to stop decontrol for the 'real working-class houses' (which were in very short supply and were likely to be so for some considerable time). Control was to remain in force until June 1938: there was thus to be no suggestion that control might be of a permanent nature.

Slum Clearance

During the first post-war decade there had thus been a great increase in the number of houses but very little direct benefit to the poorest families. At the beginning of the 'thirties a significant change in policy began to take place. One aspect of this—the more careful recasting of rent control—has been discussed. Two other changes were the start of slum clearance and the emergence of a more clearly-defined local authority housing and rent policy.

Despite increased powers, simplified procedures and the existence of Exchequer percentage grants, local authorities undertook little slum clearance during the 'twenties. As in the years following the second war it was generally felt that insanitary housing was better than none at all. Only some 11,000 houses had been demolished and replaced. But the now easier general housing situation, together with an increased concern at the inadequacy of indirect methods of improving the housing conditions of the poor, led to slum clearance becoming a topical political issue. It was an important plank in the election programmes of 1929. Ernest Simon, a former Lord Mayor of Manchester and Chairman of the City's Housing Committee, argued that a housing crisis was developing 'which will mean that no more working-class houses will be built, that the slums will remain as they are, that grave unemployment will occur in the building trade'.[51] The reasons were that the demand for private housing of the more expensive type appeared to be slackening and that current levels of costs and subsidies prevented the needs of the poor being met. This was a time when the birth rate had fallen to a very low level and when it was generally accepted that the population would soon cease to grow. Though this was falsified by events, the time seemed propitious for a policy of replacing old houses. A spate of pamphlets on 'the appalling slums' stressed the urgency of the situation and the necessity for public action.

The Labour Government, with Mr Greenwood as Minister of Health, took the lead. The Greenwood Housing Act of 1930 increased the powers of local authorities in relation to insanitary houses, streamlined the previously unwieldy statutory procedures, and introduced specific subsidies for the rehousing of families displaced by slum clearance. Instead of a fixed subsidy per house the new subsidies varied with the number of people displaced and rehoused by the local authority. Higher subsidies were payable in urban areas and additional subsidies were provided for expensive sites where housing had to be provided in flats. The rehousing could be undertaken by local authorities or by housing associations acting under arrangements with a local authority.

Five-year programmes were to be submitted to the Ministry of Health and local authorities were urged to take advantage of falling building costs to charge lower rents. (The average capital cost of a three-bedroom council house fell from £510 in 1926 to £432 in 1928 and to £411 in 1931. This trend continued until 1934 when the average cost was £361. Interest rates also began to decline—from 5 per cent in 1930 to $3\frac{1}{2}$ per cent in 1934.) Indeed it was stressed that, under the Act, the intention was to enable local authorities to provide houses at a definitely lower rent than they normally charged for their existing houses. The Act also specifically empowered local authorities to give rent rebates to poorer families.

The minority Labour Government remained in power until August 1931, when MacDonald formed his National Government. This was a period of high unemployment and financial crisis. The May Report on National Expenditure (which inflicted the final death blow on the Labour Government) forecast a huge government deficit and proposed various taxes and economies to meet it. So far as housing was concerned the 'waste' of public money on subsidies to families who could afford to pay economic rents was severely criticized. It was argued that future subsidies should be payable only for houses provided for families displaced by slum clearance.

These recommendations were accepted and, in 1933, the Wheatley subsidy was abolished. Greenwood's slum clearance policy was now to be the only centrally-supported local authority policy. Though local authorities could 'supplement' private enterprise building where necessary by providing unsubsidized houses, a Ministry of Health Circular maintained (optimistically) that 'with the re-establishment of more normal conditions, economic forces, operating in a free field, will secure a large volume and variety of production at competitive rents, and that a great number of persons and organizations will play their part; private builders, housing companies, public utility companies, finance societies and private investors will, it is hoped, all take a share in the ownership of working-class houses'.

This was (until the end of the second war) virtually the finish of local authority housing provision for 'general needs'. Greenwood's rent policy was changed from one under which local authorities could increase the total supply of modern housing at rents which individual working-class families could afford to one under which families displaced from the slums would not, it was hoped, be debarred because of financial circumstances from moving into council houses. The responsibilities of local authorities were now to be confined to dealing with the worst housing conditions. As Marian Bowley has put it, this was a return to the sanitary policies of the pre-first war period in a modern dress of subsidies and the compulsory exercise of powers by local authorities.[3]

The Housing Act of 1935, however, added another dimension to the diminished responsibilities of local authorities. Overcrowding was to be made a statutory offence and local authorities were given the duty of surveying their areas, assessing the amount of overcrowding and providing the housing which was needed to overcome it. The definition of overcrowding was an exceedingly limited one and in effect only covered very large families living in average-sized houses or average families living in very small houses. Nevertheless an overcrowding survey carried out under the Act showed that a third of a million out of the 9 million dwellings inspected were statutorily overcrowded.

The standard involved counting every habitable room as available for sleeping purposes. Had living rooms been excluded the number of 'overcrowded' families would have risen to 853,000. But though the official standard was a very low one, its importance lay in the acceptance of the principle of legal prohibition of overcrowding. As with slums a direct attack was now being made on the problems of the worst housed families—and presumably, as conditions improved the standard could be raised (though in fact it never has been!).

The subsidies for providing houses for overcrowded families were restricted to three special cases—unlike the subsidy for houses built to rehouse families displaced by slum clearance. An automatic subsidy was available for flats on expensive sites; a discretionary subsidy could be given to individual local authorities whose financial position was such that their housing programme would involve an unreasonable rate burden; and a special subsidy was available in rural areas. In all these cases the local authority was obliged to make a prescribed rate contribution. The assumption that subsidies would be needed for the relief of overcrowding only in these special cases was quite unjustified and, indeed, was abolished in 1938 when subsidies were reviewed (and reduced).

Only 24,000 houses were built by local authorities for rehousing overcrowded families before the programme was cut short by the outbreak of war. But, of course, overcrowding was only one aspect of the working-class housing problem, and the problems of overcrowding and slum conditions overlap. The 1934 slum clearance programmes of local authorities envisaged the demolition or closure of some 267,000 houses, but later programmes increased this number first to 378,000 (in 1937) and then to 472,000 (in 1939). In all, 273,000 houses were dealt with by March 1939. Inadequate though this may appear in retrospect it marked a considerable achievement: one which would have become considerably greater had not war intervened.

In 1933 new house building was running at an annual rate of about 200,000. In 1934 it rose to 267,000, and in 1935 to 327,000. The peak year of this building boom was 1937 when 347,000 houses were built —a figure never since exceeded. (See Tables 1 and 4.) This increase was almost entirely due to the growth of unsubsidized building for owner-occupiers. There were several factors contributing to this great expansion in owner-occupation. Building costs and interest rates fell, building society advances increased from 70–80 per cent of the purchase price to 90–95 per cent, and the period of repayment was extended. By 1935 it was possible to buy a house with a deposit of between £20 and £25 and with a weekly repayment of less than 10s. Increasing numbers of the better-off working-class families were now buying their own houses.

The decline in costs and interest rates also helped local authorities in their attempts to meet the more difficult working-class housing problem. Throughout the period 1934 to 1938 local authorities could provide houses to let at subsidized rents of less than 5s (though rates would be additional). Furthermore with the use of differential rent schemes these rents could be considerably reduced for the poorest families. Added encouragement to the adoption of such rent schemes was provided in the 1935 Housing Act which required local authorities to consolidate their housing accounts. Previously separate accounts had to be kept for houses built under different Acts. This was an inflexible and cumbersome system. Since each housing account had to balance, a system of differential rents could lead to a surplus on one account and a loss on another: the former would have involved either a transfer of the surplus to the Ministry or a general reduction in the rents of the houses in that particular account: the latter would have involved a rate charge. Local authorities were too astute to allow either to happen and the problem was dealt with by selecting tenants for different estates according to their rent paying capacity. The 1935 Housing Act cut through these complexities by requiring local authorities to consolidate all the separate accounts into one Housing Revenue Account. In future all rents and subsidies were to be regarded as a common pool, and the rents of individual houses could be adjusted on a common basis. More important, subsidies could be concentrated on needy tenants irrespective of the legislation under which their houses happened to have been built. Furthermore the new system freed local authorities from the complex system of central control over rents which had operated (under certain of the Housing Acts) up to this time.

Rent Control

By 1937 the total number of houses in England and Wales had increased to 10½ million: an increase of over 3 million since the war. Of these 950,000 had been provided by local authorities and virtually all the remainder by private builders. New house building was now running at the rate of about 340,000 houses a year. Even more striking was the re-emergence of private building for letting. Nearly 200,000 new private houses were let during the three years up to March 1937, of which over a half were small houses with rateable values of £13 or under in the provinces and £20 or under in London. The situation was, therefore, propitious for a further extension of decontrol, and the now traditional committee of inquiry was set up—this time under the chairmanship of Viscount Ridley.

The Ridley Committee reported in December 1937.[24] Opinions on rent control were still sharply divided. One school of thought maintained that housing was not 'a fit subject for commodity economics' but that it was 'a social service of such extreme importance [that it] ought to be controlled, the public being protected against extortion and improper treatment'. On this view control should be regarded not as a temporary expedient but as a permanent and desirable feature of 'the housing service'. This was the opinion of the minority of the Ridley Committee. The majority, on the other hand, held that rent control could be justified only to the extent and as long as there was a housing shortage. An assessment of the size and character of this shortage was, therefore, an important part of their deliberations.

Though the total number of houses in England and Wales had increased by 42 per cent since 1914, for the lowest value houses (Class C) it was only 26 per cent, whereas for middle-value houses (Class B) it was 90 per cent and for the highest-value houses (Class A) 47 per cent. Nevertheless, in absolute numbers the largest (gross) increase (1½ million) had been in Class C. It followed that the *proportion* of controlled houses, even in Class C (which were not subject to decontrol on vacant possession) was steadily declining. In 1931, 78 per cent of these Class C houses had been controlled whereas by 1937 the proportion had fallen to 57 per cent. For Class B houses the proportion controlled had declined from 60 to 32 per cent.

Evidence was presented to the Committee which suggested that there were parts of the country in which there was no longer any housing shortage—particularly of Class B houses. Indeed, there were some areas where many houses were standing empty. On the other hand there were areas, particularly in London and the large provincial cities, where the shortage was still acute. The Committee believed that the Overcrowding Survey provided an index of the shortage in each area. The average overcrowding rate in working-class dwellings was 3·8 per cent, but in thirty local government areas it was over 12·5 per cent. This led the Committee to propose a scheme of gradual decontrol operating on a geographical basis using incidence of overcrowding as an index of the housing shortage. The position in relation to Class B houses, however, was felt to be so much improved as to allow the higher value ones to be decontrolled. They therefore recommended that Class B should be split into two groups (with the dividing line at a rateable value of £35 in London and £20 elsewhere in England and Wales). This was to take the place of decontrol by vacant possession.

This latter recommendation was accepted by the Government (in the Rent Act of 1938), but decontrol by area on the basis of an overcrowding index was thought to require further examination—by yet another Committee. The advent of war in September 1939, however, involved the reintroduction of rent control (freezing rents at their current level) over virtually all privately-rented houses. The next— and last—Committee of Inquiry on Rent Control was not appointed until 1943.

THE INTER-WAR YEARS: AN OVER-VIEW

Between 1919 and 1939 4·1 million houses were built. The net increase was probably 3·7 millions. During the same period the population increased by nearly 4 million and the number of households by probably 2¼ million. The figure for the number of households can be only a rough estimate, but it is clear that, even when the backlog existing at the end of the first war is taken into account, the overall housing situation had improved very greatly. The impact on the face of the country was clearly to be seen: the private 'suburb' and the council housing 'estate' had become a common feature of the urban and suburban landscape. These housing developments were easily recognizable from pre-war housing. Terraced housing, usually without gardens, and at densities of up to 40 to the acre, had given way to the ubiquitous 'semi', with front and back garden, built at a usual density of eight to twelve to the acre. The standard of these houses—in terms of space and amenity if not durability—was considerably higher than that prevailing pre-war. Baths were a normal provision (though a few local authorities built houses without baths in the early years, and more provided a bath in the kitchen. Baths were not a statutory requirement for subsidized housing until

1923, and for non-subsidized housing until 1936). The standards proposed in the Tudor Walters Report of 1918[18] were for a minimum of 855 sq ft and an optimum of 1,055 sq ft excluding stores. The houses actually built under the 1919 Act were of a minimum of 950 sq ft. Though standards were soon reduced the majority of three-bedroom houses built by public authorities had an overall area of 750 to 850 sq ft.

One in three of all households now lived in these 'modern' dwellings, and nearly one in ten lived in a council house. This was a significant achievement by any standard. Nevertheless there were some important differences between different areas and between different classes. Some of these were partly the result (and partly the symptom) of major differences in economic activity and the standard of living which the local economy could support. The north-east of England was a very different area from Greater London, as was Merseyside from the Birmingham region. The 'depressed areas' of the outer provinces benefited greatly from the rearmament programme which began in 1936 and by the outbreak of war their 'reserves of unemployment' had been transformed from a national liability to a powerful asset. But throughout the inter-war years unemployment was endemic and even in 1938 the rate was 18 per cent in the north and 24 per cent in Wales. At the bottom of the slump in January 1933, the national average was 23 per cent and in Wales it was 30 per cent. Even relatively prosperous London had 15 per cent unemployed. Differences between smaller areas were much greater and in Jarrow (where, in September 1935, unemployment reached the fantastically high figure of 73 per cent) it was immortalized in Ellen Wilkinson's *The Town that was Murdered*.

Regional differences in economic activity and prosperity were a marked feature of the inter-war years. One response was a major shift of population. The population of the north-east (Northumberland and Durham) and of Wales actually declined: the number of emigrants exceeded the natural increase. One and a quarter million people migrated to Greater London and the south-east. Seventy per cent of the country's population growth was concentrated in the south-east and the Midlands. These were the regions where house building was the most rapid, and where private house building was the greatest.

By 1939 between a quarter and a fifth of households either owned or were buying their houses. The majority of these owner-occupied houses had been built since 1919 with the aid of loans from the Building Societies. In 1913 these societies lent about £9 million; in the late 'thirties they were lending over £130 million a year. By the outbreak of war 1½ million house buyers owed them over £700 million. Falling costs and interest rates, together with easier terms (lower deposits and longer repayment periods), brought house-ownership within the reach of increasing numbers of better-paid working-class families.

TABLE 1: *Permanent Houses Built in England and Wales* 1919–39

Year ending September 30th	Local Authorities	Private* Builders	Total
1919–20	3,502 ⎫		
1921	47,651 ⎬	73,099	210,228
1922	85,976 ⎭		
1923	25,241	53,497	78,738
1924	14,544	94,947	109,491
1925	32,090	126,936	159,026
1926	61,402	136,182	197,584
1927	113,274	159,955	273,229
1928	59,220	107,195	166,415
1929	60,367	143,076	203,443
1930	52,017	109,682	161,699
1931	63,288	131,656	194,944
1932	68,490	133,486	201,976
1933	49,213	169,100	218,313
1934	53,342	260,327	313,669
1935	43,345	275,299	318,644
1936	64,874	274,654	339,528
1937	71,339	265,795	337,134
1938	88,330	252,548	340,878
1939	78,952	201,616	280,568
Total 1919–39	1,136,457	2,969,050	4,105,507

When the local authority building programmes are examined a marked difference emerges between the bigger and the smaller authorities. The largest authority of all, the London County Council, built over 100,000 houses. Birmingham (85,000 council houses), Liverpool (41,000), Manchester (32,000), Sheffield (31,000) and Leeds (24,000) contributed another 215,000. These authorities with 6½ per cent of the 1931 population accounted for nearly a fifth of the total inter-war council housing. On the other hand some authorities, particularly in rural areas, built no houses at all. But these were a

* 43,099 private houses were built with the aid of subsidy between 1919 and 1922. The number built without such assistance during this period is not accurately known, but is estimated at 30,000. Of the total 2,969,050 private houses built between 1919 and 1939, 431,669 were subsidized.
Source: House of Commons Debates, Written Answers, Cols. 161–2, March 11, 1946.

minority. In most areas council houses had become a familiar sight.

HOUSING AFTER THE SECOND WORLD WAR

In 1939 there was a rough balance between the numbers of houses and families. The virtual cessation of house building during the war, bomb damage and destruction, and a population growth of a million, resulted in a housing shortage of enormous dimensions. As in the period after the first war the building industry was depleted (the building labour force was only a third of its pre-war strength of a million men) and the shortage of materials was acute.

The size of the problem was not known with any degree of certainty. Estimates of the shortage varied greatly—from 750,000 to over 6 millions. But though there was considerable disagreement about the scale of existing and future needs, there was no disagreement about the necessity for rapid action—action which would not lead to the disastrous inflation of costs which followed the first war. Centralized control over building was a major plank of both housing and economic policy. Furthermore a strong Labour Government was determined to control not only the production of houses but also their allocation. The great majority of houses were to be built for letting at reasonable rents to families in the most urgent need. The criterion was to be urgency of need, not ability to pay. It followed that the building of houses for sale should be strictly limited and that rented houses should be provided by an agency that could 'select occupants according to the degree of hardship they were enduring'. In short the majority of houses were to be provided by local authorities. Private enterprise was to have a strictly controlled and subordinate role. Local housing programmes were rationed and allocations to private builders were determined in the light of available resources and the size of the local authority building programme.

The first priority, however, had to be given to the repair of war damaged houses. Apart from the 200,000 houses which had been destroyed, some 3½ million houses had sustained varying degrees of damage, and of these 250,000 were uninhabitable. At first the magnitude of the problem was so great that only 'first-aid' repairs were possible. The aim was to achieve an emergency standard of 'tolerable comfort': only essential rooms were repaired and no decoration was undertaken unless it was essential for the protection of the work done.

Attempts were made to utilize to the fullest possible extent all existing accommodation. Householders with spare rooms were urgently requested to let them. The use for non-residential purposes of housing accommodation was severely limited. The powers of local authorities to requisition empty houses (originally introduced as part of the war-time evacuation scheme) was extended to meet the needs of 'inadequately housed' families. Service camps and wartime hostels were adapted for temporary housing, and, in London, huts were erected as 'emergency accommodation'.

Most of the visible signs of these emergency operations have gone, but still to be seen in surprisingly large numbers (over 80,000) are the 'temporary houses'—or 'prefabs' to give them their popular name. One hundred and twenty four thousand of these factory-built houses were provided by December 1948 when the programme (which was proving nearly 100 per cent more costly than expected) was brought to an end. The production, transport and erection of these were undertaken by the Government, but they were let and managed by local authorities in the same way as permanent houses built by them. A large number of these houses were built of aluminium and made minimum demands on the traditional building industry. (They also provided employment in an industry which was not expecting the sudden end of the Japanese war.)

By the end of 1946 about a third of a million 'family units of accommodation' had been provided: 80,000 in prefabs, 45,000 in conversions and adaptions; 107,000 in repaired unoccupied war-damaged houses; 3,000 in temporary huts; 9,000 in service camps; 25,000 in requisitioned houses; and 52,000 in new permanent houses. Additionally some $1\frac{1}{4}$ million occupied dwellings had been repaired.

The 'permanent housing' programme, during this period of adjustment from a wartime to a peacetime economy, was subordinate to more immediately clamant needs. But in 1946 it began in real earnest. Subsidies were increased, and were made available for a range of special needs. At the same time the size of a standard three-bedroom council house was increased to 900 sq ft plus 50 sq ft for out-buildings. But the rush to start new building rapidly overloaded the building industry and the national target of 240,000 houses a year had to be reduced to 200,000. In England and Wales, 127,541 houses were completed in 1947 and 206,559 in 1948. During the next three years production was held steadily at just over 170,000. The detailed story of these years of the 'housing drive' can be found elsewhere;[9, 46, 48] here we need take note of only two issues which have a more than short-term importance. Both these issues were embodied in the Housing Act of 1949. Among other things this expanded the housing powers of local authorities to provide for all social classes, and introduced a policy for the improvement of older houses.

Up to this time local authorities had legally been restricted to providing housing for 'the working classes'. The term had never been statutorily defined, nor had it been the subject of any general judicial interpretation. But in a Schedule to the 1936 Housing Act (dealing with 'Rehousing by Undertakers in Case of Displacement of Persons of the Working Classes') it was laid down that it included

> mechanics, artisans, labourers, and others working for wages, hawkers, costermongers, persons not working for wages but working at some trade or handicraft without employing others, except members of their own family, and persons other than domestic servants whose income in any case does not exceed an average of three pounds a week, and the families of any such persons who may be residing with them.

Judicial opinion held that chauffeurs could be members of the working class but police superintendents could not. In practice, however, local authorities had not been subject to any effective controls in this matter. Indeed with the major housing role played by local authorities in the early post-war years it was officially held (in disregard of the law) that 'there is no limitation other than the one which the local authority imposes upon itself in . . . the kind of income group for which it makes provision'.* Mr Bevan, as Minister of Health (and thus—at this time—responsible for housing), was personally very strongly in favour of the 'mixing' of social classes. Though this view was not always felt to be practicable it was generally agreed that the old legal restriction was outdated. As in other fields of social policy the principle was now for the social services to be comprehensive rather than restricted to particular income groups. The implications of this universalist approach were not thoroughly thought out, but they assumed a new importance in the middle 'fifties when rising subsidy bills began to raise serious questionings as to the appropriateness of the blunt system of housing subsidies.

The historical significance of the removal of this social class restriction lies in the explicit acceptance of the wide and important role of local housing authorities. Their duty 'to consider the housing conditions of their district' now applied to all housing, not merely that of lower-income groups. (Of similar interest in this Act was the extension of the powers to local authorities to make loans to intending owner-occupiers. These powers, which are discussed in Chapter XI, again reflect the 'broadening' of housing policy.)

The second significant provision made by the 1949 Act was in relation to the improvement of old houses. New powers were introduced to enable local authorities to give improvement grants to private owners wishing to improve or convert their property.

Critics argued with some irony that this 'public assistance for landlords' was necessitated by the Government's refusal to amend the Rent Restriction Acts: 'So long as the Rent Restriction Acts prevent a landlord from so increasing his rents as to make the holding of

* *House of Commons Debates,* Vol. 421, Col. 236.

property profitable, there is no way in which it can reasonably be expected that these improvements will be carried out unless a grant of this kind is made.'* Nevertheless, though there was considerable discussion on the morality of giving Government grants to landlords who had no 'need' of them, it was generally accepted that the object was a laudable one. And in the case of the reluctant landlord who was 'not sufficiently attracted' by the grants, there were the already existing powers of compulsory acquisition. The local authority could purchase the house, undertake the necessary improvements and claim the Government grant.

There were, however, the sceptics who noted in the explanatory introduction to the Bill the statement that there was to be no change in the volume of housing work, merely a redistribution of building resources. Miss Jennie Lee (ironically the wife of the Minister) believed that the whole problem of reconditioning was being tackled 'prematurely'; others pressed for an assurance—which was readily given—that a redistribution of resources in favour of reconditioning would not retard the new house building programme. This seeming impossibility was to be achieved by local authorities: they would know the needs of their districts, and just as some were able to resume slum clearance so would some be able to start or permit improvements.

Advice and instructions given by the Ministry to local authorities[26] suggested that no major programme of improvements was expected. Any work to be carried out on improvements—whether undertaken by local authorities or private owners—was to be reckoned as part of the housing programme of the local authority. New house building was to remain the top priority while ever there was a 'substantial' number of applicants. Improvements carried out by local authorities themselves should form part of 'an ordered plan'—not a 'series of improvisations'. Private improvements would depend on 'the initiative of the owner of the property and his readiness to put forward satisfactory proposals, and on the readiness of the local authority to approve these proposals as part of the housing work to be carried out in the district'. Local authorities were to decide 'whether they should take positive steps to make generally known in the district the facilities available under the Act'. All applications were to be submitted to the Ministry for approval.

MAINTENANCE AND REPAIRS

Whatever the effect of the 1949 Housing Act on improvements—a subject discussed in a later chapter—it did nothing to ease the far

* Committee Stage Debates on the Housing Bill 1949, *Standing Committee Debates 1948-1949*, Vol. II, Col. 1957.

bigger problem of repairs. The cost of maintenance had steadily increased since the war and by 1953 was at least three times the pre-war figure: but no rent increase could be made by private landlords, housing associations or New Town Development Corporations to offset this. Only local authorities were exempt from this restriction. The effect on the condition of property attracted more and more of the attention of professional bodies as the number of newly-built houses increased. The Sanitary Inspectors' Association in 1951 maintained that local authorities were finding it increasingly difficult to enforce the statutory obligations of owners either effectively or equitably.[49] Two years later they reported[50] that more than half of a sample of 128 local authorities were not using their Housing Act powers to remedy housing defects. Such powers could be used only where the necessary repairs did not involve unreasonable expense. The cost of repairs had risen so much (whereas rents remained frozen) that 'the cost of enforcing a proper standard of fitness has become unreasonable and prohibitive for a substantial proportion of the older houses'. Indeed, so great was the burden that some owners were seeking to dispose of their houses by donating them to local authorities or conveying them to 'men of straw'. A survey carried out by the Association of County Sanitary Officers in 1950[2] showed that, of a million houses inspected in rural areas, only 31 per cent were completely 'fit': 27 per cent required minor repairs, 30 per cent needed major works of reconstruction and 12 per cent were unfit. 'Hundreds' of these houses had inclusive rentals of less than 6s a week, and 'a great number' of only 3s. The National Federation of Property Owners[42] stressed the fact that many owners (33 per cent of their members) had no source of income other than the rents from their houses, and were quite unable to maintain them in good condition at prevailing rents. They pointed out 'nearly every local authority, apart from the London County Council' had found it necessary to increase the rents of their houses in order to meet the higher costs of repair and maintenance. The only alternative for the private owner was to allow his property to deteriorate.

A considerable number of proposals for 'adjusting' rents was put forward. The Royal Institution of Chartered Surveyors[47] suggested an increase related to the higher cost of repairs', with the safeguard of an appeal to the local authority if repairs were not in fact carried out. PEP[45] proposed 'increases of varying sizes, designed to eliminate the worst anomalies between houses of similar type' and suggested increased tax reliefs and direct government subsidies. The National Federation of Property Owners considered a flat rate 50 per cent increase of rents to be the simplest and speediest short-term remedy.

All these proposals fell on deaf ears. Housing policy was directed almost solely to the provision of new houses. Under the Labour

C

Government (i.e. until October 1951) the problem was viewed largely as one of organizing resources to meet a limited house building programme. Private enterprise building was stringently controlled particularly when national economic policy demanded a curtailment of the housing programme. Thus in October 1949, the Prime Minister announced a reduction of some £35 million a year, but 'by reducing the number of licences issued for the erection of houses by private persons, we shall secure that the local authority programme for the building of houses to let can proceed without any marked reduction'. Of the 900,000 permanent houses erected by the end of 1951 only 174,000 were privately built. The higher standards of the early post-war years were also reduced. Mr Bevan's insistance on two water closets in three-bedroom houses was dropped when he became Minister of Labour in 1950. The minimum standard of 900 sq ft for a three-bedroom five-person household was similarly cut—on the grounds that 'many able Architects have shown that it is possible by skilled planning to maintain [room] standards within a smaller total superficial area'.[27] It was left to the discretion of local authorities whether or not the 900 sq ft standard was to be reduced. But seven months later (following the advent of the Churchill Administration wedded to an election promise of 300,000 houses a year) it was stressed that houses built to the lower overall space standard would not only be economic in available resources but promised a 'reasonable prospect' of being completed more quickly. 'If this proves to be the case and the Authority are able to build more houses than the number allocated to them for 1952, the Minister will, later in the year, be prepared to make them an additional allocation'.[28]

THE EXPANSION OF THE HOUSING PROGRAMME

Building resources were now considerably easier but the Conservative Government's target of 300,000 a year involved an increasing pressure on the lower space standards (or, if the phrase is preferred—more skilful design). The average floor area of a three-bedroom council house declined from 1,050 sq ft at the beginning of 1951 to 984 sq ft in 1952, 923 sq ft in 1953 and 909 sq ft in 1954. Tender prices tended to rise slightly, from £1,304 in 1951 to £1,378 in 1954, but, of course, the cost per square foot rose much more—from 24s 10d to 30s 4d.

Under the Conservatives the relaxation of building controls, which had started under the Labour Government as conditions became easier, continued. Private builders were also given greater freedom and, as a result, private building increased from 21,000 houses in 1951 to 60,000 in 1953 and 88,000 in 1954. The most significant expansion, however, came in the local authority sector. The administrative control of local authority building programmes by a system of allocations was replaced by an expansionist policy of 'targets'. Instead of being given a maximum programme local authorities were given a target representing their 'minimum responsibility'. This was estimated on the basis of local capacity, but, if possible, it was to be exceeded.

The brakes were off and local authorities responded with alacrity: completions rose from 150,000 in 1951 to around 220,000 in 1953 and 1954.

It was, of course, fully appreciated that, in substituting targets for allocations, there was a danger that more houses would be started than the capacity of the building industry warranted. Nevertheless this was a risk which had to be taken if the national target was to be attained. It was hoped that the run-down of the programmes of war-damage repairs and replacement, together with the regulation of other kinds of building work where necessary, would ensure an adequate supply of labour. The limiting factor was the supply of materials. It was indeed fortunate that compact design and layout could achieve savings 'without any loss of standard or amenity'—as was stressed in the 1952 and 1953 Supplements to the Housing Manual! In commending *Houses 1953* a Ministry circular waxed lyrical of the benefits that would accrue:

> The supplement, *Houses 1953*, shows how by proper integration of house design and layout still further savings can be achieved. This is important enough with present high costs, but the supplement demonstrates that, in addition to saving money, it is possible to save valuable land, to conserve manpower and materials used for road making, reduce the danger from road traffic, especially to children playing near their houses, and, taking advantage of natural features, to give closer knit communities in happier surroundings, more akin to the traditional English town and village, than many housing estates provide today.[31]

It was not until 1961 (by which time the average size of a three-bedroom house had fallen to less than 900 square feet) that this decline in standards was arrested. The Parker Morris Report[4]—significantly titled *Homes For Today and Tomorrow*—then stressed that 'the country already possesses a large stock of houses and flats that are becoming out-of-date and cannot afford to go on building more of them'. The problem was revealed in its true light as a choice between standards and numbers built. But, though the Parker Morris Committee thought that standards should not be sacrificed in the future, the situation appeared differently in the 'fifties. It is perhaps asking too much for politicians and administrators not to make a virtue out of necessity.

The choice, if it really was one, seemed clear in the 'fifties. Had house building during the twelve years 1952 to 1963 proceeded at the 1951 rate, we would have had at the later date over 1,100,000 fewer houses than were actually built.

The 300,000 target was hit—and exceeded—in 1953 (279,000 in England and Wales, and 39,000 in Scotland). The strains on the building industry were apparent and steps had to be taken to prevent the programme from getting out of hand. Allocations for local authority building were reintroduced (though the Ministry were coy in using the term.) The programme was to be stabilized at a rate some 50 per cent higher than under the Labour Administration. But the position was now more difficult. The 'bonfire of controls' over the private sector was only just finishing: it was out of the question to reintroduce them. In any case it was part of Government policy to increase the proportion of private building in the total programme. Yet private building could not be easily assessed in advance now that licensing had virtually gone. An attempt was made by the Ministry to guess the probable size of private building output on the basis of existing trends. This was then subtracted from the national programme, and allocations for local authority building made to the Ministry's Regional Offices, who in turn divided them between local authorities, taking into account the contribution which private builders were likely to make in the individual areas.

The new procedure was not successful. House production in 1954 topped 309,000 for England and Wales and 39,000 for Scotland: a total of 348,000. Even in 1955 the total was 317,000. In short, once control had been eased in the private sector it was found impossible to control the national programme merely by restricting the contribution of local authorities. It was not until measures of an entirely different nature were taken, in 1955, that it was possible to bring down the national programme to the level intended: only in 1956 did the number of completions in Britain fall to around 300,000.

REAPPRAISAL: 'HOUSES—THE NEXT STEP'

As the house-building programme expanded the campaign waged by the professional and property owners associations to stimulate action to prevent the further deterioration of existing houses gathered momentum. Added significance was provided by the publication, in 1953, of the Girdwood Report on *The Cost of House Maintenance*.[29] This Report estimated that the cost of maintaining a house in good tenantable repair had increased by 216 per cent between 1939 and 1953. The estimate took no account of any increases necessitated by the increasing age of houses or by the need to make good deterioration which might have occurred during the war years.

Even the political parties were now turning their attention to the problem of deteriorating housing. A pamphlet published by the Labour Party in September 1952 maintained that 'it is obvious that the tenant himself would benefit from some form of revision of the (Rent Restriction) Acts which would provide for a proportion of the rent to be spent on the improvement and maintenance of the dwelling'.[17] The National Committee of the Co-operative Party recommended to the 1953 Annual Conference that they should accept 'a policy which deals with the problem of repairs and prevents a loss from the nation's existing stock of houses, however unsatisfactory many of them may be by modern standards'. Basically this policy amounted to the municipalization of privately-rented properties. A similar proposal was made in a Fabian pamphlet by D. L. Munby published in May 1952.[41]

As the pressure for action mounted the Government decided to make a 'full inquiry into the facts of the situation as a preliminary to whatever action may be decided on'. At the 1952 Annual Conference of the Association of Municipal Corporations, the Minister of Housing (Mr Macmillan) spoke of 'aspects of the housing problem which haunted him—especially as he was unable to deal with them without legislation, and perhaps police protection'. One of these was rent restriction—a 'complicated and delicate' problem on which he could never hope to obtain general agreement.

At last in November 1953 a major reorientation of official housing policy was announced. Now that the house building programme had been expanded by over 50 per cent since 1951 and was running at 300,000 houses a year, attention could be turned to the less spectacular problem of maintenance and improvement and to the resumption of slum clearance. The White Paper, *Houses—The Next Step*,[30] gave a broad analysis of 'the many aspects of the national housing problem', and outlined the Government's 'comprehensive plan' for dealing with them.

At this date there were some 13½ million dwellings in Great Britain. Of these 6¼ million were owned either by their occupiers or by public authorities. The remaining 7¼ million were privately rented. Most of the latter were very old: 2¼ million were 100 years old or more and a further 2¼ million were over 65 years old. As the White Paper pointed out, these figures of age were striking. Though there were no national data on condition it was obvious that a policy which concentrated almost solely on building additional houses should not continue any longer than was absolutely necessary. But these old houses varied enormously in quality: 'Some are in a perfectly good state of repair. Some need only minor repairs. Some are in a bad state. Some are obsolescent. Some ought to be condemned.'

In short what was required was 'a comprehensive plan of repair, maintenance, improvement and demolition which covers all types and conditions of house'. The Government's plan—a 'Better Housing Campaign'—divided houses into four classes: essentially sound, slum, dilapidated and needing improvement.

TABLE 2: *Ownership of Houses in Great Britain, 1953*

		%
Owner Occupied	3,750,000	28
Local Authority, etc.*	2,500,000	18
Privately Rented	7,250,000	54
	13,500,000	100

Age of Privately Rented Houses		%
100 or more years old	2,250,000	31
75–100 years old	1,750,000	24
65–75 years old	750,000	10
Less than 65 years old	2,500,000	35
	7,250,000	100

Essentially sound houses

The great bulk of privately rented houses were thought to be either in good condition or capable of being put into good condition if rents were raised to a sufficient level. This was not taken to imply that a general decontrol of rents was justified: the housing shortage was still too severe to allow this. Some method was needed which would enable and encourage landlords to undertake repairs, but at the same time would ensure that rents were raised only if the necessary repairs were in fact carried out. A flat rate increase was rejected on the grounds that it would have been illogical and unfair since rents varied enormously, not on the basis of differences in the value of houses, but according to the accidents of previous measures of control, decontrol and recontrol. A setting-up of rent tribunals to adjudicate on rent increases was also rejected on the ground that the administrative difficulties would have been enormous. The solution favoured by the Government was the one proposed by the Royal Institution of Chartered Surveyors in 1951. This needs a few words of explanation.

Every house has a gross value for rating purposes which is the

* Including houses owned by New Town Development Corporations, Housing Associations, etc.

theoretical annual rent that might be expected if the landlord bore the cost of repairs and maintenance, and the tenant was responsible for the rates. The net (or rateable) value—on which local rates are levied —is less than this. The difference, which is fixed by law and is known as the statutory deduction, is the amount allowed to the landlord to cover the cost of repairs, insurance and other expenses necessary to maintain the dwelling in such a state as to command the expected rent. Thus a house with a gross value of £15 would have had (at this time) a net value of £9. The difference of £6 was the statutory deduction. In other words in a free market the landlord could, for this house, expect to receive an annual rent of £15 and to spend £6 a year on maintenance and repairs. (At this date all residential values were determined in relation to 1934 rent levels.) The RICS proposal was that the statutory deduction should be used as a basis for fixing rent increases. As the cost of repairs had risen by 200 per cent since 1939 (at which date the statutory repairs deduction gave a true representation of the cost of maintaining and repairing houses) a repairs increase of twice the statutory deduction would enable landlords to repair and maintain houses to the standard they adopted in 1939. The political attraction of this scheme was that it gave landlords an increase only for that part of their rent income which was needed for repairs and maintenance: it gave them no increase in their investment income. Thus in the example already given the landlord's investment income would remain at £9 a year, but the rent income needed for repairs would be increased from £6 to £18, i.e. by £12 a year or 4s 7d a week.

So much for the arithmetic: it still remained to ensure that the increased rent was spent on repairs—and that the house to which an increase applied was in a good state of repair and decoration. Two procedures were devised to meet these requirements. To take the latter first, the legislation implementing the White Paper's proposals —the Housing Repairs and Rents Act 1954—also laid down a set of criteria for determining whether a house was 'unfit for human habitation'. Only if a house was, first, 'fit' according to these criteria, and, secondly, in a good state of repair, were the 'conditions justifying an increase in rent' fulfilled. Having fulfilled these conditions the landlord then had to show that he had actually undertaken repairs of an appropriate value. This was required 'as a test of good faith'— though once the test had been passed the increase became permanent unless the tenant could prove that the house was no longer in a good state of structural and decorative repair.

It was the Government's belief that these provisions would 'work to the mutual benefit of landlord and tenant; they should enable millions of houses to be put and kept in good repair and thus help to preserve a national asset'.

Slum houses

At the other extreme from these 'essentially sound houses' were 'hundreds of thousands' which were 'unfit for human habitation and cannot be made fit at reasonable expense, or which, by reason of their bad arrangement or the narrowness or bad arrangement of the streets, are dangerous or injurious to the health of the inhabitants'—in short, slums. The slum clearance campaign which had been interrupted by the war was to be resumed immediately. But slums were not evenly distributed throughout the country: in some areas there were very few; in others they formed a major problem which could not be solved for many years. The Government considered it 'a national duty to see that the slum houses which have to be used for years to come should be made more tolerable for the people who have to live in them until something better can be provided'. By definition these houses were both unfit for families to live in and incapable of being made fit at reasonable expense. Municipal enterprise in Birmingham had shown a way for dealing with this problem. Under (the now lapsed) powers of the 1944 Town and Country Planning Act a large area containing over 30,000 substandard houses and over 5,000 other properties had been 'designated' for acquisition. Most of the properties had been purchased, and the slum houses patched or reconditioned to a standard which was reasonable in relation to their planned life.* Profiting from Birmingham's success in this field, the Government gave general powers to local authorities to undertake similar schemes of 'deferred demolition'. Houses which could not be demolished within a reasonable period could now be acquired (at site value) and patched up to provide accommodation which was 'adequate for the time being'. Exchequer grants were made available for such schemes. Though 'novel', the Government commended the idea to local authorities: 'From the human angle the money and work involved in these operations will be well expended. There should be countervailing savings on sickness, disease, human degradation and crime'.

Dilapidated houses

Thirdly there was thought to be an intermediate class of 'dilapidated'

---

* 'The houses were divided into three categories, namely those which will be demolished within about five years from the starting date of the programme of clearance, those with a life of between five and ten years, and those that will not be required for demolition until the second half of the 20-year period. The first category receive the minimum amount of maintenance necessary to keep them weatherproof and reasonably fit for occupation; substantial work is done to the longest lifed houses but considerable renovations carried out to those in the intervening category where necessary.' H. J. Manzoni, 'Redevelopment of Blighted Areas in Birmingham', *Journal of the Town Planning Institute*, Vol. XLI, March 1955, p. 99.

houses which could be brought into the 'essentially sound' category if sufficient repairs were undertaken. Technically such houses were 'unfit for human habitation'—but at the same time capable of being made fit at a reasonable cost. Expenditure on such repairs would not of itself be sufficient to warrant a repairs increase since the 'conditions justifying an increase of rent' stipulated a higher standard than that which was used in determining mere 'fitness'. Nevertheless landlords were statutorily bound to keep their houses in a fit condition and local authorities had powers to ensure that this was done. They could even carry out the works in default and recover the cost from the landlord. These powers had been little used during the war and post-war periods, but local authorities were now to be exhorted to bring them into operation. It was hoped that the use of these powers would not only ensure that dilapidated houses were made fit but would also encourage unwilling landlords to make the 'extra effort' and bring these houses up to the higher standard of 'good repair'. There was thus both a 'stick' and a 'carrot'.

Houses needing improvement

The final category was of houses which 'could give years of good service if they were improved' or (in the case of large socially obsolete houses) properly converted into flats. Grants were already available, under the 1949 Act, to local authorities and private owners who wished to undertake improvements or conversions, but the scheme had proved ineffective: between 1949 and 1953 grants had been given for only 5,463 improvements and 624 conversions. This was thought to be due to the lack of publicity given to the scheme during the years of shortage of labour and materials which followed its introduction, and to the restrictive nature of the original provisions. The easier conditions now obtaining removed the basis of the first difficulty, and the 1954 Act made the scheme much more liberal.

The new emphasis on slum clearance, conservation and rehabilitation was only part of the new policy. Equally important was the Government's concern to foster private enterprise.

Her Majesty's Government believe that the people of this country prefer, in housing as in other matters, to help themselves as much as they can rather than to rely wholly or mainly upon the efforts of Government, national or local. . . . One object of future housing policy will be to continue to promote, by all possible means, the building of new houses for owner-occupation. Of all forms of saving, this is one of the best. Of all forms of ownership this is one of the most satisfying to the individual and the most beneficial to the nation.[30]

Within a stabilized annual building programme of 300,000 new houses a year (for Great Britain), private enterprise was to play 'an ever increasing part in the provision of houses for general needs'. Not only would this meet the demands for owner-occupation, it would also enable local authorities to concentrate on slum clearance. At the same time it would 'lighten the ever-growing burden of housing subsidies which, in the interest of the general body of taxpayers, cannot continue indefinitely at the present rate'.

The emphasis was on private enterprise building for owner-occupation, but on the Report Stage of the Bill a new clause was introduced which was designed to stimulate the private provision of houses for renting. Reference was made to 'well-to-do people living in council houses at subsidized rents'. They were not to be blamed for this since it was almost impossible for them to obtain an unsubsidized house to rent. The new clause freed from control all new dwellings (including non-grant aided conversions) built after the passing of the Act. No great hopes were entertained that this would result in a major resumption of private building of houses to rent, but the experiment was 'worth making'.

THE EFFECTS OF THE 1954 ACT

Very little information was collected by the Government on the effect of the 1954 Act on repairs. There are no figures of the number of cases in which repairs were carried out. Indeed, the only published information relates to cases in which tenants applied to local authorities for certificates of disrepair. In the first six months following the Act some 20,000 applications were made and 18,000 granted. This was the peak period: less than half these numbers were recorded in the following *eighteen* months. In relation to the four million rent-controlled houses which were thought to be essentially sound these are extremely low figures. It may have been, of course, that a very large number of rent increases were accepted by tenants. The general opinion, however, was that the provisions of the Act were too restrictive. *The Times* reported (on January 17, 1955) that, as far as could be ascertained, landlords in the north had not taken advantage of the Act since there was 'precious little return to be gained for too large an outlay'. Ironically they were inclined to quote Mr Bevan's comment of 'mouldy turnips' as being a just verdict of the results produced by the Act. These impressions were corroborated by a survey carried out by the National Federation of Property Owners in March 1955. They found sufficient indications already (six months after the passing of the Act) to 'show clearly that the great majority of owners, particularly those owning small cottage houses, consider that the repairs increase will be of little help to them owing to the conditions imposed, and do not intend to claim it'. Local authorities, it was alleged, were issuing Certificates of Disrepair on a much greater scale than was ever expected; landlords had insufficient capital to finance repairs before increasing rents; the 'twice gross value stopper' worked unfairly against owners of houses with 'artificially low rateable values'; the permitted increase was insufficient to keep up a high standard of repair; the procedure for obtaining an increase was far too complicated. In a later memorandum,[43] the Federation stated that in their view 'nothing short of a complete reform of the rent structure will solve the problem of repairs'.

The new improvement grant provisions, on the other hand, were much more successful. The easier conditions, together with increased publicity, resulted in a sharp rise in approvals. The number of grant-aided conversions and improvements in 1954 (1,202 and 12,508 respectively) was more than double the number for the whole period 1949–53. In 1955 there was a further very large increase: to a total of 2,697 conversions and 33,726 improvements. Most of the grants were given for the installation of baths and hot-water systems.

By the end of 1956, 7,328 conversions and 82,593 improvements had been grant-aided. In spite of this progress few improvements were undertaken in privately-owned *rented* property. Though no figures were published it was thought that about 90 per cent of grants had gone to owner-occupiers. Either the conditions were still too restrictive or—as was now increasingly being suggested—rented houses had ceased to be an economic asset to their owners. Certainly a major problem facing landlords was the cost of repairs which were necessary before improvements could be carried out. These did not rank for grant and naturally (even with the repairs increase) reduced the landlord's return.

In accordance with the new policy of expanding the private provision of housing, licensing control over private enterprise building was abolished in November 1954. The number of private houses increased from 60,000 in 1953 to 110,000 in 1955, representing at the latter date nearly two-fifths of the total number of houses built. This increase was, of course, intended. But if the total building programme was to be stabilized at 300,000 houses a year it followed that local authority building should decline. Local authority housing programmes were restrained by a system of allocations (yet at the same time, stimulated by housing subsidies). The retention of controls over the local authority sector was resented, particularly since (as was intended) the private sector was now free. Yet the Government could hardly free local authorities in the same way while ever they were being stimulated by a system of general housing subsidies. Indeed the freeing of private building led to an overloading of the building industry. In such circumstances controls over the local authority

sector became even more important. It seems that the intention was
to persuade local authorities to restrict their programmes to the
number of houses required for slum clearance purposes except where
it was obvious that private enterprise was unable or unwilling to
meet 'general needs'. Such a policy was not easy to enforce without
some additional means of 'persuasion'. This was provided in October
1955 by a recasting of housing subsidies.

THE 'REALISTIC RENTS' POLICY

The expansion of local authority housing programmes under
stimulation by the Conservative Government in the early 'fifties
greatly increased the cost of housing subsidies. By the end of 1955
local authorities owned 2¾ million houses and were receiving nearly
£47 million a year in Exchequer subsidies. Even with a reduction in
local authority building this Exchequer aid was likely to grow at a
rate of £5 million or £6 million a year. Figures of the distribution of
incomes on Council estates,[19] and of the rents charged by local
authorities,[37] were felt by the Government to show that in general,
council house rents were being subsidized to a greater extent than the
financial circumstances of the individual tenants required; the amount
of subsidy which the Exchequer was paying out in respect of existing
houses was unnecessarily large, and provided a margin which could
properly be used for financing some part of the future house-building
programme.

At the same time greater efforts were needed, in the Government's
view, to encourage local authorities to concentrate on slum clearance.
Direct controls were considered undesirable: they were 'extremely
difficult to work' and entailed 'a wholly unjustifiable interference in
local affairs'. The alternative was to provide a financial incentive.

Both these arguments led to the conclusion that the general needs
housing subsidy should be replaced by a system of specific subsidies
for slum clearance and other types of provision which the Government wished to encourage, such as overspill. Changes in subsidy
policy were announced by the Minister of Housing (Mr Sandys) in
October 1955. The general needs subsidy was abolished, though to
soften the impact, the Housing Subsidies Act of 1956 retained it for a
short while at a reduced rate. It was finally abolished in November
1956 except for one bedroom houses. The exception was made to
encourage local authorities to provide more dwellings for elderly and
single people. The Housing Subsidies Act also broke the tradition of
housing finance by relieving local authorities of the necessity of contributing to housing from the rates. Up to this time local authorities
had been obliged to make a 'rate fund contribution' proportionate to
the Exchequer contribution for each subsidized house.

The 1956 Act constituted part of a general policy of substituting financial measures for administrative controls. The system of allocations was abolished and local authorities were now free to determine the size of their own housing programmes. But they would receive Exchequer subsidies only for the special categories of need defined in the Act. Furthermore, two other measures were taken which formed a most effective substitute for administrative controls. First, major changes were now made in the availability of loans to local authorities from the Public Works Loan Board. During the whole period of the Labour Administration local authorities had been required (subject to limited exceptions) to raise all their loans from the Public Works Loan Board. This, in effect, provided a guarantee that finance would be available, at favourable interest rates, for all approved capital schemes. In 1952 local authorities were allowed to borrow in the open market if they preferred to do so. In 1955 local authorities were required to try to borrow on the open market before they applied for a PWLB loan. Furthermore the rates of interest for PWLB loans were now to be fixed by reference, not as hitherto to the Government's own credit, but to the credit of local authorities of good standing in the market.

At the same time interest rates generally were rising. During the period of the Labour Government, PWLB interest rates had been kept at 3 per cent or lower. The return of the Conservatives towards the end of 1951 saw the reintroduction of the whole apparatus and idea of monetary control.[53] The PWLB rate (for loans for periods exceeding 15 years) fluctuated between 3¾ and 4¼ per cent until August 1955 when it was raised to 4½ per cent. By October 1955, when the new subsidy arrangements were announced, it had been increased to 5 per cent—the highest since 1932. In accordance with the new policy of basing PWLB interest rates on those payable in the market by local authorities of good standing further increases were made in 1956, and by October of that year the rate stood at 5¾ per cent.

During the expansionist period of housing policy increases in interest rates (and in building costs) had largely been offset by an increase in subsidies. Under the new policy, however, the increased costs could be met only by increases in rents or rate fund contributions. The theoretical increase in the 'economic rent' was significant. For example the rise in interest rates from 3¾ per cent in June 1954 to 5½ per cent in March 1956 increased the annual loan charges for a house costing £1,525 from £64 1s 0d to £87 5s 0d: an addition of nearly 10s a week. But the Government argued that this *was* theoretical: if local authorities pooled their subsidies and gave rent relief only to those tenants who needed subsidies, they should be able to continue building new houses with little or no rent increases. The intention was clearly and explicitly to encourage local authorities to operate a 'realistic' rents policy within a reduced building programme designed mainly to meet social categories of need.

The new policy had a rapid effect on house-building. By the end of 1956 local authority building had declined by about a third from the 1954 level. The number of houses built in 1956 (149,139) was actually slightly lower than the number completed in 1951. Private building, on the other hand, continued to increase, and in 1956 was a third higher than in 1954. These trends continued through the remainder of the 'fifties. In 1958, for the first time since the war, the number of private houses (124,087) exceeded the number provided by local authorities (117,438). In 1961 private builders provided over 70,000 more houses than local authorities.

During the same period the slum clearance programmes of local authorities gathered momentum. The total number of houses demolished or closed rose from under 20,000 in 1954 to 47,000 in 1957 and 62,000 in 1961. This was a significant achievement, but it was below even the modest target set by the local authorities themselves. Under the Housing Repairs and Rents Act of 1954 local authorities were obliged to submit to the Ministry a return showing the number of unfit houses in their areas, and the numbers which they proposed to demolish or to 'retain for temporary accommodation' (i.e. deferred demolition) during a period of five years. These figures gave only a minimum national estimate of the slum problem. Quite apart from continuing obsolescence, some major urban authorities returned only the number of houses which they thought could in fact be demolished within, say, ten or twenty years. Even with this qualification, the number of unfit houses was estimated to be 850,000. Local authorities proposed, within five years, to patch up 88,000 for use as temporary accommodation and to demolish nearly 380,000. This gives an annual demolition rate of about 75,000: over 10,000 more than the highest figure yet recorded. Indeed in the five years 1955 to 1959 only 225,000 were demolished. The difficulties in reaching a higher figure proved to be greater than had been expected and towards the end of the period under review new measures were beginning to be taken.

'REALISTIC RENTS' IN THE PRIVATE SECTOR

The 'realistic rents' policy which accompanied the resumption of slum clearance was applied to the private sector at virtually the same time. In October 1956, the Minister of Housing (Mr Sandys) announced to the Conservative Party's annual conference that the time had come to begin a progressive abolition of rent control:

It is an essential part of our Conservative policy to restore some sanity to housing finance. Last year we halved the subsidy on council houses for general needs as a prelude to abolishing it altogether. Rent control of private houses is the other half of the problem.*

Added point to the necessity for action was provided in the following month when a White Paper was published giving figures of the rents of controlled houses. Of the 4¼ million dwellings which it was proposed to leave under control nearly a quarter had net weekly rents of 5s or less and nearly three-quarters had rents of 10s or less.

TABLE 3: *Net Rents of Controlled Dwellings in England and Wales, 1956*

Net weeky rents	No. of dwellings
Up to 5/–	983,500
5/– to 10/–	2,062,500
10/– to 15/–	835,200
15/– to 20/–	325,400
Over 20/–	43,400
	4,250,000

Source: Rent Control: Statistical Information, Cmnd. 17, HMSO, 1956. The figures exclude 750,000 dwellings with rateable values above the Rent Act limits (i.e. over £40 in London and over £30 elsewhere in England and Wales).

The Government's proposals were for the automatic decontrol of all dwellings with a rateable value of over £40 in London and over £30 in the rest of England and Wales. It was estimated that there were 750,000 such dwellings. Furthermore any dwelling below these 'control limits' would become decontrolled when let to a new tenant. For the 4¼ million dwellings remaining under control a system of rent limits based on gross values was introduced. Existing rents which were below these limits could be increased, subject to the right of tenants to challenge them on the grounds of disrepair.

These proposals were incorporated in the 1957 Rent Act—one of the most controversial pieces of legislation of the 'fifties. In retrospect the debates on the Bill have a curious air of unreality.[7] In view of the fact that the legislation was not preceded by an investigation of the problems it was designed to solve, nor even of the facts of the existing situation, this is not surprising. Government spokesmen often seemed to be stating simple lessons in economic theory. Increased freedom—and rents—would restore the market situation. The condition of rented property would be improved. Under-occupation ('caused by

* *The Times*, October 12, 1956.

artificially low rents') would be reduced by the simple process of small families in large houses moving and making way for large families previously living in small houses. For various reasons the 'supply' of privately-rented accommodation would increase: the basic reason being that it would now be profitable. But not too profitable: landlords were not the inhuman capitalists the Opposition sometimes suggested; they were reasonable men (and women) merely interested in obtaining a fair price for the commodity they wished to sell. By permitting rent increases the Government were simply restoring a measure of justice and sanity into the privately-rented market—as they were attempting to do in the subsidized council housing market by the revision of council house subsidies. Justice indeed figured largely in the debates: after all, since there were no adequate facts there was little apart from economic theory and justice to argue about! The Opposition did stress the electoral implications of the Act (forgetting that a Government can sometimes obtain support for its Party by courageously tackling an unpopular subject), but concentrated on the injustices it would create, on the wage increases and inflation that would follow from it, and on the unreality of the Government's predictions of its happy impact on the housing situation.

Several studies have been made of privately-rented housing since the Rent Act came into operation.[6, 7, 10, 13] These all show that the Act made remarkably little impact. A large number of rents were increased (but a surprising number were not), more repairs were done but they were generally minor and superficial ones, the rate of movement does not seem to have been affected, and there was no observable increase in the supply of rented accommodation—indeed, the decline in the number of privately-rented houses has continued. This was the national picture. In London the situation gave increasing cause for concern. Here housing problems were aggravated by the problems being faced by coloured immigrants and by the actions of a few unscrupulous landlords. The Rachman affair brought matters to a head. New legislation had eventually to be brought in to control 'houses in multiple occupation', and a Committee of Inquiry (the Milner Holland Committee) was set up in August 1963.[34]

GOVERNMENT AID FOR HOUSE PURCHASE

A notable feature of the housing situation in the 'fifties was the large-scale purchase by owner-occupiers of old houses which had previously been let by private landlords. Exact figures are difficult to come by, but such as are available clearly show that the growth of owner-occupation was considerably greater than the rate of completion of new non-council houses. In 1948, 33 per cent of non-council houses were owner-occupied: by 1958 the proportion had risen to 51 per cent.[13] The Social Survey Report on *The Housing Situation in 1960*[14] indicated that 43 per cent of all houses built before 1919 were owned by their occupiers.

There are several reasons for this. On the 'supply' side landlords preferred to sell their houses rather than relet them. Before the 1957 Rent Act this was thought to be mainly because of the low level of rents fixed by rent controls. Experience since the Rent Act (which freed houses from control when they were relet) and later studies[6] showed that even with a free market in rents, many landlords found the problems of managing rented property too great to make the business worth-while. In England and Wales as a whole 12 per cent of dwellings decontrolled between 1957 and 1959 became owner-occupied.

On the 'demand' side, older houses were comparatively cheap, and purchasers could obtain the benefits of tax relief on their mortgage interest payments.

Loans for older houses, however, were not always easy to obtain, particularly when the Building Societies had insufficient funds for lending to all applicants: in such times they tended to favour loans on newer properties. Nevertheless by the late 'fifties they were lending some £40 to £50 million a year for the purchase of pre-1919 houses— in addition to over £300 million a year for newer houses.

As part of the Government policy to encourage owner-occupation the House Purchase and Housing Act 1959 provided for loans from the Exchequer to approved Building Societies. Though these loans would indirectly make more money available for the purchase of newer houses, the loans were earmarked for financing the purchase of pre-1919 houses with values up to £2,500.

The agreement with the Building Societies was also linked with a new system of 'standard grants' for improvements. Anyone buying a pre-1919 house under the scheme was entitled to a loan covering his share of the cost of installing certain 'standard amenities' which were lacking in this house.

The second objective of the 1959 Act was to encourage a higher rate of improvement in older houses. The existing scheme was continued but the conditions were relaxed. Grants under this scheme had always been given—and were continued to be given—at the discretion of the local authority. This *discretionary grants* scheme was now supplemented by a new system of *standard grants*, which owners of eligible property could claim as of right towards the cost of installing a bath, a wash-hand basin, hot-water supply, a water closet and a food store.

The relaxed conditions for discretionary grants and the introduction of the new standard grants, coupled with better publicity, brought about a fourfold increase in improvements, which by 1960

D

were running at the rate of about 125,000 a year. Nevertheless comparatively few private landlords took advantage of them, even after 1961 when the Housing Act of that year increased the permitted return on the owner's share of the expenditure from 8 per cent to 12½ per cent.

The problem of old and obsolete housing received increasing attention at the turn of the 'sixties. This was highlighted by the publication of the Social Survey Report on *The Housing Situation in 1960*[14] which showed that not only were there 622,000 'unfit' houses in England and Wales, but also that 210,000 had an estimated life of under five years: a total of 832,000, compared with the official programme of demolitions amounting to 486,000 over this period. Looking slightly further ahead, nearly 2 million houses needed replacing within fifteen years. This implied an annual demolition rate of 130,000—about double the existing rate. The older houses having a life of fifteen or more years needed a considerable number of improvements: 1½ million lacked a fixed bath, wash-basin, hot water and a water closet. A further 2¾ million lacked one or more of these.

Steps were taken in the 'sixties to increase the rate of clearance and improvement, though in fact demolitions have stuck at about 60,000 a year and improvements have fallen from 125,000 to 115,000 a year.

THE ROLE OF PUBLIC AUTHORITIES IN THE EARLY 'SIXTIES

A reappraisal of housing policy was outlined in the 1961 White Paper, *Housing in England and Wales*[32]. The proposals outlined in this were incorporated in the 1961 Housing Act.

The major political debate on housing in the post-war period has been on the respective roles of public authorities and private enterprise. The 1961 White Paper—like its 1953 predecessor—looked towards an expansion of the private sector in the provision of new houses, and a concentration of public effort on slum clearance and similar problems. The specific objectives of the 1961 Housing Act were to channel Exchequer assistance to needy local authorities who were faced with problems which only they could meet; to stimulate private building for letting; and to provide new and strengthened powers for local authorities to deal with bad living conditions in houses occupied by several families.

The main tasks of local authorities were now building for slum clearance, for old people, for the relief of overcrowding or other bad living conditions, and for overspill. But the size of these problems differed greatly between different areas. Furthermore, the local resources for meeting the cost of further housing varied widely: an authority with a large number of pre-war houses (built at the comparatively very low costs then ruling) was considerably better off than one in which the majority of houses had been built since the war. It followed, in the Government's view, that radical changes were needed in the subsidy system. At the same time it could be made more flexible —by giving subsidy for all dwellings approved by the Ministry, irrespective of the purpose for which they were built.

Under the new system—which remained in operation until November 1965—there were two basic rates of subsidy: one of £24 payable to authorities who satisfied a test of 'financial need', the other of £8 payable to other authorities. The test was based on the 'potential' rent resources of each local authority, and was intended to give the most help to those local authorities who would have had difficulty in continuing to build and let new houses at rents which the tenants could afford. Clearly the new scheme constituted a logical step in the Government's 'realistic rents' policy. Indeed, it was explicitly stated in the 1961 White Paper that these subsidy arrangements would encourage local authorities to 'pursue reasonable rent policies'. Furthermore, in the Government's view 'at present, many council houses and flats which ought to be available to those who really need them are still occupied by people who, whatever their situation when they first became local authority tenants, have since become well able to make their own arrangements without need of subsidy'. It was even argued that, 'increasingly such tenants are making their own arrangements as councils adopt more realistic rent policies'.

Since the new subsidies—at both the lower and the higher rate— were available for all local authority dwellings, the purpose for which dwellings were built had to be approved by the Ministry. This had the incidental advantage that official policy could be easily geared to meet changing circumstances.

A restriction of local authority effort to particular needs was part of a wider policy of encouraging the private provision of housing. Owner-occupation was still spreading rapidly, but there had been few signs of any resumption of private building for letting. In order to stimulate this the 1961 Act initiated a 'pump-priming operation' which, it was hoped, would 'serve to show the way to the investment of private capital once again in building houses to let'. This took the form of Exchequer loans, up to a maximum of £25 million, to approved non-profit making housing associations building houses to let at economic rents.

Other provisions of the 1961 Act included minor changes in the Improvement Grants schemes, an increase in the return allowed to landlords taking advantage of these grants, and strengthened powers to enable local authorities to deal with squalid living conditions in 'houses in multiple occupation'.

One more White Paper was published and one more Housing Act was passed before the Conservative Government went out of office in

TABLE 4: *Permanent Houses Built in England and Wales, 1945–64*

	Local Authorities*	Private Builders	Total
1945–6	21,878	30,657	52,535
1947	87,915	39,626	127,541
1948	175,213	31,346	206,559
1949	147,092	24,688	171,780
1950	145,784	26,576	172,360
1951	150,497	21,406	171,903
1952	176,897	32,078	208,975
1953	218,703	60,528	279,231
1954	220,924	88,028	308,952
1955	173,392	109,934	283,326
1956	149,139	119,585	268,724
1957	145,711	122,942	268,653
1958	117,438	124,087	241,525
1959	102,905	146,476	249,381
1960	107,126	162,100	269,226
1961	98,466	170,366	268,832
1962	111,651	167,016	278,667
1963	102,413	168,242	270,655
1964	126,073	210,432	336,505
Total 1945–64	2,579,199	1,855,977	4,435,176

1964. The 1963 White Paper, *Housing*,[33] announced the Government's intention, during the next ten years, to meet 'the remaining shortages', to clear nearly all the remaining slums, to provide for growth and for workers moving to new jobs, to improve most of the houses worth improvement and to make a start on the renewal of the depressed residential areas. The output of housing was to be increased beyond the 300,000 which had been the average over the previous ten years—up to at least 350,000 (later official statements set the target at 400,000 a year); the provision of houses for letting and co-ownership was to be expanded; and improvements were to be increased to a rate of between 150,000 and 200,000 a year.

More specifically, a Housing Corporation was to be established to promote the development of cost-rent and co-ownership housing societies; local authorities in the congested industrial areas were to have expanded five-year building programmes and were to have access to technical assistance from regional offices of the Ministry;

* Includes 98,126 houses built by New Town Development Corporations, 52,337 by Housing Associations and 86,297 by Government Departments and excludes 124,455 temporary houses built by local authorities.
Source: *Housing Returns*.

house improvement schemes were to be encouraged on a street or area basis (with a certain measure of compulsion in the case of rented properties); further powers were to be given to local authorities for dealing with the problems in houses in multiple occupation; and a complete overhaul of housing subsidies was to be made.

The year 1964 saw the largest number of house completions in any year since the war: 336,000—an increase of 66,000 over 1963. In total over 4½ million houses have been built since 1945: over 2½ million for public authorities and nearly 2 million for private owners. The proportion built for public authorities has varied under different Governments, with the extremes of over 80 per cent in 1948 to rather more than a third in recent years. Local authorities now own over 3½ million dwellings and are building at a rate of well over 100,000 a year. Slum clearance is running at the rate of 60,000 a year—with over ¼ million demolitions since the war. Different Governments and different policies are likely to have only a marginal effect on the overall picture: at least in the short run. In the longer run greater changes may take place. It is only forty-six years since local authorities began to emerge as significant providers of houses. Now, a quarter of all households live in council houses, and local authorities have a housing revenue budget of nearly £400 million a year. They receive nearly £80 million a year in Exchequer subsidies and have an outstanding loan debt for housing of £4,500 million. They are currently building over 10,000 every month. As the private rented sector declines—by slum clearance and sales to owner-occupiers—local authorities are becoming the main provider of rented houses. They also have major functions in relation to the maintenance and improvement of old property, and loans to owners.

New problems are constantly arising which demand new or wider powers for and programmes by local housing authorities. The Milner Holland Committee on Housing in Greater London[34]—which cannot be regarded as hostile to private owners—clearly showed that the role of housing authorities, in the larger urban areas at least (where the majority of the population live) is not simply to be one of administering their vast estates.

POSTSCRIPT: THE 1965 HOUSING PLAN

As the 1964 election drew near housing increasingly became the major domestic political issue. Rent control, housing subsidies, assistance to owner-occupiers, control of land prices, the rating system, controls over 'unessential' building, all formed topics of debate. The Labour Party was returned to power with a very tiny majority, but wedded to an election programme of major reforms on the domestic front. By the end of 1965 new legislation included the

Rent Act, the Control of Office and Industrial Development Act, and the Housing (Slum Clearance Compensation) Act. The Rent Act of 1965 introduced a system of 'rent regulation' under which landlords and tenants of virtually all uncontrolled lettings can seek the assistance of a Rent Officer in determining a 'fair' rent; failing agreement by this means the rent is settled by a Rent Assessment Committee. The Control of Office and Industrial Development Act introduced a system of controls over new office development. In order to cover the whole field of 'less essential' building, legislation was promised for 1966 which would institute a licensing procedure for privately-sponsored construction projects of the value of £100,000 or more. The Housing (Slum Clearance Compensation) Act, which is outlined in Chapter VIII, made special provision for certain owner-occupiers of unfit property purchased for slum clearance. The Government also issued a White Paper outlining their proposals for establishing a Land Commission which would have wide powers to purchase land (compulsorily as well as by agreement) and to operate a levy on development values. The objective is 'a flexible system which, combining a levy with other operations of the Commission, will both provide an effective and fair solution to the problem of betterment and ensure a sufficient and orderly supply of land for development'.[38]

A further White Paper, *The Housing Programme 1965 to 1970*,[36] set out the main lines of the Government's housing policy.* This Paper is commonly referred to as 'The National Housing Plan', but is in fact an assessment of priorities. Indeed the Paper clearly states that it sets out only 'the first stage in the formulation of a national housing plan.' The rate of house-building is to be increased as quickly as resources and improved techniques allow. The first objective (for the United Kingdom) is 500,000 new houses a year by 1970—rising to even higher figures in the nineteen-seventies. Information about needs is inadequate and great stress is being laid on intensive research; but the broad assessment of the current situation is summarized as:

Needs existing now (1965)
  (i) About 1 million to replace unfit houses already identified as slums;
 (ii) up to 2 million more to replace old houses not yet slums but not worth improving;
(iii) about 700,000 to overcome shortages and provide a margin for mobility.

Needs arising annually
(iv) 30,000 a year to replace the loss caused by demolition—road widening and other forms of redevelopment; and

* See also Department of Economic Affairs, *The National Plan*, Cmnd. 2764, HMSO, 1965, particularly Chapter 17.

(v) 150,000 a year to keep up with new households being formed in the rising population.

Within the increased programme (which, it is pointed out, is 'modest' not only in relation to needs but also in comparison with the programmes of other advanced western countries) a larger proportionate role is to be played by public authorities—but only in the short term:

> Once the country has overcome its huge social problem of slumdom and obsolescence, and met the need of the great cities for more houses let at moderate rents, the programme of subsidized council housing should decrease. The expansion of the public programme now proposed is to meet exceptional needs: it is born partly of a short-term necessity, partly of the conditions inherent in modern urban life. The expansion of building for owner-occupation on the other hand is normal; it reflects a long-term social advance which should gradually pervade every region.

This represents a major change in the attitude of the Left to owner-occupation—a change which has been taking place gradually over the last fifteen years. In part this is itself a political readjustment to the increasing spread of owner-occupation, but it also reflects an important change in social attitudes. This change is also evident in the recognition of the need to plan *both* the public and the private house building sectors. During the period of the first post-war Labour Government private building was controlled and held back in favour of local authority building. The Conservative Government at first concentrated on expanding total house production, but once the private sector had re-established itself, held back council building for letting in favour of private building for owner-occupation. (The popular phrase at this time was 'a property-owning democracy'.) Throughout the years 1958 to 1964 local authority building fluctuated between about 100,000 and 126,000 a year, while private building rose to about 170,000, with a major increase in 1964 to 210,000 (see Table 4). The new policy attempts to plan not only the total programme but also both its main constituent parts. Local authority programmes, of course, are relatively easy to control—and, in previous years have been cut back when the overall programme appeared to be straining the available resources. But now 'forward planning' is to be introduced in the private as well as the public sector. How this is to be achieved is not yet clear, but apparently representatives of the building societies and private builders have agreed 'that it would be sensible to plan the rate to which [private building] should grow; and they are now exploring with the Housing Departments the practicability of ensuring that growth is at the planned rate—on the understanding that targets should be flexible and subject to a good measure of tolerance'. The favoured means of ensuring that private building corresponds broadly with the overall plan is through the availability of mortgages. The idea is that the building societies and other lenders will agree in advance of the amount of capital they will advance each year for new building.

The Government's 'comprehensive' approach to housing policy, as set out in the White Paper, is detailed in the relevant chapters of this book. The 'essential requirements', however, are in summary as follows:

'(a) control of less essential building to give housing top priority—along with industrial building, educational buildings and hospitals;

(b) expansion and modernization of the construction industries;

(c) making the necessary land available in good time;

(d) machinery for reviewing the forward programme and for settling the balance between houses to let and houses for owner-occupation;

(e) measures for ensuring that quantitative increase of houses built by private developers for sale is accompanied by a steady improvement in quality as well as protection for the owner-occupier against jerry building;

(f) stimulation of the planned growth of owner-occupation by financial measures designed to widen its economic basis;

(g) reorganization of the subsidy system to provide a sound financial basis for public authority housing, and to ensure that the new more generous subsidies are used to improve the quality as well as the quantity of this housing;

(h) measures to enable local authorities to take full advantage of industrialized building, and so to increase the output of the housebuilding industry;

(i) programming of local authorities' building by a system of regional and local allocations designed to give first priority to relieving shortages of houses to rent in the conurbations;

(j) measures to be worked out in consultation with the local authorities for formulating the rent and tenancy policies required to gear local authority housing to social need'.

One final comment needs to be made here on this White Paper—this relates to its refreshingly humble approach. White Papers are commonly distinguished by the way in which they present the 'answer' to the problems. The current Paper, however, stresses the fact that insufficient is known about the problems to permit adequate answers to be given. Decisions have had to be taken—particularly on the balance between building for owner-occupation and building to let—but these are short run decisions. 'For a comprehensive and firmly based plan much more must be known about the reality of housing needs—not just the crude needs in terms of slums, over-crowding, obsolescence and the increasing number of households, young and old—but needs in terms of the sort of houses people want and for which they are prepared to pay'.

The Paper ends with a series of questions which Mr Crossman, the Minister of Housing, has been repeatedly asking since he came to power—questions to which no certain answers can yet be given: 'What is the real demand for owner-occupation; in what circum-stances do people prefer to rent; what is the scope for co-operative ownership; what kinds of tenure best serve the country's economic needs, facilitating mobility of labour? Far too little research has been done into these questions; yet the answers are vital to housing policy.'

No academic—least of all the present writer—would argue against the need for more research. The need for this is embarrassingly obvious. But answers to one set of questions frequently raise further sets of questions—questions relating to administrative procedures and structures, to the tax situation, to the social security system, to the organization of the market for housing finance, for example. Some of the relevant issues are commented upon in the final chapter of this book. Here it is sufficient to note that after nearly half a century of 'housing policies' a radical reassessment is being set in motion. This reassessment may have social, economic and admini-strative implications far wider than is currently anticipated. If this view is correct the housing policies of the 1970s may look very differ-ent from those of today.

REFERENCES AND FURTHER READING

[1] Ashworth, W., *The Genesis of Modern British Town Planning*, Routledge, 1954.

[2] Association of County Sanitary Officers, *Second Interim Report on the Housing Survey in Rural Areas*, 1952.

[3] Bowley, M., *Housing and the State*, Allen and Unwin, 1944.

[4] Central Housing Advisory Committee, *Homes for Today and Tomorrow*, HMSO, 1961.

[5] Corfield, F. V., *Compensation and the Town and Country Planning Act, 1959*, Solicitors' Law Stationery Society, 1959 (Chapter I).

[6] Cullingworth, J. B., *Housing in Transition*, Heinemann, 1963.

[7] Cullingworth, J. B., *English Housing Trends*, Occasional Papers on Social Administration, No. 13, Bell, 1965.

[8] Department of Economic Affairs, *The National Plan*, Cmnd. 2764, HMSO, 1965.

[9] Donnison, D. V., *Housing Policy Since The War*, Occasional Papers on Social Administration, No. 1, Codicote Press, Welwyn, 1960.

[10] Donnison, D. V., Cockburn, C., and Corlett, T., *Housing Since The Rent Act*, Occasional Papers on Social Administration, No. 3, Codicote Press, Welwyn, 1961.

[11] Elsas, M. J., *Housing Before the War and After*, Staples, second edition, 1945.

[12] Frazer, W. M., *History of English Public Health*, Bailliere, Tindall and Cox, 1950.

[13] Gray, P. G., and Parr, E., *Rent Act 1957: Report of Inquiry*, Cmnd. 1246, HMSO, 1960.

[14] Gray, P. G., and Russell, R., *The Housing Situation in 1960*, The Social Survey, Central Office of Information, 1962.

[15] Institute of Municipal Treasurers and Accountants, *Housing Statistics*, Annual since 1949–50.

[16] Jarmain, J. R., *Housing Subsidies and Rents*, Stevens, 1948.

[17] Labour Party, *The Welfare State*, Discussion Pamphlet, 1952.

[18] Local Government Boards for England and Wales, and Scotland, *Report of the Committee on the Provision of Dwellings for the Working Classes* (Tudor Walters Report), Cd. 9191, HMSO, 1918.

[19] Lydall, H. F., *British Incomes and Savings*, Blackwell, 1955.

[20] MacColl, J., *Policy for Housing*, Fabian Society, 1954.

[21] Mackintosh, J. M., *Trends of Opinion about the Public Heath, 1901–1951*, Oxford University Press, 1953.

[22] Ministry of Health, *Final Reports of the Departmental Committee on the Increase of Rent and Mortgage Interest (Restrictions) Act, 1920* (Onslow Report), Cmd. 1803, HMSO, 1923.

[23] Ministry of Health, *Report of the Inter-Departmental Committee on the Rent Restrictions Acts* (Marley Report), Cmd. 3911, HMSO, 1931.

[24] Ministry of Health, *Reports of the Inter-Departmental Committee on the Rent Restrictions Acts* (first Ridley Report), Cmd. 5621, HMSO, 1937.

[25] Ministry of Health, *Report of the Inter-Departmental Committee on Rent Control* (second Ridley Report), Cmd. 6621, HMSO, 1945.

[26] Ministry of Health, *Circular No. 90/49*, 'Housing Act, 1949', HMSO, 1949.

[27] Ministry of Housing and Local Government, *Circular No. 38/51*, 'Housing Standards', HMSO, 1951.

[28] Ministry of Housing and Local Government, *Circular No. 70/51*, 'New House Designs—1952 Programme', HMSO, 1951.

[29] Ministry of Housing and Local Government, *Report of the Committee of Inquiry on the Cost of House Maintenance*, HMSO, 1953.

[30] Ministry of Housing and Local Government, *Houses: The Next Step*, Cmd. 8996, HMSO, 1953.

[31] Ministry of Housing and Local Government, *Circular No. 54/53*, 'Houses 1953', HMSO, 1953.

[32] Ministry of Housing and Local Government, *Housing in England and Wales*, Cmnd. 1290, HMSO, 1961.

[33] Ministry of Housing and Local Government, *Housing*, Cmnd. 2050, HMSO, 1963.

[34] Ministry of Housing and Local Government, *Report of the Committee on Housing in Greater London* (Milner Holland Report), Cmnd. 2605, HMSO, 1965.

[35] Ministry of Housing and Local Government, *Circular No. 21/65*, 'Housing', HMSO, 1965.

[36] Ministry of Housing and Local Government, *The Housing Programme 1965 to 1970*, Cmnd. 2838, HMSO, 1965.

[37] Ministry of Labour and National Service, *Report of an Enquiry into Household Expenditure in 1953–54*, HMSO, 1957.

[38] Ministry of Land and Natural Resources, *The Land Commission*, Cmnd. 2771, HMSO, 1965.

[39] Ministry of Reconstruction, *Housing*, Cmnd. 6609, HMSO, 1945.

[40] Mowat, C. L., *Britain Between The Wars, 1918–1940*, Methuen, 1955.

[41] Munby, D. L., *The Rent Problem*, Fabian Society, 1952.

[42] National Federation of Property Owners, 'Twelve Point Memorandum to Mr Bevan', *Property*, August 1950.

[43] National Federation of Property Owners, *Plan for Rent Reform*, 1955.

[44] Nevin, E., *The Mechanism of Cheap Money*, University of Wales Press, 1955.

[45] Political and Economic Planning, 'Rent Control Policy', *Planning*, Vol. XVI, No. 305, November 7, 1949.

[46] Rosenberg, N., *Economic Planning in the British Building Industry*, University of Pennsylvania Press, 1960.

[47] Royal Institution of Chartered Surveyors, *A Memorandum on Rent Restrictions and the Repair Problem*, 1951.

[48] Sabatino, R. A., *Housing in Great Britain*, Southern Methodist University Press, Dallas, 1956.

[49] Sanitary Inspectors' Association, *The Effect of Rent Restrictions on the Repair of Dwelling Houses*, 1951.

[50] Sanitary Inspectors' Association, *An Enquiry into the Repair of Dwelling Houses*, 1953.

[51] Simon, E. D., *How to Abolish the Slums*, Longmans, 1929.

[52] Umrath, H., 'Rent Policy in Western Europe,' *International Labour Review*, Vol. LXVIII, No. 3, September 1953.

[53] Youngson, A. J., *The British Economy 1920–1957*, Allen and Unwin, 1960.

CHAPTER II

The Administrative Framework

LOCAL AND CENTRAL GOVERNMENT

LOCAL AUTHORITIES ARE not agents of the central government.*
They are popularly elected, legally independent bodies with independent powers of taxation. Nevertheless they are by no means completely autonomous bodies. Though they have a wide measure of
freedom to determine how they shall interpret and operate the
powers entrusted to them, they are subject to several types of con-
straint. In the first place they are 'creatures of statute': they can do
only those things for which they have specific authority in Acts of
Parliament. In legal phraseology they must act *intra vires*. This is a
very real limitation on their powers: it can affect not merely major
issues (such as whether or not they can purchase land in advance of
their requirements) but also the precise way in which they carry out
their functions. Thus the procedures laid down for the exercise of
powers relating, for example, to the compulsory acquisition of land
must be precisely followed: otherwise those aggrieved may have the
right of appeal to the courts. Such a right of appeal exists even if the
action of the local authority has been approved by the Minister.
Similarly in condemning unfit houses the legal requirements must be
observed: a local authority cannot condemn houses just as they
please.

The justification for many of the constraints of this nature is, of
course, simply that personal and property rights of individuals are
involved, and that individuals may need protection against arbitrary
actions of public authorities just as they do against private companies. The fact that local authorities are charged with acting in the
public interest (morally if not statutorily) does not mean that they
are immune from the dangers of an over-zealous interpretation of
their role or an inadequate consideration of the rights of individuals.

* For a more extended discussion and a short historical account of the development of local government, see *Hart's Introduction to the Law of Local Government
and Administration*, Butterworth, seventh edition, 1962. See also W. A. Robson,
The Development of Local Government, Allen and Unwin, third edition, 1954,
Part II.

Secondly, many of the actions of local authorities require approval by a central government department: for housing and town planning the department concerned is the Ministry of Housing and Local Government. Some of these controls are *quasi-judicial*: the Minister's role is to ensure that, within the framework of central government policy, a just and reasonable balance is being struck between the different interests concerned. The process is not, however, simply a judicial one. Decisions are taken not on the basis of legal rules as in a court of law. They involve the exercise of a wide discretion in the balancing of public and private interest within the framework of a 'policy'. Thus when the Minister holds an inquiry into a local authority's proposal to compulsorily acquire a piece of land he is concerned not only with the case put by the local authority and the 'objections' raised by the owners of the land, but also with the general policy issues involved. These themselves may be conflicting—for instance the need to conserve green belt land while at the same time to make more land available for housing.

The Ministry's role in housing policy formulation is remarkably weak—as will be apparent from later discussion. They may 'encourage' local authorities to build more houses, to attain higher standards, to concentrate on the needs of particular categories of need, to charge 'reasonable' rents and so on. The local authorities, however, may see their local problems differently, or may interpret such concepts as 'need' and 'reasonable' in their own way. On the other hand, they may be in sympathy with the Ministry's exhortations but argue that they cannot comply with them because interest rates are too high or subsidies are too low. Special subsidies for particular types of building (such as one-bedroom houses) may be more effective, but they are difficult to devise on a national scale while at the same time meeting the differing needs of different areas.

The Ministry do, however, have formal powers of control over local authorities. Housing subsidies, for instance, are payable 'subject to such conditions as to records, certificates, audit or otherwise as the Minister may, with the approval of the Treasury, impose'. Furthermore, the Minister has power to reduce or discontinue subsidies where a local authority have 'failed to discharge any of the duties imposed on them' under the Housing Acts or have failed to observe any condition which was imposed on the granting of a subsidy. The Ministry's most powerful formal power flows from the requirement that all borrowing by a local authority must receive their prior approval. This 'loan sanction' provides a means whereby the central government can exercise an overall control over the total debt commitments of a local authority. The purpose of this is to ensure that the local authority are in a sufficiently sound financial position to undertake the loan and that too great a burden is not being placed on future generations of ratepayers. At the same time the total borrowing by local authorities can be controlled in the light of the national economic position. The control also enables the central department to check that the scheme for which the loan is required is one for which capital expenditure is properly applicable. For instance a local authority would not be allowed to raise a loan to meet a deficit on their housing revenue account: this should be met by increased rents or by a contribution from the rates. Though this is essentially a financial control the Ministry are also able to consider and, if necessary, amend the scheme for which the loan is required. Thus a proposal to build several blocks of multi-storey flats could be rejected on the grounds that the method of construction is unsatisfactory or that the amount of daylighting is inadequate.

In fact, however, the controls are not operated in this blunt way. The Ministry are reluctant to use a 'big stick' on local authorities: their position is not that of a headmaster in relation to an awkward schoolboy. Where difficulties are thought to be likely to arise local authority officials will have informal discussions with Ministry officials. This is particularly the case with costly developments such as high flats.[7] Such informal contacts can ease administrative procedures: at times they can resemble the striking of a bargain. The local authority are concerned to get approval for a development: the Ministry wish to speed the housing programme. A point conceded by one party puts them in a stronger bargaining position in relation to another point.[1] Head-on collisions are unusual: relationships are generally too gentlemanly to allow this to happen. And when they do occasionally arise the point is likely to be one of general principle on which the Local Authority Associations will (if they think the case is reasonable) take issue at a higher level. It should also not be forgotten that local authorities have in the local rates their own independent source of income: they can always finance (or threaten to finance) a scheme from revenue thus avoiding the need for Ministry approval. This is seldom done, but it remains a last-ditch way of asserting the local authority's position.

The administrative controls so far outlined are all concerned with preventing local authorities from carrying out proposals which they wish to undertake or from carrying them out in a particular way. There remains the opposite type of control: coercing a local authority into carrying out functions to which they are opposed. Apart from an order of *mandamus*, central departments have default powers under which they can take over functions which local authorities have a duty to carry out. Examples are extremely rare, but the Coventry case can be cited. In 1954 the Coventry City Council decided to disband its civil defence organization in protest against national defence policy. The Home Office transferred the City's civil defence functions to a body of three Commissioners, stopped the 75 per cent government grant, and charged the city for the whole cost of the service. The city council reconstituted its civil defence committee after one year. Mackenzie and Grove comment that this case 'suggests that the practical difficulties which face one body acting in default of another are almost insuperable unless (which is unlikely) the defaulting authority allows its officials to co-operate fully. On the other hand, the case also suggests that the financial weapon is almost certain to prevail in the long run.'[5]

So far as housing is concerned default powers over rural district councils rest in the first place with the county council. For other local authorities they rest with the Minister who may transfer the powers to himself or (except in the case of county boroughs) to the county council. These are draconian powers which are used only extremely rarely. The British system of government operates in a gentlemanly fashion. Central government departments may complain of the waywardness of individual authorities, just as local authorities may complain of the obtuseness and pedantry of ministries, but relationships are generally smooth even when they are not cordial. Though there are considerable reserves of power at the centre these are diffuse and are operated with care. Local authorities are not under the tutelage of a central Ministry of the Interior. They are not merely administrative agents; and the larger authorities in particular 'have built up local administrations that can properly be regarded as citadels of local power'. Though central government may lay down national policies, 'it is in the twists and emphases which councils give to central policies, and the degree of co-operation or unwillingness which they show, that their own power lies. They do not have the paper guarantees of local sovereignty which states in a federal system possess, but they have some of the reality of power which comes from being on the spot, knowing the special qualities and demands of the local people, and being costly and difficult to replace if the central government finds them unsatisfactory'.[6]

The power which local authorities have to raise money by levying rates on the occupiers of property in their areas is an important feature of the British local government system—one which distinguishes them from Public Corporations (and, in the field of housing, from the Housing Corporation and New Town Development Corporations). This is an extremely important power even though a very large proportion of the income of local authorities today comes from Exchequer grants. It provides a wide measure of autonomy in, for example, determining the rents of council houses. The central government may wish local housing authorities to raise their rents to a 'realistic level' and to provide subsidies only to such families as 'need' them, but local authorities which interpret their responsibilities in a way which runs counter to central policy are very difficult to influence. The ultimate control here rests with the local electorate. As will be shown in Chapter VII, council house rents are one of the few really political issues in the field of housing policy and to a large extent the political battle is in practice a local one, rather than one between central and local government. Had local authorities not had the power to subsidise rents from the rate fund (as is the case with New Town Development Corporations) the arena of controversy would have been different.

The factors which make for independence in local government are obviously important, but they should not be over-emphasised. In stressing that local authorities are not mere agents of the central government the danger is that one may suggest that they are more autonomous than they really are. Frequently the term 'partnership' is used to describe central-local relationships. This may imply rather more harmony than in reality exists, or can be hoped to exist, but it does highlight the fact that it is impossible to say who has 'the last word' and that it is not always the centre which leads while the locality 'follows'. (Indeed much of the political pressure for housing reforms have come from local rather than central government.)

THE STRESSES OF CHANGE

Yet the partnership can be broken, not by a show of force on one side, but by the establishment of new *ad hoc* administrative organizations. The stresses are already evident. There are now fourteen New Town Development Corporations in England and Wales, and a Commission for New Towns (responsible for the two towns of Crawley and Hemel Hempstead), already owning over 160,000 houses. Recent legislation has seen the establishment of a National Building Agency and a National Housing Corporation. The present Labour Government has further proposed the setting up of a National Land Commission. All these are responses to new and clamant needs which cannot be adequately met by a local government system which has remained basically the same since the 1880s. Outside the field of housing post-war trends have been even clearer and illustrate the basic conflict which can exist between, on the one hand, contemporary conceptions of a *uniformly* high standard of service and the technical needs of a service, and on the other hand, a system of truly *local* government. Thus hospitals, electricity and gas, for instance, have been transferred from local government to new organizations. Where an attempt has been made to adapt the existing local government structure to meet the needs of a particular service—as with National Parks, the result has not been conducive to rapid development.*

* See the author's *Town and Country Planning in England and Wales*, Allen and Unwin, 1964, Chapter 9.

Housing has traditionally been regarded as a local service and it may be considered unlikely that it should be taken away from local government. Nevertheless the relationship between housing and regional land use and economic planning, and the need to plan housing programmes on a large scale in order to obtain the benefits of industrialized building methods, underlines basic weaknesses in the existing structure.

The inadequacies of the present structure are to some degree recognized in the establishment of the Local Government Commission which is following a slow and tortuous procedure for re-shaping local government—but broadly on existing lines. By contrast a completely new local government system has been established for Greater London, following an inquiry by a Royal Commission.

These issues are raised here, not in order to enter into a polemic on local government, but to broaden the picture and to show first that local government is undergoing changes, and secondly, that where these changes are inadequate to meet the needs of the situation (and these may be technical, financial or political as well as purely administrative) frictions can lead, not to a realignment of forces between local and central government, but to the creation of administrative organs entirely outside the traditional arena of local government.* That this can happen in the field of housing is evidenced by developments in Scotland and Northern Ireland. In Scotland the Scottish Special Housing Association was established in 1937 to build houses in the 'depressed areas' (known at that time as 'Special Areas' and currently termed 'development districts'). Its powers have been gradually enlarged and today it owns some 50,000 houses. The Northern Ireland Housing Trust, established in 1945 to supplement the house building programmes of local authorities, has built about a quarter of Northern Ireland's post-war houses. Of course, the problems of local government in Scotland and Northern Ireland are in some ways different from those of English local government, but it should be noted that there is a government-sponsored housing organization in the North of England: the North Eastern Housing Association. This, like the Scottish Association, was set up under the 'Special Areas' legislation, but is still functioning and today owns some 17,000 houses. Suggestions have also been made for the establishment of a national housing authority which would provide houses throughout the country,[10] but though this does not appear to have been seriously considered at central government level, the importance which is attached to the development of housing societies and the establishment of a national Housing Corporation is a reflection on the inadequacy of local authority housing provision.

* See the spirited discussion of 'Local Government in Crisis' by W. A. Robson in *The Development of Local Government*, Allen and Unwin, third edition, 1954.

B

It is not only in the provision of houses that local authority housing functions are undergoing the stresses of change. There is considerable criticism of local authority rent policies, and proposals are now frequently made that some uniformity should be imposed. A family in a local authority three bedroom house may pay a rent ranging from 10s 2d and £7 13s 10d a week (exclusive of rates) depending on the local authority area in which they happen to live.[3] (In one area the rent can be reduced to nil by the operation of a rent rebate scheme.) Central government policies have been directed towards persuading local authorities to adopt 'realistic' rent policies and recent legislation has been designed with the same objective in view.*

Probably of less importance to local government (but nevertheless illustrative of the trends) is the transference of the power of making building regulations from local authorities to the central government. Though local authorities will still be responsible for enforcing the building regulations these will now be nationally determined and will take the place of the 1,400 sets of building by-laws which were previously in operation.†

It is thus clear that the role of local housing authorities is undergoing changes. The changes are gradual and piecemeal, but over a period of time they can become of great importance. The recent trend towards regionalism in economic and physical planning (and the recent establishment of regional planning boards and councils) may accelerate these changes and result in a reduced role for local government (or at least for unreformed local government). Of course local government in modern times is permanently in a period of transition, and what one writer regards as a 'crisis' may be looked upon by another as a 'reform'. And—to provide a measure of balance to the foregoing account—local government has gained as well as lost functions during the post-war period. In housing as well as in such services as education and local health, the functions of local authorities today are far greater than they were before the war. The flow of new legislation has been incessant—with an average of one *major* Housing Act every two years. Local housing authorities now operate on a vast scale. The demolition of over 250,000 slums and the erection of 2,500,000 new houses since the war is no mean achievement. Local housing authorities are currently investing over £300 million a year in new housing; they already own a quarter of the country's houses; they have given grant aid for the improvement of over 750,000 old dwellings. These are only the more obvious of their housing activities.

* See Chapter VII.
† See Chapter VI.

LOCAL HOUSING AUTHORITIES

Local housing authorities in England and Wales are distinguished by their multiplicity and their vast differences in size. Outside London all county boroughs and the three types of county districts—municipal (or 'non-county') boroughs, urban districts and rural districts—are housing authorities. In total these number nearly 1,400. They range in size from 610 (Newcastle Emlyn RD) to over a million (Birmingham CB). The position in Greater London has recently been changed by the London Government Act of 1963 (which came fully into force on April 1, 1965). This is a very large area (of 616 square miles) with a population close on eight million. In place of eighty-five local authorities of various types, thirty-two 'London Boroughs' have been set up: these are all-purpose housing authorities within their areas. However, the Greater London Council (a unique body) has certain housing functions which are, in general, supplementary to those of the London Boroughs.

Thus (ignoring parish councils) all local authorities other than county councils are housing authorities. However, county councils do have certain housing powers, for instance in connection with providing accommodation for employees, making advances for house purchase, and assisting housing associations. Hence all the 1,500 local authorities in England and Wales have some housing responsibilities. Before outlining these powers it is clearly desirable to give a general sketch of the way in which the country is divided between this very large number of authorities.

LOCAL GOVERNMENT OUTSIDE LONDON

Outside London, England and Wales is divided for local government purposes into county boroughs and administrative counties. County boroughs are 'all-purpose authorities: they are generally responsible for all local government functions in their areas. In the administrative counties, on the other hand, there is a two-tier system. The counties are responsible for major functions such as education, health and town planning, while the constituent districts (municipal boroughs, urban and rural districts) are responsible for housing, parks, sanitation, cemeteries and burial grounds, refuse disposal, and so forth. For many services, however, the division of functions is not as tidy as this suggests. In the first place larger districts frequently operate delegated powers over part of such services as town and country planning and education. Secondly, counties have certain functions which complement, supplement or overlap those of the districts. There are some differences between the three types of county districts, which can be ignored for our purposes. Mention should, however, be made of a third tier of authorities in rural districts. These are the parishes. Though they have only minor functions (in relation, for example, to footpaths, allotments, baths and washhouses) they can receive delegated powers from the rural district in whose area they are situated. In such a case the parish acts as the agent of the rural district.

Thus there are two quite distinct local government structures. In county boroughs the system is a unitary one, while in the administrative counties powers are divided between two or (in rural districts) three types of local authority.

LOCAL GOVERNMENT IN GREATER LONDON*

Local Government in Greater London is organized differently from that in any other area.[4] The Greater London Council are responsible for certain functions over the whole of the area. They are not, however, a county council: indeed they have fewer powers than a county. Nevertheless their responsibilities are wide and, particularly in view of their enormous area, very important. Ignoring certain transitional provisions relating to education, their main powers are in relation to main roads (termed 'metropolitan roads'), main sewers and principal sewage disposal works, refuse disposal, traffic control and vehicle licensing, fire and ambulance services, and research, housing and planning. So far as planning is concerned the GLC are responsible for the development plan for the whole area and for certain types of planning control. Housing is the main responsibility of the London Boroughs but the GLC are the authority for overspill housing, for maintaining records of housing applications and for providing facilities for the exchange of houses. The position concerning the provision of housing in Greater London is complicated by transitional arrangements; the intention is to restrict this to the London Boroughs (and to transfer all existing council housing to them), but to allow the GLC to assist the Boroughs on large-scale redevelopment schemes.

The GLC are thus responsible for those services which require organizing over the whole area. The Boroughs are much more 'local' authorities. Their powers are greater than those of any provincial district, though somewhat less than those of a county borough.

London local government differs from that in a geographical county such as Lancashire in that the distinction between districts and county boroughs has been abolished and the GLC have functions which can be satisfactorily administered only over a large area. (By contrast Lancashire, with a population in the geographical county of over five million, is divided first into seventeen completely inde-

* See also Chapter III, p. 85 *et. seq.*

pendent county boroughs and then into an administrative county (of 2¼ million inhabitants) and 109 districts.)

The London Boroughs range in population from 146,000 to 341,000. Only six provincial county boroughs are bigger than the largest. More striking, only twenty-nine county boroughs exceed the size of the smallest. (The City Corporation, with a population of 4,580, is insignificant in size; its special position is due to its history and wealth—and, some would say, its political sway with the Government which passed the London Government Act.)

HOUSES OWNED BY LOCAL AUTHORITIES

Nearly a quarter of the country's total stock of houses is owned by local authorities, but the proportion varies greatly between different areas. In absolute numbers the range is from less than 100 to over 250,000. The Greater London Council (previously the London County Council) are by far the largest housing authority in the country with 237,000 houses. Birmingham is second with 166,000, of which 36,000 are old houses bought for repairing to a minimum standard prior to demolition.

At the other extreme are many small (and some not so small) urban and rural districts with less than 100 council houses. Newcastle Emlyn Urban District (population 610) with twelve council houses appears to have the lowest number.

Tow Law is the only authority in the country with no council houses at all. But in fact there are 164 houses in this area which are indistinguishable from normal 'council houses': these have been built by the North Eastern Housing Association—a government-sponsored agency established before the war to assist housing authorities in depressed areas.

Generally speaking the authorities with a large number of council houses have equivalently large building programmes. London again leads with over 13,000 houses under construction at March 31, 1965. All the cities with over 50,000 council houses (and populations around or over 500,000) had over 3,000 council houses under construction. The building programmes of small authorities tend to be rather erratic, and nearly a quarter had no houses under construction. Newcastle Emlyn had thirty-six: so it will lose its place at the bottom of the 'table' to Broadwoodwidger!

These figures serve to underline the enormous differences which exist between different local housing authorities. This needs to be continually borne in mind when policies, practices and programmes are discussed in later chapters. What applies to London will not necessarily have any relevance at all for Broadwoodwidger.

TABLE 5: *Houses Owned by Selected Local Authorities, 1964*

	Population June 1963	Houses completed March 31, 1945, and before	Houses completed April 1, 1945, to March 31, 1964	Houses Acquired	Total	Houses under construction March 31, 1965
London County Council	3,178,870	103,223	119,068	14,881	237,172	13,318
Birmingham CB	1,115,630	84,667	45,222	36,429	166,318	4,578
Liverpool CB	739,740	40,822	40,461	1,195	82,478	3,264
Manchester CB	654,670	32,712	33,332	1,088	67,132	3,049
Sheffield CB	495,290	30,773	27,421	2,247	60,441	3,730
Leeds CB	513,800	24,298	28,108	3,694	56,100	3,012
Bristol CB	433,920	16,179	26,244	1,945	44,368	1,220
Crewe MB	53,180	1,983	3,271	121	5,375	72
Dover MB	36,180	1,098	1,946	179	3,223	46
Rhondda MB	100,100	330	2,465	170	2,965	98
Stratford-upon-Avon MB	17,040	404	714	2	1,120	25
Billingham UD	32,850	1,172	3,794	122	5,088	116
Fulwood UD	17,280	—	141	1	142	—
Newcastle Emlyn UD	610	—	12	—	12	36
Rotherham RD	62,380	2,507	4,100	440	7,047	144
Aysgarth RD	3,230	—	66	—	66	—
Broadwoodwidger RD	2,030	2	38	—	40	—
Tow Law UD	2,920	—	—	—	—	—

Source: Institute of Municipal Treasurers and Accountants, *Housing Statistics (England and Wales) 1963–64.*

REFERENCES AND FURTHER READING

[1] Donnison, D. V., Chapman, V., and others, *Social Policy and Administration*, Allen and Unwin, 1965, Chapter 9, 'High Flats in Finsbury'.

[2] Hart, W. O., *Hart's Introduction to the Law of Local Government and Administration*, Butterworth, seventh edition, 1962.

[3] Institute of Municipal Treasurers and Accountants, *Housing Statistics* (Annual).

[4] Jackson, W. E., *The London Government Act, 1963*, Butterworth, 1963.

[5] Mackenzie, W. J. M., and Grove, J. W., *Central Administration in Britain*, Longmans, 1957.

[6] Miller, B., 'Citadels of Local Power', *The Twentieth Century*, Vol. 162, October 1957.

[7] Ministry of Housing and Local Government, *Circular No. 61/58*, 'Flats and Houses 1958: Design and Economy'.

[8] Ministry of Housing and Local Government, *Housing Return: Appendix*, HMSO (Quarterly).

[9] Robson, W. A., *The Development of Local Government*, Allen and Unwin, third edition, 1954.

[10] Socialist Commentary, 'The Face of Britain—A Policy for Town and Country Planning', *Socialist Commentary*, September 1961.

CHAPTER III

Local Authority Housing Administration

LOCAL AUTHORITIES VARY enormously in the scale of their housing activities and it is therefore not surprising to find that administrative organizations and procedures vary also. But in fact administrative structures do not simply reflect the scale of operation. Many other factors are relevant, including history, the balance of power between different committees and different officers, and even political or personal accidents.

At the outset it is important to appreciate how 'housing' differs from many other local government services. In the first place it covers a wide miscellany of activities, all of which impinge upon, and sometimes are actually part of the work of other services. Even an incomplete list underlines the point—housing design, house building, housing repairs and maintenance, council house rents, housing management and 'welfare', improvement of old property, control of houses in multiple occupation, slum clearance, loans for house purchase, and so forth. Even if all these were the responsibility of one Housing Department and one Housing Committee, it is obvious that they would have to be co-ordinated or linked in some way with the work of other Departments and Committees, particularly Finance, Health and Planning. And it is equally clear that 'housing' may be organized as part of the Architect's or Engineer's departments, or even be split between several departments—the department of the Architect for design, the Engineer for maintenance, the Treasurer for rent collection, the Clerk for house purchase loans, and the Medical Officer of Health for improvement and slum clearance.

Secondly, while local authorities are statutorily obliged to appoint, for example, a Clerk, a Treasurer, a Medical Officer of Health, a Public Health Inspector and (except in rural districts) a Surveyor, there is no such obligation to appoint a Housing Manager. Similarly though education, health and children's authorities (i.e. counties and county boroughs) are required by law to appoint Committees for these functions there is no such requirement to appoint a Housing Committee.

Thirdly, not only do housing authorities vary in size (both of their population and of their ownership of houses), they also vary greatly in the character of their housing problems. Bournemouth and Salford have similar populations (around 150,000) but while the former has no slums, Salford has 18,000. Furthermore, as Elizabeth Layton has nicely put it, 'towns which have high architectural traditions to uphold and where the influence of historic buildings is strong are likely to stress the responsibilities of the Planning Officer and the Architect. Towns under the pall of industrial grime may have few aesthetic standards by which to judge their buildings and so pressing a need for more sanitary dwellings as to make the architectural merits of their work seem less important'.[7] It might be added that things do not always work out this way. 'Coketown' may be so aware of its environmental shortcomings as to give high priority to architecture, while 'Cathedral City' may be so sleepy as not to realize what is happening on its periphery and in its redevelopment areas.

All these factors are clearly important in determining administrative structures. And there are others which in practice may be crucial. Probably the most important of these is the historical development of local government services. Public health and civil engineering were early established as important local government functions. When the provision of working-class housing developed it was frequently just added to the responsibilities of existing well-established departments. (Many local authorities regarded the employment of architects as a luxury to be reserved for monumental civic buildings, and a quite unnecessary expense in connection with 'houses for the workers'—an attitude which has taken a long while to die.) With the expansion of house building in the inter-war years the number of architects employed by local authorities increased, but these remained generally in the department of the Engineer.

'Housing management' grew gradually, but even by the outbreak of the second war only about a fifth of local authorities had appointed housing managers—and many of these worked in the department of another chief officer. Most authorities managed their houses through the departments of the clerk, treasurer, medical officer, engineer and surveyor—either separately or in combination. Discussion on the desirability of establishing separate housing departments was confused by the existence of two professional bodies—the Society of Women Housing Managers and the Institute of Housing—the former of which stressed the social side of management, while the latter held that social service should be kept entirely separate from property management.

The end of the second war and the great expansion in civil engineering works, school building and house building saw the establishment of an increasing number of separate Architect's Departments, whose responsibilities included house building. The number of separate departments concerned with housing management also increased but, at the time of writing, though most county boroughs have such departments the majority of district councils do not.

As with the Architect's Department, Housing Departments can thus be established only if some functions are taken away from an existing department. But whereas the functions of the Architect are clear cut—to design houses—those of the housing manager are far less so. Should he deal only with housing applications and rent collection, or additionally with reporting and execution of repairs? What 'welfare' functions should he have and how should these relate to those of the Welfare Officer? What part should he play in assessing local needs and advising on the scale and character of building programmes? There is no obvious and simple answer to these questions and thus there is always a good case to be made for preserving that *status quo* or for allowing local factors and personalities to decide.

It follows that it is not a straightforward matter to give an account of local authority housing administration: practice varies far too widely. Nevertheless certain patterns do emerge and these can usefully be discussed. What follows is a summary of the latest official review of housing management and a description of the organization in several highly contrasted local authorities.

HOUSING MANAGEMENT: THE 'OFFICIAL' VIEW

The Ministry of Housing has no control over the way in which local authorities manage their houses: this is entirely a local responsibility. Nor are the Ministry at all keen to involve themselves in this field: they prefer to restrict themselves to the giving of advice. Even this is done largely through the medium of an advisory body—the Central Housing Advisory Committee (on which local authorities are well represented). This Committee has issued a number of reports on housing management of which five cover special issues such as the selection of tenants or the problems involved in moving families from slum houses—topics which are discussed in other chapters. Three reports, issued in 1938, 1945 and 1959, deal with wider issues of administrative organization. To compare these reports is to see how far social conditions have changed over a twenty-year period. The 1938 report[1] discusses such 'problems of housing management' as the prevention of bed-bugs and assisting necessitous tenants to obtain furniture—'the bare necessities of comfort at a price within his means'. Though it rejected the argument that council tenants would use their baths for storing coal it held that good management involved a form of social education and should aim at 'teaching a new and inexperienced community to be housing minded'. The 1959 report,[5] on the other hand, stressed that local authority dwellings 'represent a considerable part of the nation's wealth, and that it is the responsibility of local authorities to treat their management as an important business enterprise which must be conducted with due attention to the financial as well as to personal aspects'. Housing management has thus developed from a social service for necessitous working-class families to a major enterprise catering for a quarter of the population. In its broad sense it includes the planning and building of houses, the selection of tenants, the fixing and collecting of rents, the maintenance of estates and the repair of houses, together with a rather vaguer responsibility for the 'welfare' of tenants.

The Committee did not examine committee structures in detail but were firmly of the opinion that management should be the responsibility of a major committee and that, with the possible exception of the largest authorities, there were distinct advantages in bringing both the building and the management of housing estates under the care of the same committee. The argument here is that housing affairs are closely inter-related: if building and management are separated those responsible for new building may lose the benefit of the experience gained in managing existing estates. The danger, however, is that a single committee may become overburdened. The normal practice, however, is for the full committee to be responsible only for issues of broad policy. Matters of detail are generally delegated to smaller sub-committees. Thus a large authority might have sub-committees on allocation of tenancies, staffing and staff training, selection of sites, and so forth. In small authorities, on the other hand, the full housing committee might be responsible for everything —from the preparation of house-building programmes to the consideration of a tenant's application for a transfer.

Obviously daunted by the great number of local housing authorities, the CHAC inquiry did not attempt to discover the departmental organization in all areas. They contented themselves with an analysis of fifty-four authorities which were 'broadly representative of the different parts of the country'—together with three New Town Development Corporations. The fifty-seven departmental organizations proved classifiable into four categories:

Type of Departmental Organization	*No. of Authorities*
Housing manager in charge of a separate department, directly responsible to the housing committee for all or most aspects of management	27

Housing manager in charge of a separate section of a department, responsible under the control of another officer for all or most aspects of management   11

Housing manager not in charge of a separate department or section of a department, and responsible under another officer for part of the work only   8

No housing manager, but each of the chief officers dealing separately with that part of management most closely related to his principal function   11

The forty-six authorities with housing managers allotted varying combinations of functions to them. Nearly all dealt with applications and lettings, general estate supervision and 'housing welfare', but less than half were responsible for carrying out repairs.

Responsibilities of Housing Manager	No. of Authorities
Applications	45
Lettings	43
Rent Collection	30
Ordering Repairs	36
Executing Repairs	18
Supervision of Estates	45
Housing Welfare	42

The weight of evidence submitted to the Committee favoured the principle of a separate department, with responsibility for all the functions of management, under the direction of one suitably qualified officer. The Committee accepted this argument on the grounds that the various management functions are closely interdependent, that only with full co-ordination under a single head can the best results be achieved, and overlapping, duplication or neglect of detail be avoided. It also has the advantage that the tenant has *one* main link with his municipal landlord, instead of a number of contacts with different departments responsible for different functions.

With small housing authorities, however, it may be quite impracticable and uneconomic to establish a separate housing department. In such cases the Committee recommended a division between 'personal' and 'structural' functions. 'Personal' functions include the investigation of applications and the assessment of housing need, lettings, transfers and exchanges; the collection of rents; receiving requests for repairs; and general tenancy problems. 'Structural' functions are concerned with the carrying out of maintenance and repairs to buildings. A division along these lines gives the housing manager responsibility for all those matters which bring landlord and tenant in contact with each other, while leaving the council's engineer or surveyor with the task of maintaining the estates.

When this advice was 'commended' to local authorities by the Ministry they were not asked to report on the result of any review of management which followed. It is therefore difficult to summarize the present position. A recent circular[10] has, however, requested detailed information on management. When this is available it will be possible to give a fuller picture. In the meantime it may be noted that administrative arrangements still vary very widely. For example, there are still a few county boroughs which have not appointed a housing manager and where the work is usually undertaken by the treasurer or the surveyor; in one county borough the offices of housing manager and welfare director are combined. The majority of county boroughs have specialized housing managers, but these include cases in which the duties assigned to the housing manager are restricted and do not conform to the recommendations of the CHAC. Amongst smaller authorities the numbers without officers designated as housing managers is greater. Thus less than half the municipal boroughs list a housing manager among their principal officers. Among the remainder and the urban and rural district councils the responsibility for management usually rests with the treasurer, the surveyor or in some cases the chief public health inspector. A qualified housing manager may head a department or section under one or other of these officers, but in many cases the duties are somewhat restricted.

A short description of the administrative organization of several local housing authorities is given at the end of this chapter. First, however, it is useful to dwell a little further on the various aspects of housing management.

ASPECTS OF MANAGEMENT

Selection of Tenants

An account of the various policies followed and methods used by local authorities in selecting tenants, together with a sketch of the types of families living in council houses, is given in Chapter V. Here we are concerned solely with administrative issues.

When examining the practices of local authorities in selecting tenants one is immediately struck by the wide differences. At one extreme there are the authorities where the full Housing Committee or, more commonly, a sub-committee actually decides which individual families shall be selected for the houses available at any given time (sometimes after interviewing the applicants). In some areas this is done by a separate sub-committee for each ward or parish, or group of wards or parishes in the area. At the other extreme there are the authorities who lay down a policy of selection and delegate to their officers the business of determining the order in which individual applicants are housed: only exceptional cases which cannot easily be dealt with along pre-determined lines come to the attention of the Committee.

The former practice, though adversely commented upon in the reports of the Central Housing Advisory Committee, is strongly adhered to in certain small authorities, particularly in rural areas where individual councillors may regard the selection of tenants for houses in their part of the district as one of their most important functions. In some rural districts selection of tenants has even been delegated to the parish council.* The argument here is that parish councils are elected specifically to look after the affairs of the parish and that this principle would, in effect, be abandoned if the more remote (a favourite word!) district council were responsible for tenant selection over the district as a whole.

The argument against practices such as these had traditionally been that too much weight may be attached to local interests and too little to the wider needs of the area as a whole. Thus an applicant who has lived in the area for many years may be given preference over one who, though in greater housing need, is a relative newcomer. Or local residents may be given undue preference over 'foreigners' from other parishes who may need to move, or wish to move, into the parish for employment or personal reasons. The danger of undesirable pressure on councillors and, at the worst, downright corruption, are obvious; and even if this is in practice not a danger or is adequately guarded against, the suspicion that selection procedures are not scrupulously fair is hard to allay. Justice must not only be done: it must be seen to be done. Nevertheless the practice still remains and where it is entrenched in tradition it is difficult to change.

More commonly, even when councillors themselves select tenants, such great emphasis is laid on the principle of impartiality that applications are dealt with under a code number: councillors then cannot (usually) know which particular families they are considering. It should be added that this practice is generally welcomed by councillors: it gives them good protection against the entreaties (and worse) of individual applicants. This is particularly desirable in areas with acute housing shortages where there are many competing claims for the available council housing.

The preservation of anonymity in dealing with housing applicants does not, of course, affect the right—indeed, some would say, the duty—of a councillor to investigate a *prima facie* reasonable complaint from an applicant that he is not getting fair consideration.

Essential to all systems of selection—and, as Chapter V demon-

* See the example of Easington Rural District, p. 101 below.

strates, there are an incredible number of different systems, some of remarkable ingenuity and hence incomprehensibility—is public confidence in their fairness. It follows that there should be adequate explanation and publicity. Some local authorities publish a leaflet outlining their selection procedure, though these are not always the model of clarity which they ought to be. The 1949 CHAC Report[3] recommended that applicants who could not be satisfied in any other way that their case had had fair consideration should be given the opportunity of explaining their grievance to a committee or subcommittee of the council. It is doubtful whether many authorities would look kindly on a proposal of this nature.

Irrespective of the way in which tenants are selected a considerable amount of preliminary work by officials is usually necessary—in receiving applications, investigating the housing conditions of applicants, assessing 'need' (often the basis of a 'points' scheme, under which weights are given to defined categories of need), and, where there is a procedure for committee selection, preparing shortlists for a final decision.

Visiting of applicants is usually carried out by a housing officer, but practice varies and is sometimes done by, for example, public health inspectors. Some authorities arrange a visit shortly after an application is received. Whether or not this is done, a visit is normally paid shortly before an offer of accommodation is to be made. The purpose of visiting is two-fold—first, to check the accuracy of the information given in the written application and to assess the degree of housing need; secondly, to assess the living standard of the family, their rent-paying capacity, and their wishes in relation to rehousing. The importance which is attached to various factors depends partly on the character of the local housing situation and partly on the policy of the local authority. A few go to great lengths to assist applicants to decide what type of house they should have; others have fixed rules. Some divide tenants into social groups according to their standard of living or rent-paying capacity and allocate them to appropriate estates.

When the time comes for a family to be housed most authorities provide some choice of district and—less frequently—of type of dwelling. It is usual, however, for the size of dwelling to be determined by the family composition. In urban areas, where density is high and building costly, applicants are seldom allowed a spare bedroom, except possibly in the case of a young family. Elsewhere, and particularly in rural districts, an extra bedroom is often allowed.

Transfers and Exchanges

Council house tenants move at about the same rate as owner-occupiers and tenants of private landlords—around 7 or 8 per cent a year. Many of these moves are from one council house to another. Technically a distinction is made between 'transfers' and 'exchanges'. A transfer is the movement of an existing tenant to another *vacant* house belonging to the same local authority. An exchange involves at least two families one of whom may be living in a house belonging to another local authority or a private landlord.

Transfers and exchanges are often encouraged by local authorities since they generally bring about a better use of council houses. This is particularly so in older estates where many three-bedroom houses are occupied by elderly couples or a widow. They also enable tenants to obtain a house which is more convenient for them in location or rent.

Exchanges are usually initiated by tenants themselves and are subject to the approval of the local authority. The administrative burden is thus small, even where a local authority maintains an 'exchange register'. Transfers, on the other hand, involve a considerable amount of work particularly for those authorities who follow a positive policy of encouraging 'overhoused' families to move to smaller accommodation. Most authorities maintain a waiting list of transfer applications and some investigate these in the same way as they do normal applications. The size of these transfer waiting lists can be very large and may include tenants who have not applied for a transfer but whom the council wish to move in order to make better use of the house. Transfer lists tend to be larger in areas where local authority estates are widely scattered or include a high proportion of flats (which are frequently unpopular among families with young children). A recent review in the area of the former Metropolitan Boroughs[9] showed that the proportion of existing tenants registered for a transfer varied from 5 to 20 per cent. Actual transfers in a two-year period ranged from less than 1 per cent to over 20 per cent of the total dwellings managed by local authorities. (Exchanges averaged 1·5 per cent each year.)

The attitude of local authorities to transfers and exchanges varies greatly. While some regard them as an important and positive management function there are others who feel that they are a confounded nuisance which merely adds to administrative costs. A full discussion of all the issues involved is to be found in the Central Housing Advisory Committee Report on *Transfers, Exchanges and Rents*.[4]

Repairs and Maintenance

As is explained in Chapter 7, a 'statutory repairs contribution' has to be paid in respect of every normal council house into a Housing Repairs Account. At present the minimum such 'contribution' is £8, but most authorities exceed this figure. Rising costs have forced local authorities to examine carefully their policy for repairs and maintenance and, in particular, to transfer more responsibilities to tenants. It has long been the practice in the north of England for tenants to have responsibility for internal decoration, while in the south it has been more common for this to be undertaken by the local authority. Increasing numbers of authorities are now following northern practice. A similar trend is noticeable in relation to minor internal repairs. All local authorities, however, assume responsibility for major internal repairs, most external repairs and external decoration.

External decoration is usually undertaken at regular intervals— commonly on a five-year cycle. Inspection of the condition of properties is also frequently carried out every three to five years, often when external painting is being done. All authorities additionally have some system for dealing with day-to-day repairs. Often these are reported by tenants to the rent collector. Repairs may be carried out by a works section of the housing department, by the direct labour department, or by the engineer or surveyor. Whatever the form of organization most local authorities use direct labour for at least part of their maintenance and repair work, though some rural district councils with widely scattered estates employ local building firms for all maintenance and repair work.

It is generally held—at least by housing managers—that maintenance work should be under the control of a housing department. Otherwise there is inadequate control of work or of its cost, uncertainty in the programming of work, and duplication of administration and expense. But of course not all local authorities have housing departments, and even some of those which do cannot (with their limited number of houses) justify the expense of two works departments—one for housing and one for other services.

There are, however, good arguments for having the engineer or (where there is one) the architect in charge of maintenance. Basically the point here is that the department which is responsible for design and building should also be responsible for subsequent maintenance. There is thus a 'feed back' of experience in the quality of materials and the advantages and disadvantages of different types of design, and the likelihood of greater concern for maintenance costs at the design stage.

Nevertheless others argue that day-to-day repairs at least are an essential part of housing management and are best dealt with by the department which has the closest relationship with tenants. Tenants naturally look to this department for the satisfaction of their demands for repairs—and, if they are not carried out satisfactorily and with reasonable speed it will be the housing manager who will be blamed, even if the matter is not in fact his responsibility. The 1959 report of the Central Housing Advisory Committee[5] recommended that in cases where the housing manager was not responsible for the

F

carrying out of repairs he should nevertheless be responsible for co-ordinating requests for day-to-day repairs, for recommending their priority, for indenting for the work to be done, and for following up to see that it is properly done in reasonable time.

The relative weight given to the various arguments varies with local circumstances, the scale of operations, existing departmental arrangements, and so forth. There is no ideal solution which will meet the situation in all areas.

What is clear, however, is that maintenance is far more than 'doing odd jobs'. It is of great importance—nationally as well as locally—in preserving the stock of dwellings and in ensuring that dwellings do not have to be replaced prematurely. It also covers the care of open spaces on estates and the surroundings of flats, and so can materially affect the appearance of estates and hence their standard and reputation. It is thus of importance in landlord-tenant relationships and must be regarded in part at least as an essential part of housing management. It requires skilled organisation with high-quality administration and cost-control.

Rent Collection
Rent collection is normally carried out either by the housing manager or the treasurer. Authorities who favour the latter argue that it is more economical and efficient to separate rent collection from other management functions which can then be carried out by specialist officers. The arguments in favour of rent collection being undertaken by the housing manager are that this constitutes the primary link between the landlord and the tenant, it enables good personal relations to build up, it enables the housing manager to keep in close touch with an estate and its problems, and it provides an easy and convenient route for the tenant (who naturally regards the person who collects the rent as the 'landlord's representative') to seek information on tenancy conditions, transfers, repairs and the like. It is also argued that this system is more economical in the long run: the housing official can report on at least the simpler repairs needed, thus saving a visit from the maintenance staff; he can answer enquiries on the spot thus saving the time of housing staff in interviewing or letter-writing—and the time of the tenant; he can carry out the necessary investigation on such matters as a request for a transfer or for an alteration to the house, thus avoiding the need for a special visit by another housing official.

The argument in terms of economy is difficult to evaluate and the situation may well differ in different areas. But the weight of evidence appears to be in favour of rent collection by housing officers. Practice varies but an increasing number of authorities combine rent collection with other management functions under the charge of the housing manager—whether he is in charge of a separate housing management department or a housing management section of another chief officer's department.

Curiously this is happening at the same time as another development which might eventually make the original justification irrelevant, namely changes in the method of rent payment. Weekly rent collection by collectors calling at the door was at one time the almost universal practice, but even in the 'thirties some authorities allowed (and sometimes encouraged) payment at a central office or at local offices situated on individual housing estates. The latter practice has increased markedly in recent years as a result both of social changes (with more married women going out to work and thus not being at home when the collector calls) and of attempts by local authorities to reduce their management costs. Some authorities allow tenants to pay by cheque, banker's order or credit transfer. All these methods are cheaper and also reduce security risks in the collection and transport of money.

Increasing numbers of authorities now collect (or 'receive') rents at fortnightly or longer intervals. Indeed less than half collect all their rents weekly. Contrary to what might be expected, fortnightly collections do not appear to have significantly increased rent arrears in spite of the fact that over a third of local authorities collect all their rents in this manner.

It is interesting to note how attitudes have changed in response to changing conditions over the last twenty years. The 1938 CHAC report on housing management[1] expressed its predominant concern in bringing tenants 'into more intimate touch' with their local authority and therefore recommended door to door collections as the best system. The 1959 report, on the other hand, urged local authorities to 'ensure that their practices keep abreast of developments' and recommended fortnightly collections; the longer term aim should be 'to win the tenants to co-operate in the payment of rent at longer intervals or by cheque or order'.

Some local authorities operate a system of 'rent free' weeks. This is a rather misleading term as any treasurer will quickly point out. What it really means is that annual rents are divided into forty-eight or fifty 'weeks', with no payments being required at, for example, Christmas, and Easter. The rent payments are, of course, slightly higher than would be the case with a fifty-two-week year, but there are fewer of them. The system has advantages both for the local authority and the tenants. It avoids the administrative difficulty of collecting rents at holiday periods (and the increase in arrears which frequently occurs at these times), and, for the tenant, brings about a form of compulsory saving which is appreciated—at least in the holiday weeks when the 'rent' can be spent on other things.

Housing Welfare

There has for long been argument as to the proper scope and organization of welfare in housing management. In the 'thirties this was institutionalized in the two professional organizations—the Society of Women Housing Managers and the Institute of Housing. The Society, commonly referred to as the 'Octavia Hill School', held that social service was an integral part of good housing management and that housing managers should therefore to some extent be social workers. The Institute maintained that housing management and social service were separate functions which should be dealt with by different departments. The extension of council housing in the last two decades, the rise in the general standard of living and the development of the social services have now settled this conflict. It is now generally held that, though local authorities as landlords are interested in the well-being of their tenants, the housing department should not be providing a 'secondary welfare service' for council tenants. Though contact and liaison with the social services may be desirable in relation to a small proportion of tenants, the housing department should in no way duplicate these other services. No better evidence of the *rapprochement* between the Society and the Institute could be given than their recent amalgamation as the Institute of Housing Managers.

Nevertheless 'welfare' remains a vague concept which is capable of varying interpretations. As with so many other aspects of local authority housing policy there is a wide range of different practices. Some authorities employ special officers to assist 'problem families' (the more up-to-date term is 'unsatisfactory tenants'), or old people. Others follow a positive policy of encouraging tenants' associations, arranging garden competitions and organizing or supervising social activities in community halls and club rooms. On the other hand, some authorities regard 'welfare' as covering only *problems* (such as those arising from neglect of property, infringement of tenancy conditions or serious friction between neighbouring tenants), or even simply such matters as routine explanations of council policy, the regulation of sub-letting and lodgers, the letting of garages, the granting of permission for tenants' 'improvements' or the erection of garden sheds, and so forth. Irrespective of the scope of 'welfare' it is obvious that it cannot easily be distinguished from general management work.

Some idea of the extent of the differences between authorities can be gained from a recent report which showed that in the former Metropolitan Boroughs the number of housing management staff per 1,000 dwellings ranged from 5·12 to 12·20.[9] The authority with the lowest ratio of staff had only 14 per cent of the average for all the Boroughs taken together, while the one with the highest ratio had 60 per cent above the average. These differing staff figures largely reflect the variety of views which prevail on the scope of 'welfare'.

Some particular problems—such as those of old people and 'unsatisfactory tenants'—are discussed in more detail in Chapter XII, together with other social issues.

HOUSING ADMINISTRATION IN SELECTED AREAS

It is clearly apparent from the account given in this chapter that there is no such thing as a 'typical' local housing authority. Nevertheless it is useful to describe the organization of a few selected authorities if only to show how the various functions described in this and other chapters 'fit together' at the local level.

The authorities which have been selected provide some indications of differing practices and policies. The Greater London Council is, of course, unique, both by virtue of its vast size and the scale of its housing operations—though this may change radically if and when the 'transitional arrangements' under the London Government Act of 1963 expire. Bristol and Leeds have been selected as examples of large local authorities which are noted for their progressive housing outlook though this should not be taken in any way as a reflection on similar authorities who could easily have been chosen instead—Birmingham, Manchester, Liverpool, Sheffield, to name but a few. Smaller authorities are much more difficult to choose and the choice of Easington and Leamington Spa can be none other than arbitrary.

No attempt has been made in these sketches to provide a comprehensive picture. Rather the object has been to highlight the main administrative structure and to draw attention to selected interesting points of detail. The accounts are based mainly on information supplied by Housing Managers.

THE GREATER LONDON COUNCIL*

The Greater London Council is the largest local authority and the largest public housing authority in the world. It has a population of eight million and owns 230,000 houses. It has an annual rent income of £25 million, receives nearly £6 million a year in Exchequer subsidies and spends a further £4 million on rate subsidies. As a local authority it is *sui generis*: it can be compared with no other. Furthermore it differs from other local authorities in that it does not have sole responsibility for housing within its area. This was the case before local government in the London area was reorganized. The former London County Council had concurrent housing powers with the

* This account is largely based on information kindly supplied by Mr J. P. Macey, Director of Housing, Greater London Council.

Metropolitan Boroughs. Under the new system, it is the Greater London Boroughs who are the primary housing authorities in their own areas. In the long run, the Greater London Council will have the following permanent housing powers and duties:

(a) To provide housing in connection with its powers to clear and redevelop comprehensive development areas.
(b) To provide houses for rehousing those displaced by the GLC in connection with any of its other functions such as roads, open spaces, etc. (This is in itself quite a sizeable task which may involve rehousing 3,000 families each year.)
(c) To provide housing for normal housing purposes (but the exercise of this power is subject to the consent of the London Borough in whose area it is proposed to provide the housing or, if that consent is withheld, to the consent of the Minister).
(d) To provide housing outside Greater London. This covers not only the provision in new and expanding towns but also the development of ordinary housing estates outside the GLC area.

The housing problem in some of the inner London Boroughs is much more acute than it is in the outer Boroughs and the Greater London Council has an important role to play in providing houses, both new and relets, to facilitate the redistribution of families in such a way as to relieve the pressure in the centre.

Eventually, some of the Greater London Council's housing estates may be transferred to the local London Borough Councils, but the official central government view is that it may take several years before it is possible to assess properly the size of the pool of houses which the GLC will need to own in order to carry out its permanent functions and also to deal with housing problems arising from the development of its other services.

At its inception, the GLC took over all the powers formerly exercized by the London County Council and it will retain these powers until dates to be determined by the Minister. It has already been made clear that the GLC will continue to deal with slum clearance areas for several years to come. In practice, the GLC and the various LBCs prepare their slum clearance programmes concurrently and agree as to which authority should deal with each particular clearance area.

The LCC had powers to make improvement grants to private owners but it used them very little. Under the transitional arrangements, these powers are likely to be terminated at an early date, but the GLC will have a permanent entitlement to receive contributions in respect of improvements made to dwellings in its own ownership and this applies also to the provision of standard amenities in its own dwellings. The LCC had concurrent powers to deal with houses in multiple occupation but this task now rests wholly with the Boroughs. The GLC's powers in this connection have, therefore, already been terminated. In the meantime it has taken over the London County Council's building programme and is responsible for administering the existing stock of housing.

Obviously only the briefest sketch can be given of this vast organization; and the reader must note that the future role of the GLC is not at all clear. How far a complete *de facto* transference of its powers will take place remains to be seen.

A separate Housing Department, under a chief officer designated as Director of Housing, was established in 1954. There is a Deputy Director and six Assistant Directors each in charge of a separate Branch—Management, Development, Construction, Maintenance, Administration and Establishment, and Finance.

Since the estates are spread over a vast area (some 40,000 houses are outside the GLC area) many management functions are carried out on a district basis. The estates are divided into ten districts, each being under the control of a District Officer. Each district is further divided into a number of areas (varying from three to seven) each with an Area Officer responsible for general estate management and collection of rents. Each area also has a maintenance team under a surveyor and foreman.

Management Branch

The Management Branch is responsible for advice on housing management, policy generally, for rehousing, lettings, movement of people to new and expanding towns, and management of hostels. The local application of these functions is carried out at District and Area Offices.

The responsibility for dealing with homeless families and for operating the waiting list of ordinary applicants now rests with each individual LBC. The waiting list formerly kept by the LCC has been divided among the various LBCs under agreed arrangements. The GLC has the power to require the LBCs to furnish statistics as to the number of applicants on its waiting lists and other information in order to enable it to keep the housing situation in Greater London under continuous review.

The allocation of houses to waiting list applicants will continue during 1965 and 1966 in order to meet certain promises made to individual families by the LCC. After that, waiting list work will be replaced by an extensive system of letting houses to families nominated by the various London Boroughs. This will assist the latter with the rehousing of families from slum clearance and other housing operations, as well as with the housing of families from their waiting list.

The Housing Department of the Greater London Council

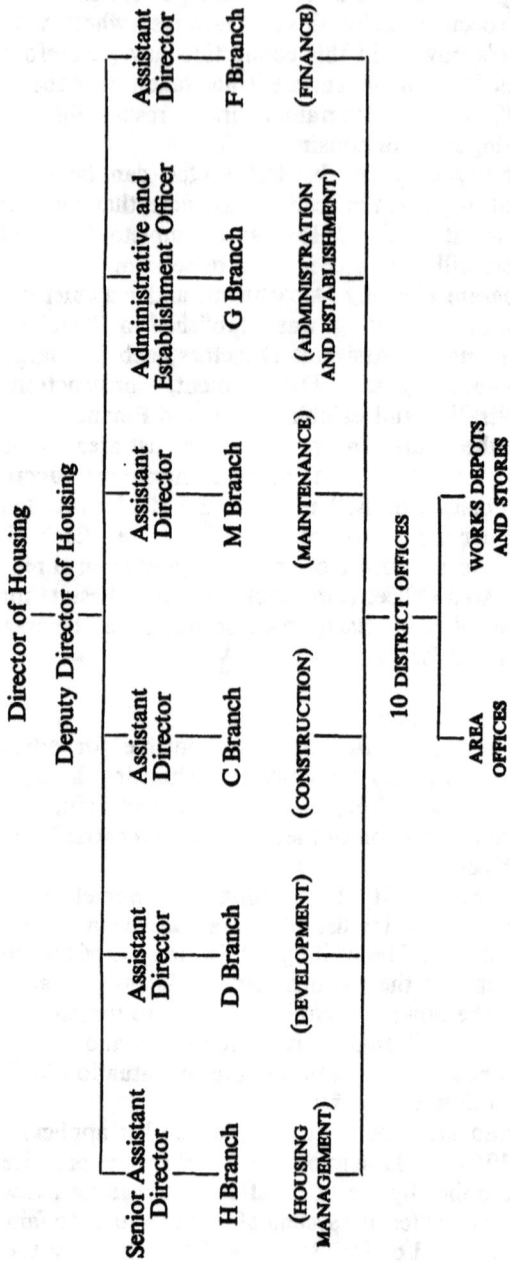

Director of Housing

Deputy Director of Housing

Senior Assistant Director	Assistant Director	Assistant Director	Assistant Director	Administrative and Establishment Officer	Assistant Director
H Branch	D Branch	C Branch	M Branch	G Branch	F Branch
(HOUSING MANAGEMENT)	(DEVELOPMENT)	(CONSTRUCTION)	(MAINTENANCE)	(ADMINISTRATION AND ESTABLISHMENT)	(FINANCE)

10 DISTRICT OFFICES

AREA OFFICES

WORKS DEPOTS AND STORES

It is also the medium by which the population can be redistributed in order to equalize housing pressures. There is liaison between the various districts so that, by transfers, Borough Council nominations and ordinary direct lettings, the houses available can be used to the best advantage. The control of the arrangements for nominations by the Boroughs will rest with the Management Branch at County Hall, but the day-to-day liaison with London Boroughs will be handled by the District Officers.

Families wishing to move to the new and expanding towns, however, are dealt with through a special Industrial Selection Scheme. This is operated in conjunction with the Greater London Boroughs. Records are kept in the Management Division of all tenants or applicants on the LBC's housing lists (together with their trades) who have expressed a wish to move to a new or expanding town. The Ministry of Labour notify the Department daily by telephone the vacancies which arise. Information about those with the necessary skills is sent to the Ministry for passing on to employers.

The District Officer is responsible for watching rent arrears in his district and for initiating action to be taken in serious cases. Officers specializing in welfare work are based on each district office. Their job is to deal with the problems of new tenants, old people, families with illness, friction between tenants and persistent rent arrears. They also help community and tenants' associations, many of which are members of the Association of London Housing Estates set up by the London Council of Social Service.

Development Branch

This Branch is responsible for advising on policy so far as the provision of new housing is concerned, for liaison with the Valuation Department in connection with new housing sites, for advice on the management aspects of design and layout and for the control of work carried out by private architects on behalf of the Housing Committee. It works in close touch with the GLC Architect's Department on management aspects of design and layout in connection with housing schemes prepared by this Department.

As its name implies the Branch also deals with all development matters affecting existing estates, such as provision of garages and clubrooms, and deals with schemes for the improvement, conversion and modernization of existing dwellings. Examples of the type of policy matters on which this Branch advises in consultation with other Branches are (a) development standards for heating, refuse disposal, sheds and stores and (b) the proportion of dwellings of various sizes and types. This is under continual review in the light of demographic trends. Nearly a fifth of the post-war housing owned by the GLC is suitable for old people. Currently the plan provides for 30 per cent of dwellings of one and two rooms, 65 per cent with three and four rooms and 5 per cent with five or more rooms.

It fixes rents for all new Council dwellings and those acquired for the Council. The rents of new dwellings were originally fixed on the principle of comparability with similar privately rented accommodation in the area, but with the growth in the number of GLC houses the basis was changed. Comparison is now made with the rents of other similar Council dwellings, with weight being given to the type and situation of the dwelling, fittings, appliances, floor area and other individual factors.

Rents at present average 36s a week with a range from 10s to 78s. Increases to be applied over three years have been approved and these figures will then be 10s to 93s with an average of 45s.

It is held that with the wide variety of dwellings and rents it is possible to meet a wide variety of needs; nevertheless, to ensure that no family in need of housing is faced with hardship in meeting the rent, a 'social aid scheme' has been introduced. A lower rent can be paid if the tenant shows that his income does not justify his paying the full rent of the dwelling. The cost of reducing the rents of those who justify it is borne by the ratepayers.

Construction Branch

The majority of dwellings built for the GLC are built by private contractors, but some 600 dwellings a year are built by direct labour, a number which it is planned to increase to 800. Responsibility for the preparation of expenditure estimates, the ordering of materials and the recruitment of labour lies with the Construction Branch. All other work, including the preparation of designs, specifications and bills of quantities is undertaken by the Architect's Department or by private architects. The greater part of the building programme carried out for the Council by private contractors is also designed by the Architect's Department.

Schemes for modernization, conversion and rehabilitation are also frequently undertaken by direct labour to plans prepared by the Architect. A long-term programme, started in 1950, aims at modernizing 6,750 older-type flats, most of them built in blocks before 1919. This modernization entails a complete rebuilding of the interior so as to provide a 25–50 per cent increase in area per flat, and amenities and standards comparable with new dwellings. By the middle of 1965, 1,400 modernized flats had been produced from 2,350 old dwellings. This programme is expected to be completed by 1972.

Schemes for rehabilitation of acquired dwellings in redevelopment areas are also carried out by direct labour. A major project of this type is at Brandon Estate, Southwark, where 10 acres of old houses are being rehabilitated, while 46 acres are being redeveloped for housing and other purposes.

Maintenance Branch

The GLC, like many southern local authorities, undertakes internal decoration of its dwellings as well as external decoration and internal and exterior repairs. It also maintains greens, shrubberies and flower beds on the estates. All this work is the responsibility of the Maintenance Branch. Most of it is carried out by direct labour, supplemented where necessary by specialist contractors. The maintenance force consists of about 6,600 building trade workers.

Requests for internal repairs are normally made to the estate officer when he calls weekly or fortnightly for the rent. He orders the work to be done by the repairs staff who usually have a depot on the same site as the area office. Major structural repairs are dealt with by a central group of specialist staff. A planned programme of decoration is undertaken—external painting every five years; internal decorations every five years; and internal painting of woodwork every ten years. Total expenditure on repairs, renewals, painting and decoration is now running at the rate of about £6 million a year—an average of rather more than £28 for each of the 210,000 dwellings in the Housing Revenue Account.

Administration and Establishment Division

This Branch is responsible for all staff work and its head, the Administrative and Establishment Officer, is responsible for advising the Director on the organization and general administration of the Department.

The volume of staff work is very considerable since the Department has some 8,500 manual employees and over 2,000 non-manual staff.

Finance Division

The Finance Division is concerned with audit and accounting over the whole range of the Housing Department's work. It is also responsible for the payment of wages, costing control of stores, payment of accounts and preparation of the annual estimates.

BRISTOL*

Of the 133,000 houses in Bristol, more than 43,000—almost a third—

* This account is largely based on an article by the Housing Manager of Bristol; Fleming, J., 'The Housing Department of the City and County of Bristol', *Housing*, Vol. 1, No. 2 (new series), June 1965; the Authority's *Housing Report* for the period 1959–64; and information kindly supplied by the Housing Manager.

are owned by the Council. There is a separate Housing Department with a chief officer (who is termed Housing Manager and Secretary) who controls a total staff of nearly 1,000—299 officers, 47 caretakers and cleaners and 623 building-trade operatives.

The work of the Department is organized in two main sections, Administrative and Technical, each under a Chief Assistant. The Administrative Section is further sub-divided into six subsections as shown in the chart on page 93.

Administrative Sub-Section

The main administrative load falls on this subsection which has a staff of 5 Administrative Assistants, 2 Committee Clerks, 1 Draughts-man, 11 Clerical Assistants, 23 Typists and Secretarial staff and 10 Trainees. All Committee work of the Housing Committee (including keeping official minutes), preparation of annual estimates and the keeping of records of property transactions, contract drawings, unfit dwellings, closing orders, compulsory purchase orders, and so forth is undertaken in this subsection. It also deals with the sale of council houses (950 sold since the scheme was introduced in 1960), advice and assistance to housing associations, administrative work in connection with the sale of land for private development, and a 'special mortgage scheme'. (This scheme is supplementary to the 'standard mortgage scheme', administered by the City Valuer, which is limited to 95 per cent advances for terms up to twenty years, based on 20 per cent of the purchaser's income. Under the special scheme loans of up to 100 per cent of valuation can be advanced on post-1919 houses over a term of up to thirty-five years. The scale of the advance is based on 25 per cent of the applicant's income, including bonuses, but excluding overtime.)

This subsection also supervises ten trainee housing managers working for the examinations of the Institute of Housing Managers. The training period lasts for four years during which time trainees work in every section of the Housing Department and relevant sections of other Departments. They also spend two days a week at the local Technical College.

Housing Progress Sub-section

This is a very small sub-section employing only two staff, but its work is considered vital in ensuring that the housing programme is completed on schedule. It is responsible for 'pre-development control' from the time a scheme is envisaged until building work commences: at this stage the City Architect assumes responsibility for supervision.

In brief, the sub-section works in the following way. About three years before the target date for the commencement of a scheme a

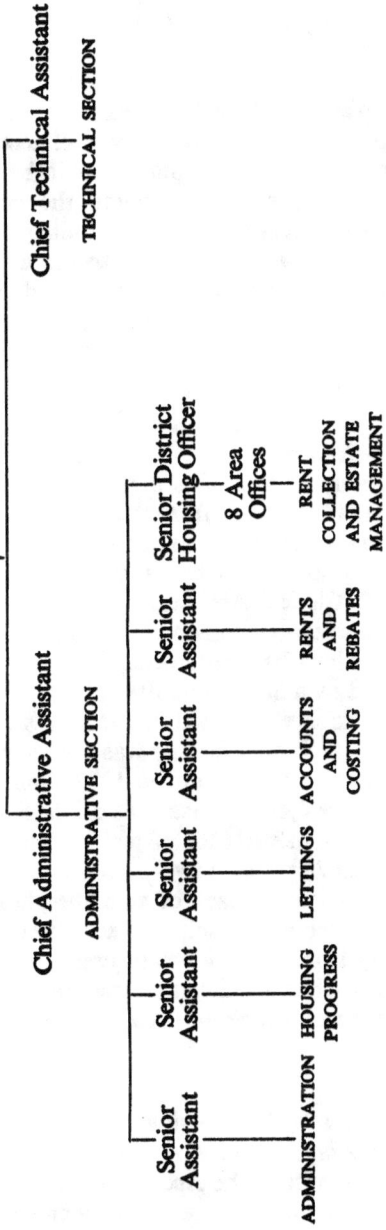

City of Bristol Housing Department

Housing Manager and Secretary

Deputy

Chief Administrative Assistant
ADMINISTRATIVE SECTION

Senior Assistant	Senior Assistant	Senior Assistant	Senior Assistant	Senior Assistant	Senior District Housing Officer
ADMINISTRATION	HOUSING PROGRESS	LETTINGS	ACCOUNTS AND COSTING	RENTS AND REBATES	8 Area Offices
					RENT COLLECTION AND ESTATE MANAGEMENT

Chief Technical Assistant
TECHNICAL SECTION

meeting is called by the Senior Assistant of senior officers of all the relevant Departments to draw up a plan of pre-development work. Thus with the City Engineer's Department, he will consider the work load of both the Engineering and Roads Section and will agree a starting date for particular operations. Similarly with the City Valuer's Department, he will agree on the dates on which properties should be purchased. With the City Architect he will agree the date when work on draft lay-out plans should be started.

A schedule is prepared, showing the commencing and completion dates for each operation, including preliminary and formal planning approval and submission to the appropriate Committees. When the schedule has been finally agreed by all concerned it becomes the formal programme. From then on the Housing Progress Sub-Section watches progress and convenes meetings to resolve any difficulties.

Lettings Sub-Section

Currently about 2,500 houses are let each year—1,500 newly-built houses and 1,000 relets. A further 1,700 transfers and exchanges are arranged. The selection of tenants is therefore a large undertaking. The Lettings Sub-Section has a staff of thirty—3 Administrative Assistants, 21 Clerical Assistants, and 6 Investigators. Tenants are selected by this Sub-Section on the basis of a 'points' scheme, though urgent cases which have insufficient points to qualify for rehousing are considered by a Sub-Committee of the Housing Committee. The waiting list, which was closed in 1957, was reopened in September 1959, during which period there was a review of all applications. A further review was carried out in 1962. Immediately following this review there were 6,480 applications on the list. At the end of March 1964 the number was 10,610, of which 17 per cent were one person households and 28 per cent two-person households. Points are given for bedroom deficiency, lack of amenities, health factors and (in the case of elderly people) 'unsuitable' accommodation. Families awaiting rehousing from redevelopment areas are dealt with separately.

A 'mutual exchange bureau' is maintained for tenants wishing to move who have no degree of need to warrant a transfer to a vacant property.

Accounts and Costing Sub-Section

There are 2 Administrative Assistants, 9 Clerical Assistants and 1 Machine Operator in the Accounts and Costing Sub-Section. The duties involve dealing with the department's payroll (now on a computer), wage rates, payment of accounts, and costing of and statistical information on repair and maintenance costs.

Rents and Rebates Sub-Section

This Sub-Section has, as its main tasks, the co-ordination of the work of eight District Officers, carrying out an internal audit, and generally supervising the operation of the rent rebate scheme. It consists of three Administrative Assistants and seven Clerical Assistants.

The total rent roll exceeds £6¼ million. Rents are pooled and are based on the size of dwellings. As an illustration of rent levels, a three-bedroom non-parlour pre-war house has a net weekly rent of 37s 6d. A parlour house of the same age is 43s 6d. Post-war three-bedroom houses are 49s and flats 41s 6d a week. There is no rate fund subsidy and the Exchequer subsidies are used mainly to meet rent rebates. About 8,500 rebates are given, averaging 14s 6d a week.

Liaison is maintained with other departments (particularly the Children's Department) in respect of welfare work where tenants are liable to eviction for non-payment of rent. A system of 'rent guarantees' is used to delay eviction in certain cases where the Children's Officer requests more time to enable his staff to carry out intensive case work to prevent the eviction. (During this period he guarantees that no further arrears will accrue; if the tenant does default the Housing Revenue Account is reimbursed.)

Decentralized Offices

Rent collection and work connected with the estates is organized through eight District Offices with a total staff of 8 District Housing Officers, 70 Housing Assistants, 17 Clerical Assistants, 37 Caretakers and 10 Cleaners. The number of properties in each district varies from about 4,000 to 8,000. The District Housing Officer is responsible for all administrative and welfare work on the estates. New tenants after being selected by the Lettings Sub-Section are 'signed up' and settled in their new homes by the district staff.

Technical Section

The Technical Section is not formally subdivided as is the Administrative Section, but its responsibilities are equally as extensive and varied. The staff includes 19 Technical Assistants, 7 Bonus Surveyors, 4 Housing Inspectors, 3 Administrative Assistants, 25 Clerical Assistants, 8 Maintenance Superintendents, 10 Foremen, 9 Depot Assistants, 9 Storekeepers and 623 Building Trade Operatives. (Additionally two firms of surveyors, employing 8 surveyors, and 70 contractors, employing about 450 building-trade operatives, are employed for work on improvement and conversion of older houses.)

Technical staff prepare schemes for the conversion and improvement of acquired properties by outside contractors and supervise the work. Housing Inspectors inspect work on dwellings where private owners have applied for Improvement Grants or loans for repairs. They also inspect private houses in course of construction on land previously owned by the Housing Committee to ensure that the dwellings comply with a minimum standard which is higher than that stipulated by the Building Regulations. Dwellings being built with the aid of a Local Authority mortgage loan are also inspected.

Bristol has now no significant slum problem—the really bad housing was cleared in the inter- and post-war years. The problem is now largely one of obsolete and sub-standard housing which can be improved with the aid of improvement grants and with selective demolition to improve layout and environmental amenities. As a result considerable emphasis is placed on encouraging owners to apply for grants. Demonstration houses have been put on show to the public, exhibitions have been held and, under the Housing Act of 1964, one area has been scheduled as a pilot 'Improvement Area'.* In one part of the city, where improvement of private property was to be encouraged on a large scale, a temporary office was set up and staffed with Technical Assistants to advise owners on procedure and improvement schemes. Street by street meetings with owners were held in this local office. (Bristol's approach to improvements has been documented in the Ministry's film 'The Bronze Horses'.)

The Technical Section is also concerned with the improvement of about 15,000 pre-war council houses. A major scheme for the programmed replacement of fittings and the addition of new facilities is under way.

Maintenance and repair of all existing dwellings is carried out by direct labour wherever practicable. However, in recent years, because of the difficulty in obtaining labour, some work is put out to contract, for example part of the external painting programme when it appears obvious that it will be impracticable to complete the work on time by direct labour. Similarly about 15,000 pre-war council dwellings are scheduled to be modernized over the next few years; many contractors are engaged on this work which would be done by direct labour if sufficient operatives were available.

The Role of the Housing Committee
The day to day executive work of the Housing Department is carried out in accordance with the policy laid down by the Housing Committee. Action taken is reported to each meeting of the Committee in the form of schedules placed on the table for inspection by members. In short the committee formulates the policy and the officials carry it out. Thus without the need of formal approval to individual cases the officers grant mortgage loans for house purchase, make grants and loans for improvements and repairs; grant leases of shops;

* See Chapter IX, p. 217 *et. seq.*

accept tenders for improvements, repairs or conversions of acquired properties and pre-war council houses; accept contracts for maintenance works; grant rent rebates; serve Notices to Quit and sign Distress Warrants; appoint junior staff; and so on.

There are three Sub-Committees. The *General Purposes Sub-Committee* deal in the main with housing applicants with apparent housing need who do not qualify under the Council's Points Scheme; applications for mortgage advances where for particular reasons a sum in excess of the scale laid down by the committee is requested; and cases of tenants who have already been served with a Notice to Quit and where the officers recommend that legal proceedings should be taken to obtain possession.

The *Viewing Sub-Committee* meets monthly to view new sites or projects where requested to do so by the officers. It also inspects areas represented by the Medical Officer of Health as one in which the houses are reaching the end of their useful life. The *Staff Sub-Committee* deals with all staffing matters.

LEEDS*

Housing management in Leeds is organized on a decentralized system; there are approximately 56,000 municipally owned dwellings in the city (out of a total of 180,000) and these are divided into eighteen Management Groups of between 1,000 and 5,000 dwellings each. Each Group is controlled by a Housing Manager whose office is situated within the Group of dwellings under his control. His staff are responsible for rent collection, ordering of repairs, dealing with tenants' difficulties and the general routine of estate management. The Manager is also responsible for maintaining a waiting list of applicants for accommodation in his Group, and deals directly with other Managers in respect of applications from existing tenants to transfer in the Group.

The Housing Department is under the control of the Director of Housing and the total number of staff employed is 254 Officers and 195 other employees; there is a Head Office with the Director and five Chief Assistants who are responsible for interpreting the Housing Committee's policies to the Housing Managers.

The City Housing Department works in co-operation with the City Architect in giving advice and comments on design of dwellings, layouts, and any other features affecting the development of housing estates or redevelopment of urban areas; maintenance and repair work is ordered by the Housing Managers on the Works Department with whom a close liaison exists within each group of estates.

* This account is based on information kindly supplied by Mr S. I. Benson, the Director of Housing for Leeds.

G

Leeds Corporation Housing Department

DIRECTOR OF HOUSING

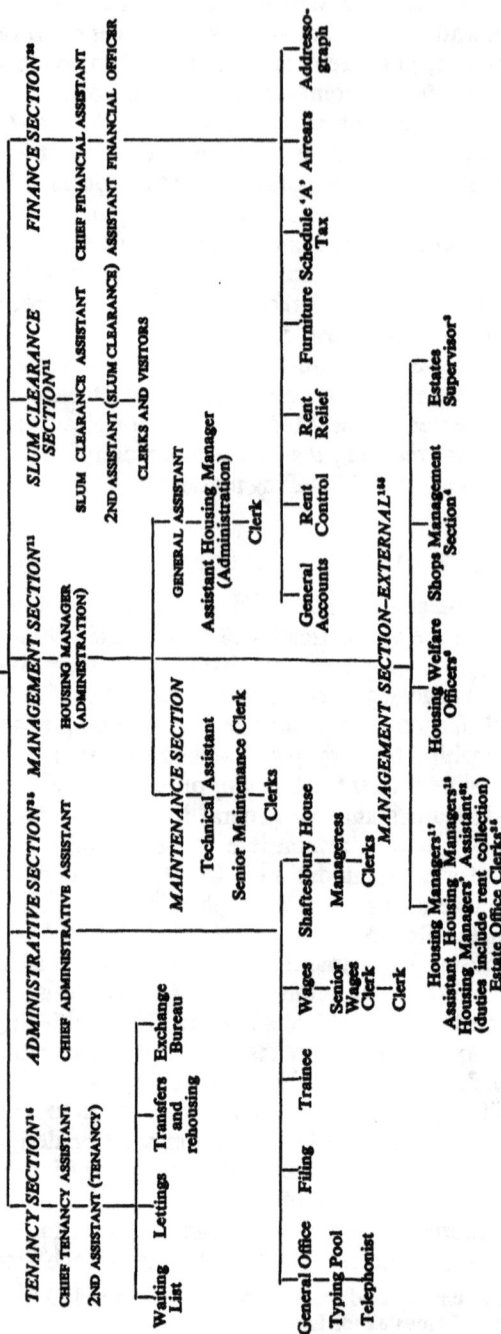

TENANCY SECTION[16]	ADMINISTRATIVE SECTION[8]	MANAGEMENT SECTION[11]	SLUM CLEARANCE SECTION[11]	FINANCE SECTION[20]
CHIEF TENANCY ASSISTANT	CHIEF ADMINISTRATIVE ASSISTANT	HOUSING MANAGER (ADMINISTRATION)	SLUM CLEARANCE ASSISTANT	CHIEF FINANCIAL ASSISTANT
2ND ASSISTANT (TENANCY)			2ND ASSISTANT (SLUM CLEARANCE)	ASSISTANT FINANCIAL OFFICER

TENANCY SECTION
- Waiting List
- Lettings
- Transfers and rehousing
- Exchange Bureau

ADMINISTRATIVE SECTION
- General Office
- Typing Pool
- Telephonist
- Filing
- Trainee
- Wages
  - Senior Wages Clerk
  - Clerk
- Shaftesbury House
  - Manageress
  - Clerks

MAINTENANCE SECTION
- Technical Assistant
- Senior Maintenance Clerk
- Clerks

MANAGEMENT SECTION
- General Assistant
- Assistant Housing Manager (Administration)
- Clerk

SLUM CLEARANCE SECTION
- Clerks and Visitors

FINANCE SECTION
- General Accounts
- Rent Control
- Rent Relief
- Furniture
- Schedule 'A' Tax
- Arrears
- Addressograph

MANAGEMENT SECTION—EXTERNAL[180]
- Housing Welfare Officers[9]
- Shops Management Section[4]
- Estate Supervisor[3]

Housing Managers[17]
Assistant Housing Managers[18]
Housing Managers' Assistants[8]
(duties include rent collection)
Estate Office Clerks[11]

(The numbers indicate the staff in each section)

On the staff of the Housing Department there are three Estate Supervisors whose tasks and functions are to ensure the general up-keep of estate maintenance, advising tenants on garden layout, siting of garages, siting of garden huts and greenhouses, and advise on their construction and use, arrangements for the gardens of elderly and disabled people to be tended, preparing specifications for ground-works, arranging programmes of repair of footpaths, re-taining walls, gates and gate posts.

There are six Housing Welfare Officers who are responsible to Housing Managers for concentrated welfare work among problem families and those elderly people who need domestic assistance. The work of this Section includes arranging the movement of people from clearance areas, often by providing transport for the elderly, showing them the district to which they are to be moved, taking them round shopping and postal facilities, and generally settling people into new neighbourhoods and environments.

Since 1934 the Housing Department has organized a training scheme to provide qualified Housing Managers for the country gen-erally. Under the present training scheme the period involved is up to five years and students may be appointed at any age over eighteen years. Those accepted are trained to take the Final Examination of the Institute of Housing Managers, although some students have opted to sit the examinations of the Royal Institution of Chartered Surveyors. At the moment there are ten Housing Manager Trainees studying and working in the Department, and the Housing Com-mittee have authority to appoint up to four each year.

The five Chief Assistants and their duties are as follows:

Housing Manager (Administration)

This Officer attends all Committees with the Director of Housing. His Section deals with all research and planning into future housing requirements and works in collaboration with the City Architect and other Departments in programming and co-ordinating new devel-opments, together with similar co-operation with regard to new dwelling types, standards and layout; preparation and submission of reports to formulate Housing Committee policy and the discussion and application of such policy through the Housing Managers. The leasing of lands, easements and wayleaves, etc., together with public relations work are dealt with by this Section.

Chief Assistant (Finance)

This Officer deals with all rent accounting and the general finances of the Department. This includes the operation of a Rent Relief Scheme, payment of wages and insurance for fire and other risks. During the year ending March 31, 1965, the total rent collected was nearly £5½ million.

Chief Assistant (Tenancies)

All matters affecting the allocation of accommodation are dealt with through this Officer who instructs Housing Managers on the detailed allocation policy, and who ensures that the waiting list is efficiently organized, and that the necessary publicity is arranged. He is also responsible for matters affecting existing tenancies, transfers, etc., and for terminating unsatisfactory tenancies or (where necessary) instituting eviction procedure. Purchases of miscellaneous properties are arranged through this Official.

Chief Assistant (Slum Clearance)

All families in clearance areas are visited by members of this Section well before rehousing, and at this point note is taken of preferences for particular districts and types of accommodation and any individual family problems.

Chief Assistant (Administration)

This is a purely administrative function covering the staffing and equipping of the Department; the staffing side tends to become complicated in a highly decentralized Department. The Section also deals with estimates, accounts, wages, filing, hostels, etc.

The Housing Committee meets once per month but has delegated certain functions to groups of members appointed for certain purposes, namely, tenancy matters; shops; redevelopment (e.g. town centres in new districts); conversions and improvements; hostels; and staff matters. These Groups of members meet as required.

The Department does not operate a points scheme but all applications are considered in date order within categories of need, thus all medically supported cases are grouped together and dealt with according to the degree of priorities recommended by the Medical Officer of Health.

The Slum Clearance Programme of 22,500 dwellings (under the 1954 Act) is almost completed, so that further dwellings that have now been classed as unfit have been added to the programme. Leeds hopes to have dealt with all the city's slums within a period of some five to ten years. There is, however, a very big problem of inadequate housing. There is a large scale improvement programme which has involved selecting large areas of suitable properties and persuading owners to 'improve', or alternatively to sell to the Council to enable improvements to be carried out.*

* This is outlined on pp. 214–15.

EASINGTON RURAL DISTRICT*

Easington Rural District is situated in the County of Durham on the north-east coast. It has a population of 85,000 and the Council owns over 8,000 of the 27,500 houses in the district. The Council houses are distributed over seventeen different villages and nearly half of them have been built since 1945. The district includes the new town of Peterlee where the allocation of houses is mainly dealt with by a Sub-Committee on which the Council is represented. Only fifty houses have been erected within the designated area of the new town by the District Council.

The District Council has no separate Housing Department and administration is divided among the Clerk, Treasurer, and Engineer, and to a smaller extent the Medical Officer's Department. The Clerk is responsible for general housing management including applications and lettings; the Accountant for rent collection; and the Engineer and Surveyor for maintenance. Any welfare work is the responsibility of the Medical Officer.

There is a small section in the Clerk's Department responsible for maintaining the waiting lists and the subsequent allocation of houses on the instructions of the various Sub-Committees of the Council; the rent section in the Accountant's Department is under the supervision of a Chief Clerk and is also responsible for following up arrears of rent and Court proceedings under the provisions of the Small Tenants Recovery Act. The Direct Labour Organization for repairs in the Surveyor's Department is under the control of a Maintenance Superintendent who is also responsible for the carrying out of improvement schemes on pre-war houses.

The selection of tenants for houses is the responsibility of the local Members in each Parish. The Council has not laid down any district policy with regard to allocations and different systems are used in each Parish. In the main the important criteria is the length of time married and resident or working within the Parish. No provision is made for regular re-registration by applicants although the lists are checked by enquiry at regular intervals.

The net rents of council houses are 13s 7d to 15s 7d (one bedroom), 27s to 31s 5d (two bedroom), 27s 1d to 33s 11d (three bedrooms), and 27s 11d to 33s 11d (four bedrooms). So far as the rate subsidy is concerned the Council has continued to give the same subsidy as they were previously statutorily required to do. Rents are collected weekly by fourteen rent collectors.

Repairs are reported direct to the Maintenance Superintendent's office by the tenant on postcards issued on request by the rent col-

* This account is based entirely on information kindly provided by D. Conyers Kelly, the Clerk of the Easington Rural District Council.

lectors. Internal decorations are undertaken by the tenants. External painting is carried out on a three year cycle by the Maintenance Department.

The annual contribution per dwelling for general maintenance is £17 plus £2 for special works, a total allowance of £19 per house, and expenditure has been well within this figure. Most of the 4,600 pre-war houses have been improved at a cost in the region of £900,000, only a very small proportion of which ranked for Improvement Grant.

There has been quite a formidable slum clearance programme which unfortunately was delayed due to the uncertainty of Town Planning land zoning. A programme commenced in 1954 envisaged the demolition of over 2,000 houses by 1966 and this programme is well advanced, and will be virtually completed by 1968.

LEAMINGTON SPA *

Royal Leamington Spa is a non-county borough situated to the west of Coventry. It has a population of 44,000. Of its 13,400 houses, 3,800 are owned by the Council; 3,000 of these have been built since 1945.

Until 1951 there was no separate Housing Department; administration was divided between the Departments of the Town Clerk, Treasurer and Engineer. In that year a Housing Manager was appointed and assumed responsibilities for all management except maintenance and repairs. In 1960, following an Organization and Methods Survey, the direct labour force of the Borough Engineer's Department was transferred to the Housing Department. This direct labour force undertakes not only housing repairs and maintenance, but also work for other Committees.

In 1963 responsibility for the initiation, co-ordination and execution of all work for the Housing Committee was transferred to the Housing Manager, who was subsequently redesignated Housing Director.

The Department is divided into two main sections. The Chief Housing Assistant, who acts as the Deputy Housing Director, is in charge of the section dealing with the keeping of the waiting list; allocation of tenancies; rent collection and accountancy, including the follow-up of arrears and Court proceedings; welfare; the rent rebate scheme, and transfers and exchanges.

The Building Maintenance Superintendent is responsible for the direct labour force; supervision of work carried out by private contractors, including new building; maintenance of estate lawns,

* This account is based on an article by the Housing Director of Leamington Spa in the March 1962 issue of *Housing* and later information kindly supplied by the Director (Mr J. Turner).

Housing Department of the Municipal Borough of Royal Leamington Spa

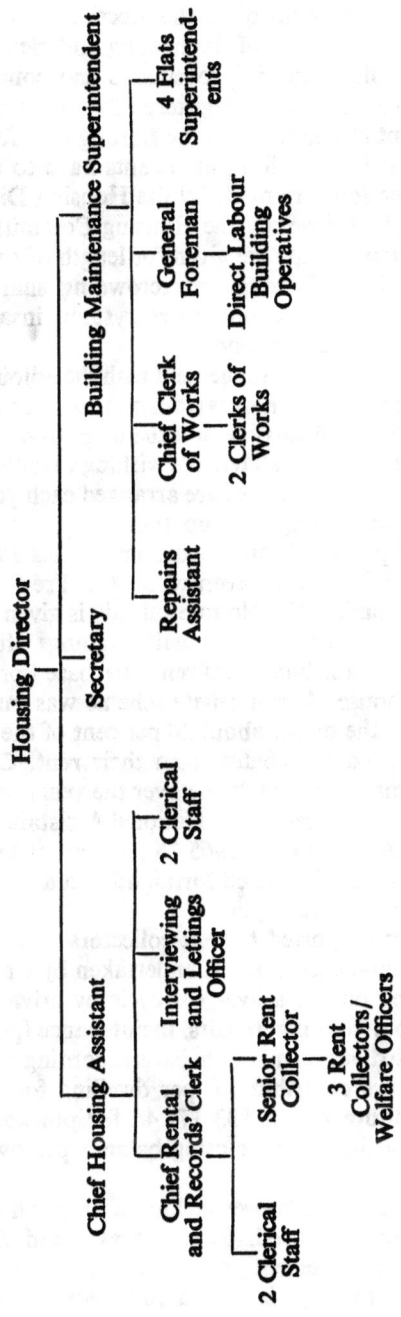

Housing Director

- Chief Housing Assistant
- Secretary
- Building Maintenance Superintendent

Chief Housing Assistant
- Chief Rental and Records' Clerk
  - 2 Clerical Staff
- Interviewing and Lettings Officer
  - Senior Rent Collector
    - 3 Rent Collectors/Welfare Officers
- 2 Clerical Staff

Secretary
- Repairs Assistant

Building Maintenance Superintendent
- Chief Clerk of Works
  - 2 Clerks of Works
- General Foreman
  - Direct Labour Building Operatives
- 4 Flats Superintendents

shrubberies, etc.; control of the erection of sheds, pens and other structures; supervision of the heating and cleaning arrangements in multi-storey flats, and improvements and conversions.

All applicants must be registered for at least two years and have been resident or employed in the Borough for four years. In order to keep the waiting list 'live', applicants have to re-register every two years. Allocations are made by the Housing Director in accordance with policy laid down by the Housing Committee. A points scheme is in operation; points are given for length of time on the list, length of residence in the Borough, overcrowding, sharing, lack of facilities, such as a bath and a hot water system, insanitary housing conditions, and medical grounds.

There is a working arrangement with the adjoining local authorities whereby a person who moves from one district to another can transfer his application and carry with it the original date of registration.

A register is kept of all tenants wishing to move for any reason, and an average of eighty moves are arranged each year, mainly to reduce overcrowding and under-occupation.

Rents of post-war three bedroom houses range from 41s 6d to 93s 8d a week with an average of 44s. Pre-war houses are rather cheaper, averaging 36s. No rate subsidy is given and the general level of rents is fixed to cover annual outgoings after deduction of Exchequer subsidies. Individual rents are based on the size and amenities of the house. A rent rebate scheme was introduced on April 1, 1956, and at the outset about 20 per cent of the tenants claimed and became entitled to rebates from their rent. Certain modifications have been made to the scheme over the years, particularly in respect of aged persons in receipt of National Assistance where a rebate of 4s is granted. At the end of 1965 15 per cent of tenants were receiving rebates. Rents are collected fortnightly on a 'forty-eight-week basis', i.e. twenty-four times a year.

Repairs are reported to rent collectors and carried out by direct labour. Internal decoration is undertaken by tenants. External painting is carried out on a five-year cycle by private contractors.

Apart from 'jobbing' repairs, maintenance (pointing, re-rendering, etc.) is carried out on an estate basis according to a maintenance plan.

The 'repairs contribution' per dwelling for 1964–5 was £10 10s and expenditure ran at £33 17s 4d for pre-war and £7 10s 8d for post-war dwellings. The closing balance per dwelling at March 31, 1965, was £17.

Over 500 pre-war houses lacking a proper hot water system have recently been improved. The cost averaged £185, part of which ranked for improvement grant. Modernization and the replacement of obsolescent fittings is also taking place in the 1919 Act houses at an average cost of £200.

Leamington Spa does not have a large slum clearance problem. The programme commenced in 1954 envisaged the demolition of 520 houses by 1960 and a further 360 later. In fact, by mid-1965, 1,000 homes had been demolished. The slum clearance programme is determined by the Health Committee on the basis of advice from the Medical Officer of Health and in the light of the current house building programme. Families are rehoused by the Housing Department. Removal expenses are paid where need exists.

REFERENCES AND FURTHER READING

[1] Central Housing Advisory Committee, *The Management of Municipal Housing Estates*, HMSO, 1938.

[2] Central Housing Advisory Committee, *Management of Municipal Housing Estates*, HMSO, 1945.

[3] Central Housing Advisory Committee, *Selection of Tenants and Transfers and Exchanges*, HMSO, 1949.

[4] Central Housing Advisory Committee, *Transfers, Exchanges and Rents*, HMSO, 1953.

[5] Central Housing Advisory Committee, *Councils and their Houses*, HMSO, 1959.

[6] Institute of Housing, 'Repairs and Maintenance of Council Dwellings', *Housing*, Vol. XXII, No. 2, September 1960.

[7] Layton, E., *Building by Local Authorities*, Allen and Unwin, 1961.

[8] Mann, P. H., 'Octavia Hill: An Appraisal', *Town Planning Review*, Vol. 23, No. 3, October 1952.

[9] Metropolitan Boroughs Organization and Methods Committee, *General Review of Housing Management*, 1963.

[10] Ministry of Housing and Local Government, *Circular No. 45/65*, 'Housing Management', HMSO, 1965.

[11] Rowles, R. J. (editor), *Housing Management*, Pitman, 1959.

[12] Waren, J. H., *The English Local Government System*, seventh edition revised by P. G. Richards, Allen and Unwin, 1963.

CHAPTER IV

Local Authority Housing and Housebuilding

THE BUILDING OF houses is by no means the only function of local housing authorities—as later chapters of this book demonstrate. It is nevertheless their most important housing function. Indeed, for district councils (which are not directly responsible for education, health or town planning) it is the most important of all their functions.

Local housing authorities have a *duty* to keep under review the housing conditions of their area and the need for additional houses. This is a general duty additional to those requiring them to provide houses for overcrowded families or families displaced by slum clearance. Powers to provide housing are very extensive. Local authorities can build new houses, or convert, improve or enlarge existing ones. These powers are not confined to the local authority's own area: they can be exercised beyond their boundaries. This is important since many urban authorities, particularly in the conurbations, have run out of building land and thus the only way in which they can 'provide for the needs of their district' is by building in the area of another local authority.

Housing development involves, of course, the acquisition of land. A local housing authority can acquire land either by agreement with the owners or, if necessary, by compulsion. Compulsory acquisition is subject to the approval of the Ministry and the price to be paid is determined by reference to the provisions of the law. These have changed radically during post-war years but at present have the effect broadly of giving the owner the market value of his land.*

Local authorities normally carry out their housing responsibilities by building houses and letting them directly to tenants. They can, however, sell or lease the land (either before or after public streets, roads and open spaces have been provided) for an approved scheme of housing development by another body. They can also build the houses themselves and then sell or lease them either to owner-

* See the author's *Town and Country Planning in England and Wales*, Allen and Unwin, 1964, Chapter 6.

occupiers or to a body intending to let them. In all these cases Ministerial approval is required, though a general consent has been given for sales to owner-occupiers. The effect of these and similar powers is that local authorities can give considerable assistance to private builders and housing associations, and, furthermore, that the houses which they build themselves do not necessarily have to remain in their own ownership.

Later chapters will discuss these and other powers in more detail. This chapter is devoted to a description of the existing stock of council houses and local authority building programmes.

COUNCIL HOUSES

According to the last Census, 3,472,027 households in 1961 rented their accommodation from a local authority or New Town Corporation—just under one in four of all households. Roughly the same number were tenants of unfurnished privately rented property. The largest group—43 per cent—owned their own houses. The remaining 10 per cent were in furnished or some type of service accommodation. These proportions have changed radically over the last fifty years, though unfortunately there are few reliable statistics to illustrate this. The vast majority of local authority houses have been built since 1918: rather more than a million were built between the wars, and most of the remainder since 1945. Probably some 200,000 houses owned by local authorities date from before the first war, but most of these have been purchased from private owners for slum clearance or improvement. Thus about the time of the First World War all but a small number of houses were in private ownership. How many of these were owned by their occupiers is not known, but it is generally believed that the proportion was not very high. However, owner-occupation spread rapidly during the inter-war years as building societies developed on a large scale as lending institutions specificially geared to this purpose. At the same time the number (as well as the proportion) of privately rented houses has declined both by sales to owner-occupiers and by the slum clearance programmes of local authorities. A third of a million houses were demolished as slums during the 'thirties. A similar number were demolished between 1945 and 1960. Since then slum clearance has averaged about 64,000 houses a year. An unknown number will have been lost by other demolitions and conversions to non-residential use. Sales to owner-occupiers are unrecorded but the number in recent years at least is thought to be high. According to the Government Social Survey Report *The Housing Situation in 1960*[9] well over 2½ million pre-1919 houses were owner-occupied in 1960. Another Social Survey Report[8] showed the proportion of *non-council* houses in Great

Britain which were found to be owner-occupied in a series of surveys increased from 33 per cent in 1948 to 43 per cent in 1954 and to 51 per cent in 1958.

The trends are thus clear: both the numbers of council and owner-occupied houses are increasing while privately rented property is declining.

The proportion of houses owned by local authorities varies in different areas. It is highest in the north and lowest in the London area. For individual local authority areas the range is very much greater. Thus Bournemouth has 9 per cent of council houses, whereas Birmingham has 35 per cent and Wakefield 44 per cent. Even within a single county the range can be very great. The extreme case is Lancashire where Southport has 6 per cent and Kirkby 91 per cent.

TABLE 6: *Tenure of Households, England and Wales, Regions, Conurbations and Rural Districts*, 1961

		Tenants of Local Authority or New Town Corporation	Owner Occupiers	Tenants of Private Landlords (unfurnished) dwellings)	Other Tenures
England and Wales	%	24	42	24	10
Regions:					
Northern	%	32	34	23	11
East and West Ridings	%	26	39	26	8
North Western	%	22	45	26	7
North Midland	%	25	42	22	11
Midland	%	30	42	19	9
Eastern	%	27	45	17	11
London and South Eastern	%	18	40	30	12
Southern	%	21	48	18	13
South Western	%	22	47	19	12
Wales	%	23	47	22	8
Conurbations	%	23	38	30	9
Rural Districts	%	20	45	17	17

The fact that most council houses have been built since 1918 means, of course, that they differ in quality from the total stock of houses of other tenures. Tables 7 and 8, based on the Rowntree Housing Survey of 1962[4] (*for England only*), illustrate this.

TABLE 7: *Tenure, Rateable Value, Type and Size of House, England 1962[4]*

	Household's Tenure of Accommodation			
	Rents from Council	Owns/is buying	Rents privately unfurnished	All house-holds†
No. of households in sample	673	1,398	1,018	3,231
	%	%	%	%
Rateable Value				
£10 or less	4	11	34	17
£11–£13	4	6	11	8
£14–£18	21	12	15	15
£19–£25	43	20	17	23
£26–£30	17	15	10	14
£31–£40	10	17	6	12
£41 or more	1	19	6	10
Not known	*	*	1	1
Median Rateable Value	£21	£25	£15	£21
Type of Accommodation				
Whole house, detached	3	19	7	12
Whole house, semi-detached	41	35	11	28
Whole house, terraced	36	38	52	41
Flat or maisonette	19	7	27	17
Part-house/rooms	2	*	4	2
Number of rooms used by household				
1–2	5	1	10	6
3	12	8	18	12
4	36	25	35	30
5	38	37	26	33
6	9	20	9	13
7 or more	*	10	3	4
Average number of rooms per household	4·33	5·03	4·16	4·55
Number of bedrooms				
1	7	3	16	9
2	32	32	47	36
3	58	54	32	47
4	4	8	5	6
5 or more	–	3	*	2

* Less than 0·5 per cent.

† In this and subsequent tables the 'all households' column includes other tenure groups, e.g. tenants of furnished accommodation.

TABLE 8: *Tenure and Housing Amenities, England, 1962*[a]

		Rents from Council	Owns/is buying	Rents privately unfurnished	All households
No. of households in sample		673	1,398	1,018	3,231
		%	%	%	%
Households having: E=Exclusive use; S=shared; N=entirely without					
Cooker with oven	E	98	99	94	97
	S	2	*	3	2
	N	1	1	3	2
Kitchen sink	E	98	99	94	97
	S	2	*	3	2
	N	–	1	3	1
Fixed bath	E	96	82	41	71
	S	2	4	6	5
	N	3	14	53	24
Flush toilet	E	97	93	79	89
	S	2	3	14	7
	N	1	3	7	4
Hot water from tap	With	95	89	58	80
	Without	5	11	42	20
Garden	E	85	81	45	69
	S	3	3	11	7
	N	12	16	44	24
Garage	With	7	34	5	19
	Without	93	65	94	81

Council housing, as may be expected, has a uniformly high standard of 'amenity'. Only a very small proportion lacks any of the basic amenities, and these are likely to be mainly old houses acquired for demolition. Uniformity is indeed a marked characteristic of this sector: in 1962 nine-tenths had two or three bedrooms and four-fifths had rateable values within the range of £14 to £30. In no other sector is there such bunching. Nevertheless changes are taking place:

* Less than 0·5 per cent.

the proportion of new council houses of the one-bedroom type increased from 5 per cent in the period 1945–50 to over a quarter in recent years and is now running at over 25,000 a year (in England and Wales). Yet this represents less than 1 per cent of the total stock of council houses (which has been increasing at the rate of about 100,000 a year) and it will therefore be many years before the size distribution of council houses is significantly affected. At the other end of the size scale only 4 per cent have four bedrooms; only 2 per cent of council houses built in recent years have four or more bedrooms.

Almost a fifth of council dwellings are flats or maisonettes. Clearly the image of the pre-war council housing estate (the 'basic social product of the twentieth century' as Asa Briggs has termed them[1]) is being considerably modified. Though many of the large cities built blocks of council flats in the inter-war years (and a few before then) most of them date from post-1945. Currently almost a half of newly-built council dwellings are flats.

CONTROL OF LOCAL AUTHORITY HOUSE BUILDING PROGRAMMES *

The duty which local authorities have 'to consider housing conditions in their district and the needs of their district with respect to the provision of further housing accommodation . . . and to prepare and submit to the Minister proposals for the provision of new houses' is necessarily much less clear-cut than their duties in connection, for example, with schools. Local authorities have a clear responsibility for providing school places for *all* children and this is only insignificantly affected by the 500,000 private school places. There is no question of a shift in emphasis from the public to the private sector (or vice versa) as there is in the field of housing. Central government policy on the balance between new house building by local authorities and by private enterprise may change from year to year, and the programmes of individual authorities will reflect not only this but also the character of the local housing situation and the local authority's assessment of the need for further council building. Indeed, though the Ministry may urge local authorities to build more—or less—houses, individual local authorities will be more directly concerned with local factors and pressures. In some areas the politics of the situation may be highly favourable towards further council house building; in others it may be quite the opposite.

The division of house-building between private enterprise and local authorities has a further implication. Whatever may be the Government's attitude towards local authority house-building as such, they

* This and the following section lean heavily in part on E. Layton, *Building by Local Authorities*, Allen and Unwin, 1961.

will have a great concern for the total size of house-building pro-gramme. When building licensing was in operation, during the early post-war years, private building could be directly controlled; since 1954 there have been no such controls—only much more indirect financial measures. It follows that if, within a given overall pro-gramme, private building expands then attempts must be made to curtail local authority building. Otherwise the strains on the building industry will give rise to increases in costs, bottle-necks in supply, and so forth. This was the position in 1954.* The alternative is to increase the total capacity of the building industry and/or to divert resources from other types of building. In recent years great emphasis has been placed on prefabricated building methods as a means of increasing total production from an industry which is chronically short of skilled labour. The Labour Government have announced their in-tention of reintroducing some form of licensing control over major construction schemes. But whatever the means employed, the essen-tial point remains that demands on building have to be kept within the bounds of the capacity to meet them.

The central Government thus exercise control over the housing programme (and, indeed, all capital expenditure) of each individual local authority. But this is not the only aim of central control. The Ministry of Housing are concerned to see that each local authority gets its 'fair share' of the limited resources and that individual housing schemes represent good value—and good economy—for money. Fair shares are obviously a matter of judgment, but equally obvious—given the uneven distribution and the housing shortage—they do not entail each authority building the same number of houses relative to population. The 1963 White Paper, *Housing*,[12] stressed the need to give priority to local authorities with large slum clearance programmes: in these areas no restraint was to be placed on the number of building starts—'though plainly they should not start more than the building industry can deal with efficiently'. This White Paper also announced that the previous practice of requiring local authori-ties to submit annual building programmes for Ministerial approval would be changed, at least for the authorities with a large slum problem. Instead, five-year programmes had been agreed: these involved an expansion of existing programmes and would be revised in the light of progress—'those who can do so will be encouraged to go still faster'. Encouragement was also given generally to local authorities to build one-bedroom dwellings 'for the very many elderly people who look to them for housing'.

The Labour Government which was returned to power in 1964 introduced a system of four-year 'rolling programmes'[13] in connection

* See Chapter I, p. 36.

H

with their policy of increasing local authority house building. Though special needs such as slum clearance were to continue to receive a high priority, local authorities were urged to build for general needs—to meet 'the scarcity of houses to let at moderate rents'. Each authority was asked to review their local housing needs and to submit to the Ministry 'housing programme forecasts' for the years 1965 to 1968 inclusive. A revised forecast is required each year for the subsequent four years.

TABLE 9: *Local Authority Dwellings Built Since The War—Number of Bedrooms for Houses and Flats*[16]

All Dwellings	One bedroom No.	Two bedrooms No.	Three bedrooms No.	Four or more bedrooms No.	Total No.
1945–62	255,612	659,905	1,246,834	53,046	2,215,397
1963	27,079	31,347	36,539	2,050	97,015
1964	32,952	41,291	42,740	2,485	119,468
1965–1st Qtr.	9,156	11,047	10,589	629	31,421
2nd Qtr.	8,533	10,969	10,731	611	30,844
	%	%	%	%	%
1945–62	11·5	29·8	56·3	2·4	100·0
1963	27·9	32·3	37·7	2·1	100·0
1964	27·6	34·6	35·8	2·0	100·0
1965–1st Qtr.	29·1	35·2	33·7	2·0	100·0
2nd Qtr.	27·6	35·6	34·8	2·0	100·0

Total						
Houses	No.	99,309	425,989	1,238,031	50,983	1,814,312
	%	5·5	23·5	68·2	2·8	100·0
Flats	No.	234,023	328,570	109,402	7,838	679,833
	%	34·4	48·3	16·1	1·2	100·0
All	No.	333,332	754,559	1,347,433	58,821	2,494,145
dwellings	%	13·4	30·2	54·0	2·4	100·0

Houses and Flats

	Houses %	Flats %	Total %
1945–60	77·4	22·6	100·0
1961–2	56·4	43·6	100·0
1963	52·2	47·8	100·0
1964	50·7	49·3	100·0
1965 (to June 1965)	48·1	51·9	100·0
Total post-war	72·7	27·3	100·0

Where a return shows projected building averaging more than fifty dwellings a year, the Ministry settle with the authority a programme of work for which loan consents will be given in due course. The extent to which a firm programme can be fixed for the whole four-year period depends on the degree of priority which is attached to the particular authority's needs. The first priority is being given to relieving 'the acute shortage of houses to rent in the conurbations— especially in areas which attract newcomers including immigrants from the Commonwealth—and to clearing the great concentration of slums'.[14] Nevertheless, the intention is that each authority will be told, as precisely as possible, what programme they can confidently plan over the four-year period. The same applies to authorities with smaller building plans, but clearly these are to receive a lower degree of priority.

The means for controlling council building programmes is basically that local authorities are required to obtain 'loan sanction' for any loans which they wish to raise, though the importance of the level of interest rates should not be underestimated, particularly in relation to smaller authorities. This procedure also gives the Ministry the opportunity of assessing whether particular schemes meet recommended standards and are not too costly. In practice this is a more difficult field in which to operate controls and there is the common conflict between the desires to raise standards and at the same time to keep costs down. There are at least two other important relevant factors. First, local authorities tend to be very cost-conscious, if only because higher costs mean higher rents or rate-fund subsidies. Secondly, housing schemes come before the Ministry—formally at least—only at the stage when the designs and layouts have been completed. To attempt to achieve economies at this stage involves delay and, in any case, major reductions in cost are usually not practicable. Outright rejection is seldom resorted to because of the political repercussions. In practice central control tends to operate mainly in relation to small authorities (who need—and frequently seek—official assistance or guidance at an early stage) and, to a lesser extent, larger authorities building tall blocks of flats (here informal contacts with Ministry officials can be close).

It is difficult to give an accurate picture of the controls actually operated by the Ministry. Much may depend on the size of the local authority (London, Birmingham, and the larger cities obviously cannot be treated in the same way as a small district council), the calibre of the local authority staff, the scale of the local authority's housing problem, and the political climate. But clearly the Ministry does not have the strong power—or at least does not use the strong power—of control which might be appropriate if local authorities were subservient agents of the central Government. And in practice local authorities tend to react to changing political and economic situations in line with the central Government. A severe economic crisis or a popular demand for faster slum clearance and rebuilding will be felt in the Town Hall just as it is in Whitehall.

BUILDING BY AND FOR LOCAL AUTHORITIES

Though it is usual to distinguish between local authority and private house building the distinction is of importance mainly in relation to the intended form of ownership rather than the agency of building. In fact the great majority of local authority houses are erected by private builders. The normal procedure, after a scheme has been designed, is for the local authority to advertise for tenders. Usually there is open competitive tendering: any contractor can then put in a tender. With some schemes, however, there is selective tendering: certain selected contractors are invited to submit a tender. This is frequently done with big schemes or high flats. Some authorities maintain a list of 'approved contractors' and periodically invite contractors to apply for inclusion in this list—which records the size of contract which can be handled, their experience and any particular specialist capacity. The number of contractors who are invited to tender varies both with the size of the scheme and the practice of different authorities. Elizabeth Layton[10] quotes one authority which has a scale which is finely graduated for smaller schemes:

Value of Contract	Number of firms invited to tender
Below £50	1
Between £50 and £150	2
Between £150 and £350	3
Between £350 and £500	4
Between £500 and £20,000	6
Between £20,000 and £100,000	8
Over £100,000	10

The lowest tender is always accepted except where there is very good reason for not doing so—for example unsatisfactory previous work. Competitive tendering is well-established as a traditional practice. It has proved an invaluable method of guarding against corrupt or dubious methods of awarding contracts and ensures that a local authority gets its work done at the lowest costs in the prevailing conditions. The procedures for advertising or inviting tenders and for opening them on the appointed day are rigorously controlled.

Recent developments in building technology and specialist building techniques, however, have led to an increasing use of negotiated contracts. These have not been unknown in the past, particularly where a scheme adjoined one on which a contractor was already working and thus had his site organization gathered together and conveniently located. In such cases a 'continuation' contract had obvious economic advantages. The increasing need to use non-traditional methods, however, means that the contractor has to be selected in advance not only of tendering but also of designing the scheme. The authority has to decide which of the proprietary methods to use and then negotiate the price with the particular contractor. A form of selection can be used, particularly by authorities undertaking large schemes, by inviting preliminary offers from a number of specialist contractors.

INDUSTRIALIZED BUILDING

The advantages of industrialized building methods can only be realized with continuous programmes of work. Yet of all the 1,400 local housing authorities in England and Wales only 250 build more than 100 houses a year. For this reason considerable emphasis is now being given to co-operation between housing authorities in order to facilitate forward programming. This allows full economic use of industrialized methods, rationalization of plan types and the bulk of ordering of components. By the end of 1963, thirteen local authorities had formed 'housing consortia' based on Yorkshire and the Midlands: the Yorkshire Development Group (Hull, Leeds and Sheffield) and Midlands Consortium (Coventry, Derby, Dudley, Leicester, Smethwick, Stoke-on-Trent, Walsall, West Bromwich, Wolverhampton and Worcester). Further consortia were formed in 1964 after the Ministry of Housing, in collaboration with the Association of Municipal Corporations and the Urban District Councils Association, had organized a series of conferences with 435 housing authorities who had sizeable house-building programmes but had not yet entered such groups. At the end of 1964, thirteen consortia had been established, comprising 120 authorities.

This movement followed the highly successful CLASP experiment in school building (Consortium for Local Authorities Special Programme),[11] and similar ventures. About £125 million (1963 figures) is spent on educational building. Five building consortia had already been established by the end of 1963, of which thirty-five local education authorities, responsible for about 45 per cent of the total school building programme, were members.[17] But housing is, in many ways, different from schools. There are ten times as many housing authorities as education authorities and whereas school design is recognized as a field for experts, housing design is a field in which every councillor and officer feels competent to advise and judge. Small modifications in design which a councillor or local authority architect may feel strongly about can significantly affect costs. Furthermore, critics have pointed to the 'fashion in consortia' and the uncritical acceptance of the idea that they automatically bring about considerable economies. A recent survey by *The Builder*[2] states quite clearly that it is not self-evident that the diversion of time, effort, enthusiasm and skilled manpower into the formation and development of consortia has been justified by the results. It also argues: 'The White Paper *A National Building Agency* gives too much scope to those with preconceived notions based on inadequate evidence of what consortia should do to push the consortium movement in the direction they think it should go. There should be greater clarification of government policy on consortia, more public discussion and more information made available, especially to housing committees and architects' departments and to the building industry generally, about the results so far achieved by consortia.'

There is no absence of a critical outlook with Government Departments. Indeed it was in recognition of the need for greater knowledge and experience of the new techniques (as well as the need for an assured and well organized demand) that the National Building Agency was set up by the Minister of Public Building and Works in 1964. Its purpose is to encourage positive ways of achieving a greatly increased building output from the given labour force without loss of quality or substantial increases in costs. The Ministry of Housing has an Industrialized Building Group which is now working closely with the agency in appraising building systems and providing professional advice to local authorities who are unable to provide them from their own resources. The Ministry of Housing also has a Research and Development Group which, among other things, has designed the '5M Flexible House'—a lightweight factory produced system which is especially devised so as not to need elaborate site organization or expensive machinery.

There is thus a considerable amount of research and development under way on industrialized building methods. Even if developed methods do not prove cheaper than traditional methods, there seems no doubt that they are here to stay. There is no other way of meeting the ever-increasing demand for building (for both social and economic purposes—not only houses, but also universities, colleges, schools, hospitals, factories and so forth). These demands are expected to increase by 50 per cent in the next decade.

The proportion of industrialized dwellings in tenders approved by the Ministry rose from 15·3 per cent in the first half of 1964 to 25·5 per cent in the first half of 1965. The 1970 target is 40 per cent.[14] Flats built by industrialized methods are now slightly cheaper on average than those built by traditional methods, but traditional building is still rather cheaper for houses. A greater degree of standardization in house designs is being encouraged. It is hoped that this, together with firmer forward programmes, will increase the cost advantage of industrialized dwellings in flats and reduce the cost disadvantages of houses.

'DIRECT LABOUR'

If discussion of industrialized building is heated, debates on direct labour tend to be at boiling point. These debates are at times so acrimonious and emotional that it is difficult to gain any balanced sense of proportion. So far as new house building is concerned the facts of the situation are that about 10 per cent of local authorities build by direct labour, i.e. labour which they directly employ. Only a quarter of these authorities build by direct labour alone. In terms of housing output about 9 per cent of council houses are built *by* the direct labour organizations of local authorities. (By contrast about 90 per cent of local authorities use direct labour for all or part of their housing maintenance and repairs.)

The arguments surrounding this issue are mainly political, but they frequently take the form of complaints by private builders that direct labour is 'unfair competition' since—it is argued—the true overhead costs are not charged to individual schemes, but are 'lost' in various departmental accounts. Fortunately it is not necessary here to pass judgment on this issue, but it needs to be pointed out that the controversy is fanned by the paucity of cost data. Elizabeth Layton[10] adds that, though it is impossible to be dogmatic, such figures as were available to her suggested that direct labour is neither markedly cheaper nor markedly dearer in first costs (i.e. excluding overheads), and that the balance of advantage, if any, is to be found elsewhere.

Building by direct labour was restricted under the Conservative Government and local authorities were required to offer one in every three contracts for open competition. The aim here was to provide a check on costs, but the disadvantage was that since a direct labour organization was tied to one type of building and also to competitive tendering it had to submit the lowest figure every time it tendered or else face the risk of going short of work even if the local building industry as a whole was overloaded.[15] Moreover, it is argued, there is some artificiality in applying the competitive tendering technique to local authority direct labour organizations since they are not empowered to make a profit or a loss on individual contracts. For these reasons, the Labour Government abolished the 'three in one' rule, thus enabling the planning of continuous programmes. Local authorities have been urged to develop their own methods of keeping a check on costs.

REFERENCES AND FURTHER READING

[1] Briggs, A., *History of Birmingham*, Vol. 2, Oxford University Press, 1952.

[2] The Builder, *Consortia of Local Authorities: Advantages and Disadvantages*, 1964.

[3] The Builder, 'The Direct Labour Controversy', *The Builder*, November 13, 1959.

[4] Cullingworth, J. B., *English Housing Trends*, Occasional Papers on Social Administration, No. 13, Bell, 1965.

[5] Cullingworth, J. B., *Town and Country Planning in England and Wales*, Allen and Unwin, 1964.

[6] Deeson, A. F. L., *The Comprehensive Industrialized Building Systems Annual 1965*, House Publications, 1965.

[7] Donnison, D. V., Chapman, V., and others, *Social Policy and Administration*, Allen and Unwin, 1965, Chapter 9, 'High Flats in Finsbury'.

[8] Gray, P. G., and Parr, E., *Rent Act 1957: Report of Inquiry*, Cmnd. 1246, HMSO, 1960.

[9] Gray, P. G., and Russell, R., *The Housing Situation in 1960*, The Social Survey, Central Office of Information, 1962.

[10] Layton, E., *Building by Local Authorities*, Allen and Unwin, 1961.

[11] Ministry of Education, *The Story of CLASP*, Building Bulletin, No. 19, June 1961, HMSO.

[12] Ministry of Housing and Local Government, *Housing*, Cmnd. 2050, HMSO, 1963.

[13] Ministry of Housing and Local Government, *Circular No. 21/65*, 'Housing', HMSO, 1965.

[14] Ministry of Housing and Local Government, *The Housing Programme 1965 to 1970*, Cmnd. 2838, HMSO, 1965.

[15] Ministry of Housing and Local Government, *Circular No. 50/65*, 'House Building by Direct Labour Organizations', MHLG, 1965.

[16] Ministry of Housing and Local Government, *Housing Returns*, HMSO, (Quarterly).

[17] Ministry of Public Building and Works, *A National Building Agency*, Cmnd. 2228, 1963.

[18] Ministry of Public Building and Works, *Preparing to Build*, Research and Development Building Management Handbook, No. 1, HMSO, 1965.

[19] Ministry of Public Building and Works, *Selective Tendering for Local Authorities*, Research and Development Building Management Handbook, No. 2, HMSO, 1965.

[20] Needleman, L., *The Economics of Housing*, Staples Press, 1965, Chapters 4 and 5.

[21] Rosenberg, N., *Economic Planning in the British Building Industry, 1945–49*, University of Pennsylvania Press, 1960.

[22] Sabatino, R. A., *Housing in Great Britain 1945–49*, Southern Methodist University Press, Dallas, 1956.

CHAPTER V

Council House Tenants

LOCAL AUTHORITIES have virtually complete autonomy in the selection of tenants for their houses. There is no statutory income limit or residential qualification which authorities have to observe. The only statutory provision requires them to give 'a reasonable preference to persons who are occupying insanitary or overcrowded houses, have large families or are living in unsatisfactory housing conditions'. Obviously this is so wide as to constitute no restriction at all. Before 1949 the concern of local authorities was supposedly restricted to the 'working classes', but this was never defined. The 1949 Housing Act, which deleted reference to the working classes, merely gave statutory recognition to the current practice of selecting tenants according to their housing need. But 'housing need' is capable of widely differing interpretations and, in any case, the housing situation varies so markedly between different areas that no standardization of selection procedures is possible—even if it were desirable. A family who might be considered by a local authority in a small provincial town as being in urgent need might not even be accepted on the waiting list of a big city.

When attention is turned to the families who are currently living in the 3¾ million council houses it must be remembered that a considerable number of them will have been council tenants for a very long time. Indeed, the 'under-occupation' of family-type houses by elderly tenants constitutes a major management problem in some areas. Nevertheless, households living in council houses are on average considerably larger than households living in owner-occupied and privately-rented property. Their average size is 3·81 persons, compared with 2·93 for owner-occupiers and 2·74 for private tenants. Most council houses contain four or five rooms and so there is a remarkably high density of occupation. While on average all households live at a density of 0·67 persons per room, for council house tenants the figure is 0·88 persons per room.

The high average size of council households is due to the proportionately large number of children they contain. Thirty-six per cent contain two or more children compared with the average of 23 per

TABLE 10: *Tenure, Household Size and Persons Per Room, England, 1962*[e]

| | Household's Tenure of Accommodation | | | |
	Rents from Council	Owns/is buying	Rents privately unfurnished	All house-holds†
No. of households in sample	673	1,398	1,018	3,231
No. of persons in household	%	%	%	%
1	7	11	18	13
2	19	34	35	31
3	20	25	20	22
4	25	18	15	19
5	13	8	7	8
6 or more	16	4	5	7
Average number of persons per household	3·81	2·93	2·74	3·05
Persons per room				
0·33 or less	5	20	19	16
0·34–1·49	87	80	76	80
1·50 or more	8	1	5	4
Average number of persons per room	0·88	0·58	0·66	0·67
Average number of persons aged 60 or more per household	0·40	0·53	0·53	0·49
Average number of children per household	1·28	0·68	0·58	0·78
*Household type**	%	%	%	%
Individuals under 60	2	3	4	3
Small adult households	7	17	18	15
Small families	22	23	18	21
Large families	24	9	9	12
Larger adult households	29	24	21	23
Older small households	16	25	30	23
Age of housewife				
Under 25	2	4	7	5
25–44	47	36	28	36
45–59	30	33	31	31
60 or over	20	27	33	27

† Including other tenure groups.

This and subsequent tables are taken from the report of the Rowntree Trust Housing Study and relate to England only. (*English Housing Trends*, 1965.)

cent for all tenure groups. About a quarter of council households are 'large families'. This is a reflection of the selection procedures followed by local authorities since the war—with a high priority being given to growing and large families. With the easing of the overall housing situation and the higher priority now being given to slum clearance an increasing proportion of new council tenants will be smaller households, particularly old people. At present council households contain an average of only 0·40 persons aged 60 or more, compared with 0·53 for owner-occupiers and private tenants. But the proportion of old people in council houses is steadily increasing. The Rowntree Trust Housing Study showed an increase from 0·34 elderly persons per household in 1958 to 0·40 in 1962.

Only 11 per cent of the heads of council households have non-manual jobs: the administrative, professional and managerial groups are particularly under-represented, as are farmers, shopkeepers and small employers. Two-thirds are in manual occupations and a fifth retired or unoccupied. In terms of the weekly take-home pay of the chief economic supporter, three-quarters are in the £7 10s 0d to £15 0s 0d groups; only 8 per cent have higher net incomes than this. These are the incomes of the chief economic supporter only. Two-fifths have at least one additional earner with a paid job for thirty or more hours a week and over a half have additional earners with any kind of paid job. These are relatively high proportions.

Council tenants differ from other tenure groups in the frequency with which they change their houses and in their 'satisfaction' with their accommodation. Taking the latter first, it is clear from Table 12 that council tenants are less satisfied than owner-occupiers, but more satisfied than private tenants. 'Housing satisfaction' is, of course, difficult to measure. A family may like their house but be dissatisfied with the neighbours, the neighbourhood, the separation from relatives or the journey to work—or vice versa. The house may be most unsatisfactory, but the cost of the desired alternative may be beyond the financial means—or inclinations—of the family. Alternatively the

---

* 'Household Types' are based on the size and age-structure of the household, as follows:

	Number of persons aged:	
	Under 16	*16 and over*
Individuals under 60	Nil	1 ⎫ None aged
Small adult households	Nil	2 ⎭ 60 or over
Small families	1 or 2	1 or 2
Large families	3 or more	any number
	or 2	3 or more
Larger adult households	0 or 1	3 or more
Older small households	Nil	1 or 2 (at least one aged 60 or over)

present accommodation might be well-liked but so costly that a move to a cheaper one is imperative. The answers given to a simple question on attitudes must therefore provide only a limited and crude measure. An analysis of movement is more useful in that it deals with concrete actions. But it should be noted that some moves are taken for non-housing reasons (e.g. in connection with employment) or are involuntary (e.g. are caused by eviction or demolition). Table 12 shows the year in which housewives in different tenure groups moved to their present (1962) accommodation. In interpreting this table it is important to remember that length of residence is obviously affected by the age of the housewife and that the age-distribution for each tenure group is different. For this reason the figures of the age of housewives are also given in the Table. Furthermore well over a half of council houses have been built since 1945, and thus the proportion of very long-residing council tenants must be small. Nevertheless nearly a fifth of council tenants have lived in their present houses since before the war —compared with 28 per cent of owner-occupiers and 36 per cent of private tenants. Nearly a half of council tenants first occupied their present houses in the period between the end of the war and the passing of the Rent Act (July 1957). This is a considerably higher proportion than for other tenure groups. During recent years, however, the proportion of households moving into houses in each of the three main tenure groups has been very similar. These figures relate to *present* tenure. The lower part of Table 12, however, shows the rate of movement by *previous tenure*. This reveals that, during the period January 1960 to April 1962, households in each of the three main tenure groups moved at virtually the same rate. This is an important finding since it is commonly argued that subsidized council housing tends to reduce mobility. Apparently it does so only to the same extent that owner-occupation and private tenancies do! Nevertheless, council tenants move considerably shorter distances than do other tenure groups. Only a relatively small proportion appear to move outside the area of their local authority. This is, at least in part, a consequence of the 'residential qualification' imposed by many councils: this is discussed later in this chapter.

SELECTION PROCEDURES

The selection procedures of local housing authorities vary far too widely to allow a picture to be given of a 'representative' scheme. At one extreme a local authority may select its tenants simply on the basis of length of time on the waiting list and the availability of houses of the required type. At the other extreme there are highly sophisticated procedures which defy description. Many authorities use a 'points scheme'. Essentially such schemes aim at providing a

TABLE 11: *Tenure, Earners, Occupation and Income, England, 1962*[6]

| | Household's Tenure of Accommodation | | | |
	Rents from Council	Owns/is buying	Rents privately unfurnished	All households
No. of households in sample	673	1,298	1,018	3,231
No. of persons with paid job	%	%	%	%
30 or more hours per week				
No persons	13	19	22	18
1 person	45	53	45	49
2 persons	25	22	24	23
3 or more persons	17	6	9	9
No. with paid job at all				
No persons	11	17	19	16
1 person	34	45	41	42
2 persons	33	28	29	29
3 or more persons	22	9	12	13
Occupation of Head of Household				
Administrative, professional and managerial	3	18	6	11
Farmers, shopkeepers and small employers	1	8	4	5
Clerical workers and shop assistants	7	9	6	8
Foremen and skilled workers	44	31	34	35
Other manual workers and personal service	24	10	21	17
Retired and unoccupied	19	23	26	23
Unclassified	2	1	3	2
*Weekly Income of Chief Economic Supporter**				
No. in sample giving income	548	1,014	826	2,508
	%	%	%	%
Up to £5	12	11	22	15
Over £5 to £7 10s	6	7	9	8
Over £7 10s to £10	24	15	24	20
Over £10 to £12 10s	29	18	21	21
Over £12 10s to £15	21	19	13	17
Over £15 to £20	7	17	7	12
Over £20	1	13	4	7

* Income is defined as 'the weekly income, net of income tax, surtax and national insurance contributions, of the person with the largest gross annual income'.

more objective basis for selection. Certain factors relative to housing conditions, family circumstances and health are scored: the total score then determines the priority to which the application is entitled. Thus a scheme might award points for sharing, overcrowding, lack or sharing of WC, sink, or bath, for tuberculosis, for war service or disability, for length of residence in the area and length of time on the waiting list.

TABLE 12: *Satisfaction with Present Accommodation by Tenure, Year Housewife Moved to Present Accommodation, and Age of Housewife, England, 1962*[*]

	Household's Tenure of Present Accommodation			
	Rents from Council	Owns/is buying	Rents privately unfurnished	All households
No. of households in sample	673	1,298	1,018	3,231
Satisfaction with present accommodation	%	%	%	%
'Completely satisfied'	43	60	33	47
'Fairly satisfied'	39	32	39	36
'No feelings either way'	4	2	5	4
'Rather dissatisfied'	8	4	13	8
'Completely dissatisfied'	5	1	10	5
Year housewife moved to present accommodation				
1929 or earlier	4	10	13	9
1930–9	15	18	23	18
1940–5	4	7	14	8
1946–June 1957	47	34	25	33
July 1957 to 1959	16	17	14	16
1960	7	6	5	6
1961 to April 1962	8	8	8	9
Age of housewife				
Under 25	2	4	7	5
25–44	47	36	28	36
45–59	30	33	31	31
60 or over	20	27	33	27

Movement by previous tenure

Tenure of Accommodation in 1959	No. of households in sample	Per cent who moved Jan. 1960–April 1962
Owned/was buying	1,386	14
Rented from Council	662	14
Rented privately, unfurnished	1,002	13

In some schemes a fixed number of points is given for each factor, while in others the number is variable according to the degree of seriousness or hardship caused. The number of points given for each factor will, of course, reflect the importance attached to them. This can vary greatly depending on the local housing situation and the policy of the council. The reports of the Central Housing Advisory Committee contain a detailed examination of several schemes and underlines the differing weights attached by different local authorities to the various factors. An examination of several schemes showed that a family which under one scheme would have been second in order of priority in a list of thirty applicants would have been eleventh under a different authority's scheme and twenty-seventh under yet another scheme.

Points schemes have often been criticized for giving too much weight to factors not directly affecting housing need, such as length of residence in the area or length of time on the waiting list. But this is not a criticism of points schemes *per se*: it is a criticism of the policy of the local authority which is reflected in them. More substantial is the argument that such schemes tend to become rigid and take insufficient account of the relative importance of different factors in individual cases. In fact, however, many schemes provide for a number of 'discretionary points' which can be used for determining the final order in which applicants are offered a tenancy. In these cases the points scheme is used as a sieve for sorting applications rather than as a mechanical means of selection.

Another method of selecting tenants—which may be combined with a points scheme or used as an alternative—is to divide applicants into broad groups, e.g. living in insanitary housing; sharing; overcrowded; and so forth. Some authorities allocate houses to each group according to the proportion which it represents in the total waiting list. Others group applications according to the number of bedrooms needed.

Far less common are schemes which select tenants solely by the date of registration. But perhaps the oddest scheme is the one referred to in the 1949 CHAC Report on *Selection of Tenants*[a] under which tenancies were 'allocated by ballot'—a system which the Committee thought to be hardly appropriate for a responsible authority!

In some areas the size of the waiting list together with the shortage of building land have created an attitude almost of despair and, as a result, the housing list has been closed entirely to new applicants. Others have such a large slum clearance programme that few houses are available for applicants on the normal waiting list.

Families displaced by slum clearance have priority in all areas. This is obviously necessary if the slum clearance programme is to go ahead. (Local authorities have a duty to rehouse families displaced from clearance areas if sufficient accommodation does not already exist. There is no such statutory obligation in relation to individually condemned houses, but all authorities accept an equal moral obligation.)* If the scale of the clearance programme is so large that it requires the allocation of all vacancies and new dwellings to the displaced families, the local authority have the unenvious task of choosing between slowing down slum clearance or—in effect— refusing to rehouse families on the waiting list. In the congested inner areas of some of the major conurbations this is an acute problem— particularly since any new building is dependent upon the clearing of sites. Relief to a situation such as this can be obtained only through 'overspill' to other areas.

The waiting lists of some local authorities are open to all who wish to register, but many impose restrictions. Some refuse to accept applications from families who do not live within the administrative area, or who have not lived there for a specific number of years, though exceptions are commonly made for those who work (or were born) in the area. One of the main reasons for imposing such a 'residential qualification' is that it is often thought to be fair to give preference to local families—a view which families on the waiting list may strongly hold. Another reason is to discourage people moving into the area obtaining inadequate accommodation (either purposely or because none other is available), and then 'jumping the queue' of long-established local residents.

Some authorities, though imposing no restrictions as to the classes of applicant who may register, maintain 'deferred lists' of those who are householders or who are not regarded as having a serious rehousing need; applicants on such lists are not considered for re-housing until those on the main lists have been accommodated.

The residential qualifications imposed by local authorities have received increasing criticism during recent years—in reports of the Central Housing Advisory Committee,[2, 3, 4] in reports of Committees of Inquiry,[9] by MPs and—by implication at least—in the National Economic Plan. The problem is nicely summed up in the White Paper on *The Housing Programme 1965 to 1970*:

> The responsibility for allocating tenancies is a local one. Rightly so, since local knowledge must guide those who have the difficult task of deciding an order of priority among families whose housing needs differ only in the degree of hardship under which they are living. But the allocation of local authority houses can give rise to considerations which are not wholly local in character. An exces-sively local approach to need—especially an insistence on a lengthy period of residence in the area as a condition for getting a

* See Chapter VIII.

tenancy—can operate harshly. This applies particularly to the housing of immigrants and ex-servicemen. Insistence on residential qualifications must also impede industrial mobility.

This is a matter on which local feeling runs high. It may be socially desirable to house immigrants, it may be economically desirable to house workers from other areas, but the pressure on local councillors is from families who have been on the waiting list for a number of years—and in this, they are supported by local electorates. Hence any Minister of Housing is reluctant to do any more than exhort local authorities to take a wider view. In any case, without a change in legislation, the Minister's powers are limited, and it is unlikely that an attempt would be made to curtail this jealously guarded local power. The furthest a Minister might go is to draft model rules for the allocation of council houses and urge local authorities to adopt them.

A basic question remains, however. If local authorities are not to meet the needs of 'newcomers', who is? The *National Plan* comments that 'very little has been done, except in the new and expanding towns, to help the mobility of labour by building rented houses where expanding employment most needs them'. May not this be another case where the inadequacy of local authorities points to the need for a new type of agency?

THE HOUSING OF OLD PEOPLE*

Increasing emphasis has been placed in recent years to the housing of 'special groups'—particularly the elderly. Many local authorities maintain separate waiting lists for such households and have special building programmes for one-bedroom dwellings. During the early post-war years only 5 per cent of local authority dwellings were of the one-bedroom type. Today the proportion is well over a quarter.

The increasing need for this type of accommodation arises from the changing structure of the population and the low number of small dwellings in the national housing stock. (There are $6\frac{1}{2}$ million one- and two-person households, but only 750,000 one- and two-room, and 1·4 million three-room dwellings.) Elderly households are commonly not in 'housing need' on a housing space standard. On the contrary they frequently have far more space than they need. (But a relatively high proportion of them live in houses without a fixed bath or hot water supply.) By rehousing them a local authority thus not only provides them with accommodation more suited to their needs but also frequently frees a family-type house for another household.

The basis for selecting tenants for one-bedroom dwellings is

* See also Chapter XII.

I

frequently different from the normal procedure, and a separate waiting list is often kept. Except for cases of special hardship (e.g. inability to climb stairs) more emphasis tends to be placed on length of registration—on the grounds that differences in need are slight. Some authorities allocate the majority of their one-bedroom dwellings to existing tenants. This allows them to use the vacated dwellings for a family from the waiting list. It is also often found that a relatively high proportion of households displaced by slum clearance (many of whom may not be on the waiting list) require one-bedroom dwellings.

SIZE OF DWELLINGS ALLOCATED

Local authorities frequently have stringent rules concerning the size of dwellings which should be allocated to families of different sizes. These rules vary, but the following example (from Sheffield) is illustrative:

Family Type	Type of Dwelling Allocated
Single person	1 bedroom
Couples without children	1 or 2 bedrooms
Couples (wife over 40) with one child	2 bedrooms
Couples (wife under 40) with one child	2 or 3 bedrooms
Couples with two children	3 bedrooms
Couples with more than two children	3 or 4 bedrooms

The speed at which families of different types will be rehoused will thus depend in part on the available supply (relets and new building) of the particular type of dwelling which is considered appropriate. But, in turn, the character of the building programme will be determined in the light of the needs of the families requiring to be rehoused or transferred from under-occupied council properties.

REFERENCES AND FUTURE READING

[1] Central Housing Advisory Committee, *Management of Municipal Housing Estates*, HMSO, 1945.

[2] Central Housing Advisory Committee, *Selection of Tenants*, HMSO, 1949.

[3] Central Housing Advisory Committee, *Transfers, Exchanges and Rents*, HMSO, 1953.

[4] Central Housing Advisory Committee, *Residential Qualifications*, HMSO, 1955.

[5] Cullingworth, J. B., *Housing in Transition*, Heinemann, 1963, Chapter VIII, 'Municipal Housing' (in the City of Lancaster).

[6] Cullingworth, J. B., *English Housing Trends*, Occasional Papers on Social Administration, No. 13, Bell, 1965.

[7] Cramond, R. D., *Allocation of Council Houses* (Scotland), University of Glasgow, Social and Economic Studies, Occasional Papers, No. 1, Oliver and Boyd, 1964.

[8] Department of Economic Affairs, *The National Plan*, Cmnd. 2764, HMSO, 1965.

[9] Ministry of Housing and Local Government, *Report of the Committee on Housing in Greater London* (Milner Holland Report), Cmnd. 2605, HMSO, 1965.

[10] Ministry of Housing and Local Government, *Circular No. 60/65*, 'Housing for Ex-Servicemen', HMSO, 1965.

[11] Ministry of Housing and Local Government, *The Housing Programme 1965 to 1970*, Cmnd. 2838, HMSO, 1965.

[12] Rowles, R. J. (editor), *Housing Management*, Pitman, 1959, Chapter 5.

CHAPTER VI

Standards for New Housing

IN THIS CHAPTER we are concerned with the standards laid down or recommended by the State for the design, equipment and size of new houses. There are, in fact, two quite separate systems which need to be discussed. On the one hand there are the building by-laws and regulations designed to prevent the erection of buildings which endanger safety and health. On the other hand there are the standards of design, space and equipment which are recommended in the Housing Manuals and other Reports issued by the Ministry of Housing.

Building by-laws and regulations have the force of law. Buildings which contravene them can be required to be altered or even pulled down. This power stems from the fact that building by-laws and regulations are devised to protect public safety and health. By contrast, recommended standards of 'adequate' or 'desirable' housing are, in principle at least, designed to encourage the building of houses of high quality, comfort and convenience. Though often couched in terms of 'minimum acceptable standards' (possibly on the ground that, at any point of time, what is considered to be an optimum standard is unattainable in general), the 'minimum' here refers to household needs rather than the requirements dictated by considerations of safety and health. Thus a building regulation will specify that 'the roof of any building shall be weather proof and so constructed as not to transmit moisture due to rain or snow to any part of the structure of the building which would be adversely affected by such moisture' or that 'any larder for the storage of perishable food (other than an enclosed space having means of refrigeration) shall (unless it is adequately ventilated by mechanical means) be ventilated to the external air'. The Parker Morris official report on *Homes for Today and Tomorrow*,[6] on the other hand, deals with the influence of increasing affluence and social changes on the types of houses which are needed.

But in truth, this distinction between minimum standards and desirable housing standards is a very blurred one, both in practice and conceptually.

So far as practice is concerned the building regulations deal not only with such matters as structural stability, safeguards from fire risks and so on, but also with the height of rooms, thermal and sound insulation. (The Scottish Building Regulations go much further: they lay down that all new dwellings shall have a kitchen, a ventilated larder, a bath or shower, wash-hand basin and wc; that blocks of flats of more than four storeys shall have a lift; that living-rooms shall be of a minimum size of 170–305 sq ft and that kitchens shall be of a minimum size of 45–75 sq ft—depending upon the total size of the house.)

It is difficult to justify all such regulations in terms of danger to the public. The Report of the Committee on Building Legislation in Scotland,[7] published in 1957, has an interesting—if not wholly convincing—section which discusses the purpose and scope of building control. It is pointed out that underlying the basic objectives of ensuring that occupants, neighbours and passers-by are adequately 'protected' there is a further implicit qualifying condition—'regard to the economic use of the nation's resources. This can be seen to be implicit in some building requirements in the past which may have had the effect of requiring the erection of a better, stronger or more desirable building than the owner of his own accord would have wished or than was strictly essential for the health and safety of the public.'

But once it is admitted that considerations other than public safety and health are relevant the only limit to the extension of building controls is economic and social practicability. And this is precisely the same issue which confronts the framers of desirable housing standards. Thus the Guest Committee conclude that 'the building standards which prevail at any time must of necessity be the result of some compromise between what would be perfect and what is practicable, and must take into account the state of development of building and design techniques and what the nation can afford'. Similarly the Parker Morris Report, which proposes some notable increases in officially recommended housing standards, emphasizes that these standards are at a *minimum* level and argues that if real incomes continue to rise 'and if building research leads to advances in technique, we believe there will be a demand for a progressive upgrading' of the new minimum standards.

In the final analysis, therefore, no clear division can now be made between the matters dealt with under building regulations and those dealt with under recommended housing standards. The distinction is simply between those minimum standards which it has been considered reasonable to make mandatory and those rather higher standards which are (at the present) merely recommended as being desirable. Even this distinction can become blurred when account is taken of the powers which are available under Town and Country Planning legislation. The trend has been for minimum enforceable standards to rise (both in relation to new buildings and to existing houses), and for increasing emphasis to be placed on standards of amenity, convenience and comfort.[8]

BUILDING BY-LAWS AND REGULATIONS

Building by-laws and regulations have their origins in the sanitary legislation of the nineteenth century. Indeed, the relevant legislation is still largely that of the Public Health Acts. Under these Acts build- ing by-laws are made and operated by local authorities (the same local authorities as are housing authorities, viz. county boroughs and districts). Anyone proposing to build, alter or reconstruct a building must submit plans for the approval of the local authority. This approval is normally given only if there is strict compliance with the by-laws. These by-laws relate to site drainage, preparation of sites, prevention of damp, stability of foundations, resistance of walls to weather and damp, fire resistance, protection of roofs against weather, resistance of floors to moisture, and materials and construction for chimney flues. The siting of dwellings is controlled by regulations requiring minimum space which varies with the height of the building. Ventilation is regulated by minimum standards of openable window areas. Regulations also govern the height of habitable rooms, thermal insulation, the installation of fittings, roof drainage, private sewers, sanitary conveniences, wells and rainwater tanks, fireplaces, stoves and waterheaters.

Plans can be rejected if sites are impregnated with offensive matter; if construction is proposed over sewers or drains, or on inadequately drained sites; if building plans show inadequate watercloset accom- modation, pure water supply or access for removal of refuse; if buildings are to be constructed with short-life materials; if the provision for food storage is inadequate; or if each dwelling does not have a bathroom with a fixed bath or shower and suitable provision for both a hot and cold water supply.

Provisions of this nature are, of course, quite inadequate unless backed by penalties for contravention. By-laws can be enforced by injunctions requiring removal or alteration; by notice to an owner for demolition or conformance (in cases of default, the local authority can undertake the necessary work); and by legal proceedings.

Building by-laws are at present (1965) made by the local authorities themselves, though these are commonly based on 'model by-laws' recommended by the Ministry. They are also subject to Ministerial approval, and in practice substantial deviations from the model by-laws are rarely allowed. Nevertheless unnecessary variation between local authorities can handicap the building industry and hamper the development of new and more economical building methods. Furthermore the system under which 1,400 separate local authorities are involved in making sets of by-laws, publishing them and having them confirmed by the Ministry is cumbersome in the extreme. Keeping these by-laws up to date with new concepts of minimum standards and with technical progress constitutes an enormous administrative task. Thus in 1959 the Ministry proposed new standards of thermal insulation in domestic buildings.[17] Local authorities were urged to amend their building by-laws accordingly and to submit draft amendments to the Ministry. The 1960 Annual Report of the Ministry gave a note on progress to the end of 1960. The amending by-laws of 347 authorities had been confirmed and preliminary drafts had been agreed in a further 371 cases. Presumably the other 700 local authorities were still considering the new standards.

Steps were taken to sweep away this archaic procedure in the 1961 Public Health Act. This contains provisions for repealing the power of local authorities to make building by-laws and empowers the Minister to make building regulations for the whole of England and Wales. (In Scotland building by-laws made by local authorities were replaced in 1963 by building regulations made by the Secretary of State under the Building (Scotland) Act, 1959.) A Building Regulations Advisory Committee was set up in 1962 to advise the Minister 'on the exercise of his power to make building regulations and on other subjects connected with building regulations'. It was also announced that a comprehensive review of building law was to be instituted, primarily through the Committee, just as soon as work on the regulations had been taken far enough to allow this to be done. The Building Regulations Advisory Committee reported in 1964.[23] It is not proposed to discuss their recommendations here particularly since the wider review of building law is now under way. The need for this is underlined in the Committee's report. The new Building Regulations were issued in July 1965.[26, 24]

The present situation is thus one of rapidly moving events involving the adaptation of a basically out-dated code of building control to modern requirements. Responsibility for building control has now been transferred from the Ministry of Housing to the newly reorganized Ministry of Public Building and Works.

RECOMMENDED HOUSING STANDARDS

Prior to the First World War working-class dwellings were almost entirely provided by private enterprise. Public action was largely confined to the maintenance of minimum sanitary standards and the repair and clearance of unfit housing. The provision of housing by public authorities—though undertaken by a few municipalities, mainly in the big cities—was generally regarded as being undesirable. The limited provision of local authority housing for the poorer sections of the working classes was justified on the ground that they were unable to pay rents at a level which would provide sufficient inducement to private builders. But even this argument was strongly contested. Given this climate of opinion there was obviously little scope for officially recommended standards for new housing. Housing reformers might argue that it was obvious that the comfort and welfare of families 'both morally and physically are much better provided for when each house has at least three bedrooms',[2] and that separate toilet, washing and cooking facilities would prevent the moral deterioration of families and reduce crime, but of what relevance were these standards if families could not afford the rents and if housing subsidies were politically impracticable? Philanthropic housing societies attempted to show the way by building 'model' houses which provided good housing for working-class families at a reasonable profit, but it was clear that they could not meet the needs of the really poor. Indeed, despite a reduction in standards and the abandoning of the principle of self-contained accommodation their main achievement was not in providing a 'model', but in demonstrating the impossibility of providing decent housing for the poor without radical changes in housing policy.

As we have seen, the First World War precipitated this. Though there was no general agreement on the objectives or scope of housing policy it was agreed that the 'abnormal' conditions of the early post-war period demanded a new approach—with the direct provision of houses by local authorities and the payment of subsidies from both the Exchequer and the local rates. It was no longer the 'really poor' who were the avowed concern of policy-makers. On the contrary there was now a serious shortage of all kinds of houses. And since private builders could not be expected to meet these needs in the early post-war years of scarcity and high prices the responsibility had to pass—temporarily at least—to local authorities. As the Tudor Walters Report[9] noted, 'this fact must materially affect the types of houses which it is most economical to build, and the standard of accommodation and equipment which should be provided'. Furthermore the standard of housing demanded by the better-paid working class families was rising, and the influence of war conditions was expected to increase the force and extent of this demand for an improved standard.

THE TUDOR WALTERS REPORT

For the first time, therefore, policy was being directed not to dealing with minimum standards or poverty-line housing, but towards the provision of houses which would be of a 'high' standard. Indeed, the Tudor Walters Report argued that it was uneconomical in the long run to add to the already large supply of houses which would soon be inadequate to meet rising standards: 'it is only wise economy to build dwellings which, so far as may be judged, will continue to be above the accepted minimum, at least for the whole period of the loan with the aid of which they are to be provided, say 60 years'.

This is now a familiar argument, though in practice it has to be tempered by practical possibilities—by the size of the gap between the cost of what people can afford and what is desirable in the long run, and by the choice which has to be made between quantity and quality.

In the optimistic climate of 1918 the Tudor Walters Committee recommended housing of a type, size and layout which was strikingly different from pre-war building. Two-storey houses (in distinction to flats) were urged as the most economical type of development; densities of twelve houses to the acre in urban and eight houses to the acre in rural areas (then being recommended by the Local Government Board), though low in comparison with pre-war densities, would allow a more suburban type of development involving less costly construction in roads and footpaths. The most serious scarcity was of houses having at least three bedrooms. (The normal pre-war working-class dwelling had two bedrooms.) It was not 'sound economical policy' to reduce the cost of buildings by cutting down unduly the size of rooms; recommended plans for three-bedroom houses averaged 855 sq ft, though it was strongly urged that a considerable proportion of larger three-bedroom houses (with parlours) should be built: these averaged 1,055 sq ft excluding fuel and other stores.

The desire for a parlour (or 'third room') was, according to the evidence received by the Committee, remarkably widespread. Though the provision of a living-room of adequate size and of a separate scullery in which meals could be cooked would go some way towards meeting the wishes of many tenants, 'nevertheless it is the parlour which the majority desire' in spite of the extra rent this would involve. A parlour could be obtained more cheaply by reducing the size of the living-room and scullery, or even by adopting the old type of house with combined living-room and scullery (thus making the parlour the 'second room'). The Committee were, however, 'struck by the fact that none of those who spoke on behalf of either working men or women (this was, of course, before the day of consumer or 'user-needs' research) regarded such alternatives as desirable; and while they were emphatic as to the need of the addition of a small parlour, they were equally emphatic that the parlour should not be given at the expense of the necessary accommodation and area of the living-room and scullery, but should either be given in addition to these or omitted altogether'.

The evidence strongly stressed the desire of working-class families 'to eliminate from the living-room the dirty work and particularly the cooking of meals'. Particular dislike was expressed of the common house-type which had a front parlour and a combined back kitchen and living-room which contained the cooking-range, the sink and often the copper. The difficulty of achieving the separation was that it involved two fires—one for cooking in the scullery and one for heating in the living-room. Where gas was available at reasonable cost the difficulty was partially overcome by placing a gas cooker in the scullery. In such cases 'a modified form of fire is sometimes used in the living-room, the grate having an open fire but at the same time having a little oven and a small hob with which minor cooking operations can be carried out'.

This problem had to be met according to local circumstances. The provision of a parlour was the simplest solution; where this was not possible 'the tendency to transfer cooking, etc., from the living-room to the scullery should be given due weight' in deciding upon the equipment to be provided.

Perhaps the biggest single advance recommended by the Tudor Walters Committee was that every house should be provided with a bath (or, where there was no water supply, space for one to be later installed). At this date very few houses had baths, though it was becoming more common in new houses. In the smaller types of houses it was frequently placed in the scullery, where drainage was available and where hot water could be obtained from the copper without the necessity for any circulating system. Though obviously cheap, this was becoming increasingly disliked and inconvenient as the cooking of meals moved from the living-room to the scullery. Various methods were suggested for improving the situation but the preferred method was to have a separate bathroom fitted with hot and cold water: this would afford 'full satisfaction of the desire which undoubtedly prevails among the artisan class and the more cleanly sections of all classes'. Where 'the probable class of tenant', the limitation of water supply, or financial factors precluded the provision of a hot water supply from a boiler, the copper could be placed at a level which would allow the hot water to flow through a pipe into the bath.

Much of the discussion on this subject now appears rather quaint, but it resulted in a very marked improvement in living conditions. (The Housing Act of 1923 made it a statutory obligation to fit 'fixed baths' in subsidized housing, but it was not until 1936 that the statutory obligation was extended to all new houses.)

The optimism implicit in the Tudor Walters Report was general. Indeed, the official housing manual issued in 1919 recommended even higher space standards—averaging 900 sq ft for a three-bedroomed non-parlour house and 1,080 sq ft for a parlour house. The standards were actually implemented—and even exceeded—in the earliest post-war years. Unfortunately the strain on the building industry led to very high costs which the system of subsidies (under which local authorities were shielded from all 'losses' in excess of a penny rate) did nothing to discourage. In the event there was a rapid reassessment of policy. It is striking, however, that though there were major changes in the subsidy scheme and in the role of local authorities in the total house-building programme, standards were maintained at a high level. Even the Departmental Committee on the High Cost of Building Working Class Dwellings, which reported in 1921, gave the opinion that the housing standards adopted were 'in no way extra-vagant' in spite of their superiority in size, construction, amenity and equipment.

Nevertheless the new standards had to be somewhat reduced. The 1923 Housing Act fixed space standards for subsidized three-bedroom houses at a normal minimum of 620 sq ft and a maximum of 950 sq ft. Though standards varied somewhat with economic circumstances (reaching their lowest in the early 'thirties) the majority of houses built by local authorities between 1923 and 1939 had three bedrooms and an overall area (exclusive of stores) of 750–850 sq ft. Virtually all had an electricity supply, a toilet, a separate scullery, a bath and a garden.

THE DUDLEY REPORT

The end of the Second World War saw the setting up of another committee to review housing standards—the Dudley Committee. Their report, *Design of Dwellings*,[3] was published in 1944 and stressed the changes which had taken place since the time of the Tudor Walters Report. The general standard of living had increased and there was a growing desire for and appreciation of good housing. In particular there was a rising demand for convenient domestic arrangements and labour-saving fittings. In a typical inter-war local authority house the ground floor consisted of a large living-room (180 sq ft), a small scullery with a copper for laundry (80 sq ft), a combined bathroom and wc, and a fuel store. Cooking on the coal range was almost universal until the widespread extension of public services made possible—and popular—the use of a gas or electric cooker. This was usually placed in the scullery which tended to become the location for all kitchen equipment and (despite its unsuitability) for the eating of meals. For these functions the traditional scullery was far too small. The taking of meals in the kitchen was due not only to the greater convenience of eating in the same room in which the food was cooked, but also to the increasing use of the living-room as 'a quiet place for study, social intercourse and recreation'. These needs could not be adequately met in a room which was constantly used for meals. Stress was laid on this, and it was pointed out that the number of separate meal-times for a working family was much greater than was generally realized. A not unusual timetable for an average working family was given as:

7 a.m.	Breakfast for husband
8 a.m.	Breakfast for children
12.30 p.m.	Lunch for children
4.30 p.m.	Tea for children
6 p.m.	Tea for husband
7–8 p.m.	Supper for children
9 p.m.	Supper for husband

But if a kitchen was to be designed as a living-room it had to be pleasant, large and easy to run. Laundry and dirty household work would require a small separate 'utility room'. The common practice of putting the bathroom on the ground floor, though cheaper, was thought to be inconvenient and disliked. In any case, if the living space on the ground floor was to be enlarged, the bathroom could not remain there without producing a larger area than was required on the first floor for bedrooms.

The bedroom standards recommended by the Tudor Walters Report (150, 100 and 65 sq ft) were thought to be generally acceptable, though it was recommended that the second and third bedrooms should be slightly enlarged.

In total the floor area required to give effect to these recommendations was 900 sq ft. This was about the same as recommended by Tudor Walters for a non-parlour house (855–900 sq ft), but considerably less than the 1,055–1,080 sq ft for a parlour house. It is interesting to note that there was virtually no discussion in the Dudley Report on 'the parlour problem' which so exercised the minds of the Tudor Walters Committee. Indeed the only reference to the term noted that it carries 'an implication which is old-fashioned and obsolete'. With the development of the scullery into the kitchen and then into the living-kitchen and utility room, the problem was thought to be solved. All that was needed was 'a clean, cheerful room where meals could be taken with the maximum of convenience to the housewife who does the cooking but which is kept free from the dirty work of washing clothes and another more private room for other activities'. That this was not the end of the matter will be apparent from later discussion.

The equipment provided in an inter-war house normally consisted of a bath, a water-closet, a sink, one draining board, a copper in the

TABLE 13: *Housing Standards Recommended by the Dudley Committee, 1944*
(*Three-bedroom, five-person house*)

Ground Floor

Alternative 1	Minimum Area sq ft
Living-room	160
Kitchen for meals	110
Utility room	35
Total	305
Unallocated	25
Minimum aggregate area	330

Alternative 2

Living-room with dining space	210
Working kitchen	100
Total	310
Unallocated	20
Minimum aggregate area	330

Alternative 3 (for areas where cooking will continue to be done on a coal range)

Kitchen living-room	160
Scullery	50
Sitting-room	110
Total	320
Unallocated	10
Minimum aggregate area	330

First Floor

Best bedroom	135
Double bedroom	110
Single bedroom	70
Total	315
Unallocated	15
Minimum aggregate area	330

scullery, a coal range in the living-room (and, increasingly in the 'thirties, a cooker in the scullery), a dresser in either the living-room or scullery, a built-in ventilated larder, and about 20 sq ft of shelving. Apart from these normal provisions some local authorities added a wash-basin in the bathroom. Hot water was frequently provided from the copper and the supply to the bath was by means of a gravitation feed or a pump. Sometimes, however, the hot water supply was provided by a circulating system from the back boiler of the range.

The Dudley Committee commented that this amount of equipment looked quite impressive on paper, but was deficient in relation to contemporary needs. In particular there was a strong case for better heating arrangements, constant hot water, better cooking facilities, better kitchen fittings, better arrangements for washing and drying clothes, more efficient plumbing and sanitary fittings, more storage space, more light and power points, and better daylighting.

POST-WAR HOUSING STANDARDS

Following the Dudley Report an official Housing Manual[10] was published which recommended plans for a three-bedroomed, five-person house having a maximum floor area—excluding stores—of 800 to 900 sq ft (as compared with the Dudley *minimum* of 900 sq ft). But with the advent of the Labour Government (and the appointment of Aneurin Bevan as the Minister responsible for housing) the minimum area was raised to the full Dudley standard.

The houses built in the early post-war years were of considerably higher standard than the typical pre-war house. The three-bedroom, five-person house had a total floor area (including outbuildings) of over 1,000 sq ft. A hot water supply to bath, sink and wash-basin had become a normal provision. Heated linen cupboards were commonly provided. A second WC, additional cupboards for brooms and dry goods, more and better-fitted cupboards in the bedrooms, larger dressers, more shelving, more light and power points, a larger area of paths and paved space around the house, were common improvements. Other items frequently included towel rails, meter cupboards, rustproof steel windows, built-in flap tables, lagging to pipes and tanks, insulated jackets to hot water tanks, improved fireplaces, built-in electric fires, two-way light switches on staircases, bath panels, serving hatches, immersion heaters, cold shelves in larders, stainless steel sinks, an extra sink in the washhouse and double draining boards.

Not surprisingly all these improvements added considerably to housing costs. In 1947 prices the increase in costs due to additional equipment and other improvements averaged £127. Extra internal floor space added £129 and outbuildings added a further £72. The Girdwood Committee[12] estimated that of the total 1947 cost of a standard three-bedroom house (£1,242) over a quarter (£328) was due to higher standards and equipment. They calculated that had the pre-war size of house been retained and certain items of the current equipment omitted, labour and materials might have been released on a scale sufficient to build from 10 to 15 per cent more houses.

Closer control by the technical officers of the Ministry was successful in offsetting some of the inflation in building costs during the next two years. Indeed the average floor area of a three-bedroom house increased from 1,029 sq ft in October 1947 to 1,050 sq ft in October 1949 at a cost of only £16. Savings amounting to £41 were achieved by simplified design and specification. Nevertheless, increases in the cost of materials resulted in an overall increase of £79 to an average of £1,321. By 1951 average costs had risen to £1,450.

Standards were now being pared down, and they fell markedly as the total house-building programme was expanded in the early and mid-'fifties. Ministry circulars and Supplements to the Housing Manual urged the adoption of economic designs which would 'help local authorities to reduce building costs without prejudice to essential standards'. The average area of the recommended design for a three bedroom house was 900 sq ft, though the overall minimum area criterion was abolished. The new, smaller dimension house, known as 'the People's House', rapidly became the norm. Increasing emphasis was placed on smaller type houses—two bedroom and three-bedroomed four-person houses.

Standards of equipment were also reduced. Local authorities were exhorted to economise 'not merely in the design of the house but also in the services and equipment to be installed in them'. A second WC was no longer required by the Ministry in houses for five or more persons and most local authorities abandoned it. But proposals which were mooted for reverting to the pre-war practice of placing the bathroom on the ground floor did not prove generally acceptable.[1]

Unfortunately standards of design were also often reduced. The plans published by the Ministry in the 1952 Supplement to the Housing Manual accepted bulkheads cutting through a bedroom floor, flues projecting just inside a bedroom door and awkward splayed-off corners to rooms and lobbies. As Cleeve Barr comments, 'these measures were adopted as expedients in the process of cutting the floor area to the limit, and dwellings which have been built to these standards will always contain these inconveniences as a permanent record of the economy era in which they were built'.[1]

TABLE 14: *Summary of Fluctuations in the Minimum Area of the Three-bedroomed, Five-person House (1919–57)**

Source	Living-room	First bedroom	Second bedroom	Third bedroom	Aggregate living-space (where stipulated)	Overall area exclusive of stores
	sq ft	sq ft	sq ft	sq ft	sq ft	sq ft
Tudor Walters Report, 1918, and Manual of Local Govt. Board, 1919	180	150	100	65	–	Non-parlour types 855–900, parlour types 1,055–1,080
Houses built under 1919 Act	180	150	100	65	–	950–1,400
Houses built under 1923 and subsequent Acts	180	150	100	65	–	750–850
Dudley Report, 1944	160–210 plus kitchen of 100–110	150	110	70	330	900 min.
Housing Manual, 1944	160–180 plus dining-kitchen of 110–125, or 180–200 plus working kitchen of 90–100	135–150	110–120	70–80	–	800–900
Circular 200, 1945, and Housing Manual, 1949	160–200 plus dining-kitchen of 110–130, or 180–220 plus working kitchen of 90–110	135–150	110–120	70–80	–	900 min.
Circular 38, 1951	160 plus dining-kitchen of 110, or 180 plus working kitchen of 90	135	110	70	320	Overall minima abolished
'Houses 1952' and 'Houses 1953'	160 plus dining-kitchen of 110, or 180 plus working kitchen of 90	135	110	70	320	Plans range from 820–860, emphasis also on three-bedroom four-person types from 695–740

* Barr, A. W. Cleeve, *Public Authority Housing*, Batsford, 1958, p. 54.

TABLE 15: *Average Area and Building Cost of Three-bedroom Local Authority Houses, 1938–9 to 1964*

	Average floor area (including out-buildings) sq ft	Average cost £
1938–9	800	380
1947	1,029	1,242
1949	1,050	1,321
1951	1,050	1,450
October-December 1951	1,011	1,460
October-December 1952	921	1,410
October-December 1953	917	1,405
October-December 1954	916	1,390
October-December 1955	909	1,442
October-December 1956	909	1,488
1957	908	1,486
1958	903	1,485
1959	897	1,515
1960	897	1,611
1961	898	1,786
1962	907	1,967
1963	917	2,129
1964	920	2,303

The figures for 1938–9 to 1951 are estimates taken from the reports of the Girdwood Committee on the Cost of House-Building[13]. The estimated costs are based on actual final costs. The remaining figures are taken from the Annual Reports of the Ministry of Housing and Local Government. For the period since 1954 the costs relate to average tender prices.

The average size and cost of three-bedroom local authority houses built in 1938–9 and since 1947 are shown in Table 15. By the end of the 'fifties space had been reduced to less than 900 sq ft. But by this time mounting criticism of the low standard of local authority housing was bringing about an acceptance of the need for a reappraisal. As a result a Sub-Committee of the Central Housing Advisory Committee was set up 'to consider the standards of design and equipment applicable to family dwellings and other forms of residential accommodation, whether provided by public authorities or by private enterprise, and to make recommendations'. The report of this Sub-Committee was published in 1961 under the title Homes for Today and Tomorrow,[6] though it is more commonly known, from the name of the Chairman, as the Parker Morris Report.

K

THE PARKER MORRIS REPORT

Great changes had taken place since the Dudley Committee reported in 1944. Increased real incomes, full employment and the development of social services had created a 'social and economic revolution'. This was partly manifested in a large increase in material possessions—motor cars, washing machines, television sets, vacuum cleaners and refrigerators. For all these possessions more space was needed. But social changes were equally important. Children were staying longer at school; housewives had less drudgery and more free time; family life had become more home-centred. An increased range of activities was carried on in the home: 'teenagers wanting to listen to records; someone else wanting to watch the television; someone going in for do-it-yourself; all these and homework too mean that the individual members of the family are more and more wanting to be free to move away from the fireside to somewhere else in the home'. More space was needed for these activities, but the space had to be usable—in winter as well as in summer. Better heating installation was therefore essential. More space and better heating: this is the main theme of the Parker Morris Report.

Additional floor space was given first priority. The growing need for more space could be met at a comparatively small cost and 'a good house or flat can never be made out of premises which are too small.' Larger dwellings were a good long-term investment since they were more adaptable to future needs. Given the greatly increased rate of social and economic change the ideal would be 'the adaptable house'—a house which could easily be altered as circumstances changed. Unfortunately such a house did not appear to be practicable, but much more flexibility could be achieved if the idea of minimum room sizes was replaced by minimum space standards for the activities which are carried on in a house. The Dudley Committee had recommended minimum room standards but with overall dwelling sizes which gave a sufficient margin to allow for the rooms to be of satisfactory shape and for the circulation space to be adequate. This margin was whittled away during the 'fifties and resulted in a standardization and a lack of variety in internal design. Emphasis on room sizes had focused undue attention on working out a pattern of room areas which would comply with the standards, and insufficient regard to the satisfaction of the requirements of the occupants. Furthermore, the labelling of rooms for specific uses—bedroom, living-room, working-kitchen, dining kitchen—tended to assume a conventional arrangement of the dwelling and the particular way in which rooms were to be used. This inhibited the flexibility of both the design and the subsequent use of a dwelling.

The Parker Morris approach was to look at the needs as a whole of the intended occupants of a dwelling and then to set minimum sizes of the whole dwelling which they believed these needs implied. Such an approach leaves the designer a considerable freedom in determining how best to arrange space and equipment to meet the requirements of particular household types. This flexibility allows the questioning of widespread assumptions—for instance that the floor area designed for sleeping, dressing and sanitary needs should be equal to that devoted to all other needs put together, or that houses should generally have two storeys rather than one, one-and-a-half, two-and-a-half, or three.

The report contains a large number of detailed recommendations based on the Committee's view of the functional and performance requirements that future houses ought to satisfy. But in order to provide reasonably satisfactory safeguards a series of minimum over-all floor areas were recommended, related to different household sizes. These are set out in Table 16, together with recommended general storage area and provision of wcs. The Committee stressed that these are *minimum* floor areas, for although satisfactory dwellings could be built at these space standards, 'it may well not be possible to include within them some desirable features which may come to be generally required in the future'.

Considerable emphasis is given in the report on the need for better heating: 'the key to the design of the home'. The capacity of dwellings to provide privacy for individual activities such as reading, writing and following particular hobbies has been considerably handicapped during the winter because of the lack of adequate heating. If the Committee's recommendations are followed the standard foreigners' joke about the cold English bedroom will become outdated. It is certainly justified at present: 'at least half the rooms in most dwellings have been relegated for sleeping only—a habit which has set the pattern for the rest of the year as well. It is strange that half of what we build, and therefore half of what we pay for, is reserved for use during the hours of darkness when we are unconscious of our surroundings'. That the Englishman is not constitutionally wedded to the idea of a cold house is proved by the increasing demand for better heating: home sales of electric heaters doubled between 1954 and 1960; and at the latter date about three in every five households had paraffin heaters.

The minimum recommended heating standard is for an installation capable of heating the kitchen and the areas used for circulation to 55°F and the living areas to 65°F, when the outside temperature is 30°F. Where a dwelling is equipped for this standard it is not greatly inconvenient or costly to top up bedrooms. But the increasing requirements of families will make a more expensive installation capable of heating bedrooms to 65°F a 'better value for money'.

TABLE 16: *Housing Standards Recommended by the Parker Morris Committee*, 1961

	House designed for the following number of persons:					
	6	5	4	3	2	1
Net Floor Area[a] (*in sq ft*)						
3-storey house[b]	1,050	1,010	–	–	–	–
2-storey centre terraced house	990	910	800	–	–	–
2-storey semi or end house	990	880	770	–	–	–
Maisonette	990	880	770	–	–	–
Flat	930	850	750[c]	610	480	320
Single-storey house	900	810	720	610	480	320
General Storage Area[d] (*in sq ft*)						
Houses[e]	50	50	50	45	40	30
Flats and Maisonettes:						
Inside the dwelling	15	15	15	12	10	8
Outside the dwelling	20	20	20	20	20	20
WCs[f]						
One-level dwellings	2	1s	1s	1	1	1
Two-level (or more) dwellings	–	2	1s	1	1	1

(a) *Net floor area* is the area on one or more floors enclosed by the walls of a dwelling and is measured to the opposing unfinished faces. It includes the area occupied by partitions, the area taken up on each floor by any staircase, the area of any chimney breast or flue, and the area of any external wc. It excludes the floor area of any general store, dustbin store, fuel store, garage or balcony; any area in rooms with sloping ceilings to the extent that the height of the ceiling does not exceed 5 ft; and any lobby open to the air.

(b) These figures require modification if a garage is built in.

(c) 720 sq ft if balcony access.

(d) *General storage area* is measured to exclude floor area occupied by any dustbin store, fuel store, or pram space, and any space required inside terraced houses as access from one side of the house to the other—taken as 2 ft 3 in. wide. If there is a garage integral with or adjoining the house any garage area in excess of 130 sq ft should be allowed to count for general storage. Where a garage for a flat is integral with or adjacent to the block, any excess garage area may be counted in respect of the external storage requirement. But because the required 20 ft minimum is too small to be useful if split up, the excess garage area should count only if it is 20 sq ft or more.

(e) Some of this may be on an upper floor; but at least 25 sq ft should be at ground level.

(f) In two or three storey houses, a second wc with one of them on the entrance floor is preferred whatever the size of family. The table gives only the recommended *minimum* satisfactory provision. For dwellings designed for 3 or less persons the wc may be combined with the bathroom, but for 4 and 5 person

Other recommendations are that flats should have standards of accommodation and storage comparable with those for houses; that the general appearance of housing layouts should be greatly improved; that gardens should have a reasonable degree of privacy; that terrace houses should be arranged in such a way as to provide suitable access from one side of the house to the other; that play space must be the first call on available space around flats where there are children (at least 20–25 sq ft *per person*, omitting one and two-person dwellings); and that estates should generally be planned on the basis of one car per dwelling plus provision for visitors.

The cost implications of the Parker-Morris recommended standards are set out in appendices to the Report. Table 17 below summarises the extra cost for four- and five-person two-storey houses. A five-person three-bedroom house costing, in 1961, about £1,900 (including

TABLE 17: *Cost Implications of Parker Morris Standards Estimated Total Extra Costs*
(Average Costs based on Provisional Prices for Local Authority Housing at mid-1961)

	2-storey house	
	5 person	4 person
	£	£
Floor space (including storage space)	113*	90
Wash-basin in wc Compartment	14	–
Heating	33	32
Kitchen Fittings	25	25
Socket Outlets	13	13
Bedroom cupboards	11	–
	209	160

site development but excluding land) would increase by between £163 and £287—an average of £209. This would involve a rent increase of about 5s or 6s a week. Provision for one car space per dwelling would, of course, increase this still further, at least at housing densities above sixty habitable rooms per acre. Average cost figures are not very meaningful here, since they will vary according to the type of provision made (£36 for hardstanding to £1,000 for communal basement garages) and the density and type of development.

---

dwellings where only one wc is provided this should be separate (marked *s* in the table). In dwellings where two wc's are provided one should be separate from the bathroom. Separate wcs should be provided with a wash-basin except where there is an adjoining bathroom.

* This figure includes the cost of a second wc.

Various examples provided in the Report give an average cost per dwelling of around £250.

These are considerable increases—particularly at a time when land and building costs are rising (the average tender price for a 900 sq ft house rose from £1,957 in 1962 to £2,269 in 1964). Reactions to the recommendations have ranged from 'exceedingly modest' (Town and Country Planning Association) to 'extremely idealistic' (*The Estates Gazette*). The Committee themselves state that 'enough people are now willing to pay more for a really good home to make our proposals workable and realistic, expensive though some of them are'. The report was commended to local authorities by the Ministry[19] 'as a basis for making a fresh assessment of the sort of houses they should build in the future'.* The new standards are in no way mandatory on local authorities, and no additional Exchequer subsidies are given for houses built to them. Indeed it was pointed out that publication of the report comes 'at a difficult time when the country is engaged in a financial struggle'. Until recently the only advice given by the Ministry was that provision of higher standard houses would involve the need to adopt realistic rent policies: 'If better and more convenient houses are to be provided, this must be reflected in the rents. Some authorities are indeed already building houses up to the standard now recommended and are charging higher rents for them, while using their cheaper houses to accommodate less well-off tenants.' The 1965 White Paper,[21] which also announced increased housing subsidies, marks a change in attitude:

> The Government intend that the improved subsidies should be used to raise housing standards. They will expect local authorities, new town corporations and housing associations normally to incorporate in new designs the space and heating standards recommended by the Parker Morris Committee. A growing number of local authority houses already incorporate them—46 per cent of dwellings approved in the first quarter of this year were designed to the full space standards and 61 per cent to the heating standards. The Government believe that many families will increasingly be prepared to pay higher rents for better (and warmer) houses, and that long before the life of today's houses come to an end the Parker Morris standards will be regarded as the minimum which every house should reach.

ENVIRONMENTAL STANDARDS

The Parker Morris Report argued that 'housing can become obsolete

* See also MHLG, *Space in the Home*, Design Bulletin No. 6, HMSO, 1963. This is a guide to the design of houses based on Parker Morris standards.

in its layout just as surely as in its internal design and facilities'. An adequate examination of the standards of housing layouts and of environmental planning would, unfortunately, take us far beyond the scope of the present book. Reference should be made, however, to two points of major importance—density and provision for traffic.

Questions of density have long formed a matter for controversy in Britain: from Unwin's *Nothing Gained by Overcrowding* (1912) to the Architectural Press onslaught on 'subtopia' in *Outrage* (1955) and other recent writings on 'urban sprawl' and 'prairie planning' on the one hand and 'metropolitan barracks' on the other hand. As the very terms suggest the arguments tend to be emotionally coloured. Even the cost analysis of different densities is a subject of some considerable disagreement, particularly since Britain seems unique (in Europe at least) in being able to provide houses more cheaply than flats—even when the cost of services is taken into account. It is not proposed to enter into these arguments here.*

A Study Group of the Ministry of Town and Country Planning, whose report was incorporated in the 1944 Dudley Report,[3] recommended net residential densities ranging from 30 to 100 (and, in special cases, 120) persons per acre.

A much more detailed study published in 1952 (*The Density of Residential Areas*)[13] reiterated the advisability of densities recommended in 1944. Full communal facilities could be provided within a gross density range of 30–40 persons per acre. The corresponding range of net accommodation density, allowing reasonable standards for other land use, was 55–90 rooms per acre. It was suggested that within this range there were densities applicable to large parts of most towns.

Considerably higher densities have been attained in some developments. The Loughborough Road Estate, in Lambeth, has 122 rooms (135 persons) per acre; Churchill Gardens, Pimlico, has 181 rooms (200 persons) per acre; and Park Hill, Sheffield, has 200 rooms per acre.

The recommendations of the Ministry are not mandatory on local authorities: each planning authority decides its own densities, and these will vary according to the land availability in the area, the attitude of the authority towards 'losing' population, and a wide range of other technical and political issues. Currently the Ministry is encouraging local authorities to achieve higher densities, particularly in the 'pressure areas'. The 1962 Planning Bulletin, *Residential Areas: Higher Densities*,[18] states that the aim is not, however, to obtain 'wholesale increases at all levels of density'. Not only is this regarded as undesirable, it also brings rapidly decreasing benefits, as

* See the author's *Housing Needs and Planning Policy*, and the references quoted therein.

TABLE 18: *Land Needed for a Residential Neighbourhood of 10,000 Persons (1944)*

Use	Open Development	Outer Ring	Inner Ring	Central	Central
Housing	Acres 333	Acres 200	Acres 133	Acres 100	Acres 83
Primary schools (3–11 years of age) (School and playing field area)	17	17	17	17	17
Open space	70	70	60	50	40
Shops, offices, etc.	9	8	7	6	5
Community centre, churches, etc.	7	5	4	3	3
Public buildings	4	3	2	2	2
Service industry and workshops	7	6	5	4	4
Main roads including half boundary roads, up to a maximum of 20 ft, and parking	35	28	20	17	14
Totals	482	337	248	199	168
Average net residential density* (persons per acre)	30	50	75	100	120
Gross neighbourhood density†	21	30	40	50	60

* *Net residential density* is the average number of persons per acre of housing area; which comprises the curtilages of the dwellings, access or internal roads and half the boundary main roads up to a maximum of 20 ft, where these are contiguous to residential property.

† *Gross density* is the average number of persons per acre of the whole neighbourhood, the acreage of which is shown by the totals.

Source: Site Planning and Layout in Relation to Housing—Report of a Study Group of the Ministry of Town and Country Planning (published as an appendix to the Dudley Report, *Design of Dwellings*, HMSO, 1944).

Table 19 illustrates. 'The need for, and the advantages to be gained from, increased density are greatest at the lower end of the density scale.' This is due to the simple fact that the amount of land needed for open space, schools, shops and so on increases with the number of people living in an area: an increase in the number of people on a given *housing* site thus increases the amount of land which must be reserved around it for other purposes. Nevertheless an increase from a low to a moderate density can achieve significant savings in land. By raising the net density from twenty-four to forty persons to the acre (i.e. from about eight to thirteen houses—which allows about 3,000 sq ft of land for each house and garden) it is possible to save 17 acres of land for every 1,000 population. This is sufficient

TABLE 19: *Land Needed for Housing 1,000 People at Various Densities* (1962)[18]

Gross population density (persons per acre)	Net population density (persons per acre)	Housing Land (acres)	Total Land Requirements* (acres)	Land saving as density increases (acres)
20	24	42	50	–
30	40	25	33	17
40	59	17	25	8
50	83	12	20	5
60	115	8·6	16·6	3·4
70	159	6·3	14·3	2·3
80	222	4·5	12·5	1·8

to house another 500 people at the same density and with the same provision for open space and other uses.†

In conurbations densities of between twelve and thirty dwellings are recommended as being generally acceptable. In 'areas of growth' compact development is recommended with a minimum density for new development of twelve dwellings to the acre: 'densities between twelve and twenty (and higher in selected areas) should be encouraged'.

* Assuming 8 acres per 1,000 people for other land uses (see footnote below).
† This calculation, and Table 19, exclude such land uses as industry, central business and commercial areas, railways, sewerage works, etc. These are always excluded from 'gross residential areas'. To include them would obscure the genuine land savings made by moderate increases in net density.

The figures are calculated on the assumption that 1,000 people are to be housed and provided with four acres for open space and four acres for primary schools, local roads, shops, etc. The Ministry add that 'most authorities consider that four acres of open space are not really sufficient, but is as much or more than most towns have, especially in their inner areas, and in this sense the table is more realistic than one based on optimum standards'.

A wider assessment of the quality of the environment is now being stimulated by traffic considerations. The Buchanan Report[25] stresses the needs to integrate land use and transport planning and to achieve a balance between the needs of traffic and the quality of urban life. This balance between *accessibility* and *environment* is involving a reappraisal of the form of housing layouts and the standards of housing density. The Buchanan Report stresses the need for 'primary road networks' and 'environmental areas':

> There must be areas of good environment—urban rooms—where people can live, work, shop, look about and move around on foot in reasonable freedom from the hazards of motor traffic, and there must be a complementary network of roads—urban corridors—for effecting the primary distribution of traffic to the environmental areas.

A Joint Urban Planning Group, serving the Ministry of Housing and Local Government, the Ministry of Transport and the Scottish Development Department is currently engaged on developing the techniques required for implementing the concepts outlined in the Buchanan Report.

REFERENCES AND FUTURE READING

[1] Barr, A. W. Cleeve, *Public Authority Housing*, Batsford, 1958.

[2] Birch, J., *Examples of Labourers' Cottages, Etc., with Plans for Improving the Dwellings of the Poor in Large Towns*, Blackwood, 1872.

[3] Central Housing Advisory Committee, *Design of Dwellings* (Dudley Report), HMSO, 1944.

[4] Central Housing Advisory Committee, *The Appearance of Housing Estates*, HMSO, 1948.

[5] Central Housing Advisory Committee, *Living in Flats*, HMSO, 1952.

[6] Central Housing Advisory Committee, *Homes for Today and Tomorrow* (Parker Morris Report), HMSO, 1961.

[7] Department of Health for Scotland, *Report of the Committee on Building Legislation in Scotland* (Guest Report), Cmnd. 269, HMSO, 1957.

[8] Hole, V., 'Housing Standards and Social Trends', *Urban Studies*, Vol. 2, No. 2, November 1965.

[9] Local Government Boards for England and Wales, and Scotland, *Report of the Committee on the Provision of Dwellings for the Working Classes* (Tudor Walters Report), Cd. 9191, HMSO, 1918.

[10] Ministry of Health and Ministry of Works, *Housing Manual 1944*, HMSO, 1944.

[11] Ministry of Health, *Housing Manual 1949*, HMSO, 1949.

[12] Ministry of Health, *The Cost of House Building* (Girdwood Reports), First Report, 1948; Second Report, 1950; Third Report, 1952, HMSO.

[13] Ministry of Housing and Local Government, *The Density of Residential Areas*, HMSO, 1952.

[14] Ministry of Housing and Local Government, *Houses 1952*, HMSO, 1952.

[15] Ministry of Housing and Local Government, *Houses 1953*, HMSO, 1953.

[16] Ministry of Housing and Local Government, *Flats and Houses 1958*, HMSO, 1958.

[17] Ministry of Housing and Local Government, Building By-laws: Thermal Insulation; Flue Pipes, *Circular No. 63/1959*, HMSO, 1959.

[18] Ministry of Housing and Local Government, *Residential Areas: Higher Densities*, Planning Bulletin, No. 2, HMSO, 1962.

[19] Ministry of Housing and Local Government, *Circular No. 13/62*, 'Homes for Today and Tomorrow', HMSO, 1962.

[20] Ministry of Housing and Local Government, *Space in the Home*, Design Bulletin, No. 6, HMSO, 1963.

[21] Ministry of Housing and Local Government, *The Housing Programme 1965 to 1970*, Cmnd. 2837, HMSO, 1965.

[22] Ministry of Local Government and Planning, *Housing for Special Purposes*, HMSO, 1951.

[23] Ministry of Public Building and Works, *Building Regulations Advisory Committee: First Report*, Cmnd. 2279, HMSO, 1964.

[24] Ministry of Public Building and Works, *Guide to the Building Regulations 1965*, HMSO, 1965.

[25] Ministry of Transport, *Traffic in Towns* (Buchanan Report), HMSO, 1963.

[26] *The Building Regulations 1965*, Statutory Instrument, 1965, No. 1373, HMSO, 1965.

CHAPTER VII

Housing Finance

LOCAL AUTHORITY housing is normally financed over sixty years. Loans are raised mainly by stock, mortgages, bonds, and directly from the Government through the Public Works Loan Board (as well as by temporary borrowing). There is a number of controls over local authority borrowing: these change with the current national economic situation and the political outlook of the Government of the day. From 1945 to 1952 local authorities were generally prohibited from borrowing from any other source except the PWLB. This was a post-war innovation: before the war only smaller authorities normally borrowed from the Board. The change was made in order that the large volume of local authority capital expenditure on reconstruction could be financed in an orderly manner and as cheaply as possible. The system in effect provided a guarantee to all local authorities that they would be able to borrow money at low rates of interest for all approved capital schemes. The rate of interest for housing loans was 3 per cent. Following the return of the Conservative Government local authorities were allowed to borrow in the market, though the facilities of the PWLB remained open to them. In 1955, as a result of an increasing pressure on Exchequer funds, restrictions were placed on borrowing from the PWLB, and local authorities had to show that they could not borrow at reasonable terms in the market. Rates of interest were fixed by reference to the credit of local authorities of good standing in the market and not, as hitherto, by reference to the Government's own credit. Rates of interest rose substantially at this time and in September the long-term rate reached 5 per cent for the first time since 1932. Further changes were made in subsequent years and PWLB loans were restricted to local authorities able to show real difficulty in obtaining their requirements in the mortgage or the stock market. The long-term PWLB rate fluctuated between $5\frac{3}{4}$ and $6\frac{3}{4}$ per cent, and the proportion of total local authority loans obtained from the PWLB (for all periods and for all purposes) fell from the 1951–2 figure of 85 per cent to 61 per cent in 1955–6, to 22 per cent in 1956–7, and to 8 per cent in 1958–9.

In recent years local authorities have found some difficulty in obtaining long-term funds for their expanding programmes of capital expenditure.[13] By 1962 their borrowing for new works was about £550 million; in addition about £370 million was borrowed for re-financing maturing long-term debt. Temporary borrowing was about 15 per cent of their total loan debt (as compared with less than $3\frac{1}{4}$ per cent in 1955). Borrowing on this scale created difficulties not only for the Central Government's own borrowing operations, but also for monetary conditions generally. Short-term borrowing in particular was getting out of hand: its rising cost could not be held in check because the only alternative for local authorities was to commit themselves for a longer term at rates even higher than the high rate of temporary loans. In short the growth of local authority capital expenditure led to the growth of a huge volume of short-term debt that was insensitive to interest rate policy. As a result controls were introduced over local authority temporary borrowing and greater access to the PWLB was allowed.

But the problem remained acute. Local authority borrowing (for all purposes) increased by 56 per cent between mid-1963 and mid-1965 and at the latter date the proportion financed in the temporary market was over a fifth. (In the first quarter of 1965, temporary debt amounted to £1,847 million, of which £1,239 million was repayable within seven days.) At the same time a severe balance of payments deficit had to be dealt with. Measures were therefore taken to slow down the rate of expenditure on all capital projects except housing and school-building.[14]

This priority for housing and school-building (together with industrial building) was a major plank of the Labour Government's domestic policy. Apart from financial measures, controls were introduced to reduce the demands on the construction industry—mainly by a licensing procedure for privately-sponsored construction projects (outside development districts) costing £100,000 or more.[15]

Local authorities can raise loans only with the consent of the Ministry of Housing and Local Government. This control was originally introduced in the early part of the nineteenth century to ensure that local authorities borrowed money only for the purposes which the law permitted, and that they did not borrow more than their financial resources warranted. But it is now used as a part of the machinery for regulating the aggregate amount of public investment and, as was shown in Chapter IV, as a means of restraining the inflation of building costs and influencing local authority housing policies in a variety of ways.

Housing is the largest item in the outstanding loan debt of local authorities. At the end of the financial year 1962–3 (the last year for which figures are available) the total loan debt stood at £6,292 million, of which £4,056 million was for council housing. Loans raised for improvement grants, for giving mortgages to owner-occupiers, and for other housing purposes raised the total housing loan debt to £4,623 million.

The enormous growth in the loan debt of local authorities during the post-war period is illustrated in Table 20. Between 1949–50 and 1962–3 the total increased from £1,540 million to £6,292 million—an increase of 309 per cent. For council housing the increase was from £1,244 million to £4,056 million—226 per cent.

TABLE 20: *Local Authority Loan Debt*[16]

	At end of year			During year
	1949–50	1961–2	1962–3	1962–3
	£m	£m	£m	£m
Housing				
Council housing	1,244	3,846	4,056	268
Improvement grants	–	46	56	11
Other housing	10	16	19	4
Loans for house purchase	27	445	492	84
Other Services				
Education	114	771	838	120
Sewerage	66	267	306	51
All other services	79	462	525	89
Total	1,540	5,853	6,292	627

For most local authority services annual loan charges form only a small proportion of total expenditure. Wages and salaries are generally much more important than loan charges. This is illustrated in Table 21. Thus for example in welfare services, children's services and police, loan charges are only a small fraction of total expenditure. The bulk of expenditure on these services is accounted for by wages and salaries. Even for education, which is a heavily capitalized service, loan charges form less than a tenth of total expenditure. Loan charges for housing, on the other hand, account for 72 per cent of expenditure. (In the table, which is taken from the official return *Local Government Financial Statistics*, rate fund contributions are regarded as income.)

Housing differs also in that a high proportion of the cost is met by the users of the service, i.e. the rents paid by council tenants. This is shown more clearly in Table 22 which gives a breakdown of the housing revenue accounts of those local authorities (about two-thirds of the total) which are included in the *Housing Statistics* published by the Institute of Municipal Treasurers and Accountants. On average about three-quarters of income comes from rents: the remainder is largely met by Exchequer and rate fund subsidies.

TABLE 21: *Revenue Account—Rate Fund Services, 1962-3*[16]

	EXPENDITURE			INCOME		
	General £m.	Loan Charges £m.	Total £m.	Fees, rents, recoupment, etc. £m.	Government grants and reimbursements £m.	Balance of expenditure not met out of specific income £m.
Housing						
Council housing	89	227	317	236	64	16
Improvement grants	1	5	6	0·2	5	1
Other housing	5	1	6	2	1	2
Loans for house purchase	4	23	27	30	—	Cr. 3
Other Services						
Education	853	77	930	51	69	810
Sewerage	29	25	54	3	1	49
Welfare Services	45	3	48	16	0·7	32
Children's Services	27	1	28	2	1	24
Highways and Bridges	139	10	149	9	37	104
Police	142	4	146	8	69	70
Registration of electors	2	—	2	—	—	2
All other services	339	26	365	48	17	300
Total	1,675	402	2,078	405	265	1,407

TABLE 22: *Analysis of Local Authority Housing Revenue, 1963–4*[6]

	County Boroughs %	Metropolitan Boroughs and City %	London County Council %	Non-County Boroughs %	Urban Districts %	Rural Districts %
Rents	74·7	56·6	68·0	77·0	75·9	76·3
Exchequer Subsidy	18·8	22·0	17·5	18·1	19·4	20·2
Rate Subsidy	5·8	20·7	13·5	4·1	3·7	2·5
Other Income	0·7	0·7	1·0	0·8	1·0	1·0

HOUSING ACCOUNTS

Local housing authorities are statutorily required to keep a special Housing Revenue Account, and a separate Housing Repairs Account. The items which are to be included in these are laid down in instructions issued by the Ministry.[10, 12] Broadly speaking all the income and expenditure relating to subsidized housing has to be included in the Housing Revenue Account, but transactions relating to such matters as advances for house purchase and improvement grants to private persons and housing associations are excluded. The main items in the Housing Revenue Account are:

Expenditure Loan charges
Supervision and management
Repairs contribution
Income Rent income
Exchequer subsidies
Rate fund contribution

Expenditure on repairs is not met directly from revenue but via the Repairs Account to which an annual contribution for each dwelling is made from the Revenue Account. The purpose of the separate Repairs Account is to allow the building up of a surplus in the early years of the life of a house in order to maintain a steady annual charge to revenue over the life of the property.

Two illustrative Housing Revenue Accounts are reproduced at the end of this chapter.

INTEREST RATES AND HOUSING SUBSIDIES

Four factors have greatly increased the cost of housing during the post-war years—higher standards, increased costs of construction, increased land values, and higher interest rates. The first two factors have been discussed in Chapter VI. The cost of land purchased by local authorities has risen markedly since the Town and Country Planning

Act 1959 restored fair market value as the basis for compensation.*
Adequate figures are difficult to come by, but in the former London
County Council area the cost of land purchased by housing authorities
rose by 275 per cent between 1959 and 1965; in the remainder of
Greater London the rise was 330 per cent.† Interest rates are very
much easier to document. Throughout the period of the Attlee
Government the PWLB rate for sixty-year loans was 2½ or 3 per cent.
During the 'fifties interest rates rose steadily, first to 5 per cent and
later to over 6 per cent. These high rates have continued and at the
time of writing have climbed to nearly 7 per cent.

An average council house built in 1965 at a total cost (including
land) of £2,700 would, with an interest rate of 7 per cent, have to bear
loan charges of about £190 a year. At 3 per cent the charges would be
less than £100. In practice the actual rents charged by local authorities
do not necessarily have to reflect the current cost of borrowing. Many
local authorities have large numbers of existing houses built at lower
costs and financed with cheaper money. By a system of 'pooling', the
rents of new houses can be reduced to well below the current full cost.

There have been too many changes in subsidies to allow a digest-
ible historical account to be given here, but it may be useful if the
first post-war subsidy is briefly discussed. The standard subsidy for
houses was fixed in 1946 at £16 10s 0d a year for sixty years on the
following assumptions:

	£	s
Loan charges based on 3½ per cent half-yearly annuity for 60 years on a capital cost of £1,070	39	12
Repairs, maintenance and management	8	8
Total outgoings	48	0
Estimated rent at 10 per cent of average wages: 10s a week	26	0
Deficiency	22	0
Subsidy:		
Exchequer	16	10
Local authority	5	10

Higher subsidies were payable for expensive sites and for flats with
lifts.

* For a short account of post-war policy in relation to compensation for
compulsory acquisition of land see the author's companion volume on *Town and
Country Planning*. A fuller discussion, and some data on the increase in land values,
can be found in Hall, P. (editor), *Land Values*, Sweet and Maxwell, 1965.

† *House of Commons Debates*, June 22, 1965.

L

These subsidies were increased twice before being fundamentally changed in 1956. The Housing Subsidies Act of that year abolished the requirement that local authorities had to pay a subsidy from the rates (the 'statutory rate fund contribution') and restricted Exchequer subsidies to certain special needs such as slum clearance and 'overspill' housing. The 1961 Act recast the whole subsidy structure and provided for two basic rates of subsidy, the higher of which was given to local authorities who satisfied a test of 'financial need'. Ignoring the detailed complexities, the test was based on a comparison of each authority's income and expenditure on the Housing Revenue Account. But though *actual* expenditure was taken, the income was calculated on a *notional* basis, namely twice the gross value of all the dwellings in the Account plus the Exchequer subsidies already granted for existing dwellings. The reason for this was simply that the higher rate of subsidy was intended only for those authorities who, though charging 'reasonable' rents, would still have had a deficit if no subsidies were given for new houses. If the actual rent income had been taken all local authorities would have been able to qualify for subsidy simply by ensuring that their rents were sufficiently low—precisely the opposite objective to that of the Act.

If the total 'income' calculated in this way was less than the actual expenditure an Exchequer subsidy of £24 a year was paid for all approved houses; if the income was greater the subsidy was only £8.[12] This test of financial need was applied annually and thus took account of changing circumstances. Authorities which initially received only the lower rate of subsidy could become entitled to the higher amount if, as a result of further building, their housing revenue accounts began to show a deficit.

These were the two rates of 'basic' subsidy. Additional subsidies were payable for the building of flats in blocks of four or more storeys (i.e. with lifts); towards the cost of precautions against subsidence and of building in special materials; for expensive sites; for agricultural dwellings; and for overspill and the housing of key workers.

INTEREST-RATE SUBSIDIES

In spite of a statement in the 1965 Housing White Paper[15] that 'the whole question of housing finance needs much deeper study than this Government has yet had the time to give to it', there has already been a radical change in housing subsidies.* This is geared to allow local authorities to cope financially with a greatly expanded house-building

* This account is based on the provisions of the Housing Subsidies Bill published in November 1965. These may be changed somewhat during the passage of the Bill through Parliament.

TABLE 23: *The Cost of Housing Subsidies, 1948–9 to 1963–4*

| | Exchequer Contributions | | | Local Authority |
	Under pre-war legislation £m	Under post-war legislation £m	Total £m	Rate-Fund Contributions £m
1948–9	12·9	5·4	18·3*	8·3
1953–4	11·7	23·8	35·5	14·7
1958–9	11·0	46·7	57·7	17·3
1963–4	9·4	58·6	68·0	19·8†

programme. More particularly, it aims at providing a stable financial basis for housing programmes by eliminating uncertainty about interest rates and also provides proportionately higher subsidies for housing developments which involve high costs.

The new subsidy makes up the difference between the annual charges on the cost of houses completed each year at the current rate of interest and the charges which would have resulted from an interest rate of 4 per cent. Supplementary subsidies continue to be available (in a modified form) for special needs and particularly high costs such as expensive sites and high flats. The new subsidies do not apply to existing houses: these continue to attract the subsidies which were payable under earlier legislation.

The 4 per cent 'interest rate subsidy' is, in effect, a percentage grant —the actual percentage depending on the ruling rate of interest. The amount of the subsidy also obviously varies with the capital cost of dwellings (including the cost of land and site development). Since it also varies according to the current interest rate it is not possible to make a simple direct comparison with former subsidies. However, an illustrative example in the White Paper shows a median *basic* subsidy (assuming a borrowing rate of 6½ per cent) of £64 for dwellings up to three storeys, and £81 for dwellings over three storeys. This is a large increase on the previous subsidies. If interest rates continue at about 6½ per cent and the planned expansion of local authority building takes place, the cost of subsidies to the Exchequer will increase from £79 million a year in 1965 to £90 million by 1969 and £98 million by 1970. Thereafter the annual increase would be about £9 million. By contrast under the previous subsidy system the increased public sector programme would have involved an annual increase in Exchequer subsidies of about £6 million a year.

These rough calculations take into account the changes in supple-

* Excluding capital grants for post-war houses constructed by non-traditional methods. A total of £25 million was given in grants for this purpose between 1946–7 and 1959–60. £15 million of this was paid in the year 1948–9.
† This figure relates to 1962–3 and is the latest available figure.
Sources: *Annual Report of the Ministry of Housing and Local Government for 1964*, Cmnd. 2668; and *Local Government Financial Statistics* (Annual).

mentary subsidies, some of which have increased greatly. Major
changes have been made in the subsidies for high buildings and
expensive sites. Under the previous system supplementary subsidies
were given amounting to £8 for flats in blocks of four storeys; £14
for flats in blocks of five storeys; £26 in blocks of six storeys; and
then £26 plus £1 15s 0d for each storey in excess of six. There is no
change in the rate of subsidy for flats in blocks of four to six storeys,
but the 'loaded' subsidy for taller blocks has been abolished. Flats in
blocks of six *or more* storeys now receive a flat rate of £26 per dwelling. One reason given for this is that, owing to improvements in
industrial methods, building costs for the taller blocks no longer
increase proportionately with height—as they did when the old scale
was introduced. There is also a feeling that high building should not
be indiscriminately encouraged. Where high land costs have been the
major factor leading to high building, however, the new subsidy
structure provides much greater financial assistance. Under the
previous system an expensive site subsidy was given where the cost of
acquisition and site development exceeded £4,000 an acre. This
amounted to £60 plus £34 for every £1,000 (or part of £1,000) by
which the cost per acre exceeded £5,000. The 'floor' of £4,000 per
acre remains unchanged but site development costs no longer rank
for subsidy. For very expensive sites, however, the subsidy is
increased to £40 for every £1,000 by which the cost exceeds £50,000
an acre. This will be of assistance to authorities in the large conurbations, particularly London.

Where the combination of the basic and the expensive site subsidy
exceeds 75 per cent of the calculated loan charges on the site, the
payment of the margin over 75 per cent is at the Minister's discretion,
depending on the rent or rate burden likely to be involved.

The Minister also has discretionary powers to pay additional subsidies for two special categories of special need. The first is where
there is 'an urgent need for more dwellings which will only be met if
the dwellings are provided by the local authority'. The second is
where dwellings are required for 'a substantial transfer' of industry or
workers but could not be provided without an unreasonable increase
in the local authority's rates or rents. Both these subsidies are payable
at a rate and for a period to be fixed at the discretion of the Minister,
but the maximum under either (or both together) is £30 per
dwelling.

Other subsidies are payable towards the additional costs incurred in
taking precautions against subsidence (maximum £2 a year) or in
building in special materials in order to preserve the character of the
surroundings (maximum £10 a year). Finally, special subsidies are
available for dwellings provided under town development schemes.
These are schemes under which families are moved from a congested

town to an 'expanding town'.* (The maximum additional subsidy is £12 for ten years, matched by a similar contribution from the 'sending' authority.)

Most subsidies are payable for sixty years, but there is provision for 'possible review from time to time'. This provision was first introduced by the Conservative Government in the 1961 Housing Act. It allows a Minister to reduce or even abolish subsidies on houses built under the 1961 (and now the 1966) Acts. When originally introduced the purpose was said to be 'purely precautionary'; it was intended to enable account to be taken of any major change in the need of housing authorities for financial assistance which would make it unjustifiable to continue paying subsidies on the original scale for the whole of the normal sixty-year period. A major rise in real earnings or a fall in the value of money could clearly have a major effect on the rent paying capacity of tenants.

THE FINANCE OF REPAIRS

As has already been stated, local housing authorities are required to keep a special Housing Repairs Account into which annual contributions are made from the Housing Revenue Account. The theoretical basis of this system is that the annual contribution should be fixed at a level which will secure an equalization of repair costs over the lifetime of the house. Such a theory has little practical applicability in a period of rapidly rising costs, and in practice all that can be achieved is a stabilization of contributions over a comparatively short period.

The statutory minimum repairs contribution is £8 per dwelling. This figure was originally fixed in 1952 (before then it was £4) but is now quite unrealistic. Very few authorities make such a low contribution. A figure double this amount is quite usual and some authorities in the London area make contributions of over £40. The highest in 1963/4 was £45 19s 0d in Westminster. But even with high contributions—indeed, almost irrespective of the amount of the contribution—most authorities spend more than this on their pre-war dwellings. The range is enormous: in 1963/64, from £2 4s 0d to £68 4s 0d. The figures for any one year can be misleading but the averages for different types of authority given in Table 24 show (with the exception of the London County Council) a consistently higher expenditure than contribution for pre-war dwellings. Expenditure on post-war dwellings is naturally lower, but it is generally uncomfortably close to the contribution; and the average closing balance is less than one year's contribution. Clearly the intention of accumulating adequate reserves

* For a fuller account see the author's *Town and Country Planning in England and Wales*, Chapter 11.

TABLE 24: *Local Authority Housing Repairs Accounts—Average Figures 1963–4*[6]

	County Boroughs		Metropolitan Boroughs		London County Council		Non-County Boroughs		Urban Districts		Rural Districts	
	£	s	£	s	£	s	£	s	£	s	£	s
Average contribution per dwelling	15	1	28	8	36	0	15	18	14	11	14	1
Average expenditure per dwelling												
pre-war	21	3	37	5	31	19	24	3	23	0	20	7
post-war	13	2	24	11	28	3	13	11	12	12	12	11
Average closing balance per dwelling	8	14	24	0	26	15	9	6	10	0	12	3

for the future (higher) maintenance costs cannot be achieved at current levels of contribution.

THE COSTS OF MANAGEMENT

It is difficult to understand why there should be such a wide range of repair costs. The same applies to costs of management. The range of costs—from £1 6s 0d to £23 2s 0d per dwelling per year—is huge. Partly this reflects differences in policy, in standards and organization, in geography and location, in the size and layout of estates and in the proportion of high flats. But it also reflects differences in accounting practices: there are widely varying practices for the allocation of salaries and wages, the calculation and apportionment of central administrative expenses and similar overheads, and for the range of work which is included under the heading of 'supervision and management'.

In an attempt to bring about greater uniformity of practice (without which comparison is useless) the Ministry has drawn a distinction between *general* and *special* expenditure. The latter includes such items as the running costs of central heating plant, the costs of lighting courtyards and staircases, the wages of caretakers, the running costs of lifts and the cost of maintaining estate lawns and grass verges. Even so, the published figures are virtually meaningless for comparative purposes. They may enable an individual authority to keep a check on trends in expenditure, but they are quite inadequate

TABLE 25: *Local Authority Dwellings—Costs of General Management,* 1963–4[6]

	Cost of Supervision and General Management per Dwelling		
	Average per Dwelling £ s	Lowest £ s	Highest £ s
County Boroughs	4 13	2 8	9 0
Metropolitan Boroughs	11 2	7 0	23 2
London County Council	5 17	–	–
Non-County Boroughs	4 18	2 0	16 6
Urban Districts	4 3	1 7	12 7
Rural Districts	4 1	1 6	9 10

for any other purpose. The 1959 Report of the Central Housing Advisory Committee, *Councils and their Houses*, commented on this, rightly pointing out that a standard method of costing was essential if valid comparisons were to be made and if local authorities were to be provided with a yardstick against which to measure their costs.

Following their recommendation a Working Party was appointed. The report, *Costing of Management and Maintenance of Local Authority Housing*,[13] was published in 1964, and set out a basis on which uniform cost records could be kept. It should be noted that the Ministry of Housing (unlike, e.g. the Ministry of Health in relation to hospitals) has no official rôle in this field. All the statistics which are available are produced on a voluntary basis by the Institute of Municipal Treasurers and Accountants. This Institute has agreed to collect and publish returns made by those authorities who decide to comply with the Working Party's report. The first such return has not yet been published.

RENTS

It needs to be stressed that the Ministry has very little effective direct control over local authorities' rent policies. The legislation merely requires local authorities to charge 'reasonable' rents, to review rents 'from time to time' and to make such changes 'as circumstances may require'. They are also specifically empowered to give rent rebates on such terms 'as they may think fit'. The Minister does have default powers which he can use following a public local inquiry, but these have never been used. (More subtle and gentlemanly powers of persuasion are preferred. The position in Scotland is rather different. There the low rents charged by several authorities have led to public inquiries, following which the authorities concerned agreed to increase their rents to a more reasonable level.)

It is this absence of direct Ministerial control, and reluctance to use means other than those of persuasion that led to the complicated subsidy system under the 1961 Act. The objective was to devise a system of subsidies which would 'encourage' local authorities to charge 'reasonable' rents. But it was also geared to a situation in which it was held that 'the great majority of housing authorities (though needing for the time being to carry on some building for one purpose or another) will progressively be able to diminish their efforts, particularly as they come to the end of their slum clearance activities'.[11] The greatly expanded programmes of local authorities envisaged in the Labour Government's housing plan required a major reorientation of subsidy policy. But emphasis continues to be laid on the need for local authorities to charge reasonable rents:

> Rent policies are for local decision. But if the extra subsidies now to be provided are to be used, as they should be, to relieve those with the greatest social need, these policies should reflect the fact that the financial circumstances of tenants vary widely. This means that subsidies should not be used wholly or mainly to keep general

rent levels low. Help for those who most need it can be given only if the subsidies are in large part used to provide rebates for tenants whose means are small. A number of authorities have had the courage to adopt thorough-going rent rebate schemes and have found that it does not entail raising general rent levels beyond the means of the majority of their tenants. The more generous subsidies now to be provided create an opportunity for all authorities to review their rent policies along these lines. In doing so, they will be able to take into account the higher standards of accommodation which will increasingly be provided with the aid of the new subsidies.[15]

One result of the Ministry's lack of direct concern for local authority rents is that there is no officially provided information or even statistics on rents (though the Scottish Office publishes an annual return of the rents of Scottish local authorities). Once again therefore one is forced back on the statistics published by the Institute of Municipal Treasurers and Accountants. These show an almost unbelievable range of rents. To give one example, the weekly rents of post-war three-bedroom houses range (in 1963–4) from nil in Sheffield to £7 13s 10d in Hammersmith. These, of course, are extremes presumably due to the operation of differential rent schemes. (The averages for post-war three-bedroom houses in these authorities are respectively 32s and 82s 6d.) Table 26 shows the averages for several categories of dwellings in county boroughs, the former metropolitan boroughs and rural districts.

Clearly rent policies vary enormously. There are numerous factors involved here, quite apart from the obvious one of the political line taken by individual authorities on the level at which rents should be set—and the amount of subsidy which should be paid from the rates. (About a third of authorities now contribute no rate fund subsidy.) Of particular importance is the rent pool: an authority with a high proportion of pre-war houses, built at costs which are very low in comparison with those ruling today, can raise the rents of the pre-war houses and use the income to offset part of the high cost of new houses. An authority with a predominance of post-war houses, on the other hand, has to charge considerably higher rents.

The types of rent scheme are legion. The basis can be the gross annual value or rateable value of the dwellings, annual costs, or size and amenities. It can vary between houses and flats, between different estates (depending e.g. upon their 'amenities', or the distance from the town centre). It can take the incomes of tenants into account or ignore them altogether. Differentiation between pre-war and post-war houses is common, sometimes on the ground that pre-war houses are inferior and sometimes as a matter of policy so as to enable houses

TABLE 26: *Weekly Net Rents of Two- and Three-bedroom Council Dwellings in Selected Authorities, March 1964*[6]

	County Boroughs		Metropolitan Boroughs		Rural Districts	
	Lowest s d	Highest s d	Lowest s d	Highest s d	Lowest s d	Highest s d
Two-bedroom Houses						
Pre-war: average	9 6	35 0	18 4	36 6	9 11	32 0
Post-war: average	18 8	43 9	26 6	71 6	13 6	49 2
lowest	Nil	–	15 0	–	4 3	–
highest	–	62 7	–	71 6	–	65 6
Three-bedroom Houses						
Pre-war: average	13 6	42 3	23 1	41 1	11 0	36 0
Post-war: average	21 6	47 7	30 4	89 5	16 6	43 9
lowest	Nil	–	12 1	–	6 9	–
highest	–	88 8	–	153 10	–	96 6

to be let to all classes of tenants without the necessity of a differential rent scheme.

Differential and rent rebate schemes vary even more: some are simple, others are so complex as to defy summary. Some apply to all tenancies while some are of very limited application. Nevertheless it is possible to discern two basic types. In a simple *rent rebate scheme*, the 'standard' (often unsubsidized) rent is reduced for tenants with low incomes. A complete *differential rent scheme*, on the other hand, involves all tenants paying income-related rents. The former type of scheme aims solely at assisting the poorer families, whereas the latter aims at relating all rents to the tenants' means, and thus charging richer families higher rents. In practice, the two types of scheme merge into each other. If a high standard rent is charged under a rebate scheme, a scale of differentiation is needed to relate the rebates to the needs of families of different incomes. At the extreme, the standard rent may be so high that nearly all tenants qualify for a rebate. Only where the standard rent is very low can a rebate scheme be readily distinguished from a differential rent scheme.

Any income-related scheme involves a determination of what income should be regarded as assessable, and what proportion of assessable income should reasonably be required for rent payments. There are two main methods by which a family's ability to pay rent could be assessed. The first is to take a fixed proportion of total income. The second is to calculate for each family a subsistence income and to regard any 'surplus' as assessable for rent. The latter, though perhaps the fairest method so far as poor tenants are concerned, is cumbersome and costly to administer. If it is to be operated efficiently it requires frequent revision to take account of changes in the cost of living. In practice a considerably refined version of the first method is most common. Family allowances and disability benefits, for example, are frequently ignored, as is a part of the wife's earnings. For other earners in the household, a fixed amount is commonly added to the rent—in preference to regarding their earnings as part of the family 'income-pool'. Difficulties arise with overtime pay. The principle is generally accepted that regular overtime pay should be assessable, whereas occasional extra earnings should not—though the determination of what is regular and what is casual is not always easy.

Obtaining accurate information on a family's income is the biggest administrative problem in income-related rent schemes. Indeed, this problem is commonly used as a major argument against the introduction of a scheme. Presentation of wage packets or corroboration from employers is frequently required.

There is no generally accepted opinion as to the 'proper' proportion of assessable income which should be allocated to rent—particularly since assessable income is defined in different ways. An examination of selected schemes shows variations from one-fifth to one-eighth, with one-seventh being the most common. But some local authorities further refine their schemes by making allowances for dependants (others consider that this type of allowance is adequately covered by social security schemes). Many make additional charges for lodgers. (Indeed, a large number of authorities with no income-related scheme operate a 'lodger charge'.) It is, of course, obvious that a rent equal to one-seventh of a very small income is quite different from an equal proportion of a high income. For this reason some authorities have a variable proportion, while others charge a proportion of the amount by which the assessable income exceeds a given sum. Many make special *ad hoc* allowances in cases of hardship.

This summary is by no means exhaustive. Nevertheless all schemes are based on one or more of the features outlined. The main principle underlying many schemes is that the best use should be made of the available subsidies. In the words of the Ministry, 'subsidies should be given only to those who need them and to the extent of their need'. But need implies a political judgment and principles must be reconciled with some degree of administrative convenience and simplicity —both for the local authority and the tenants. A highly complex scheme may be very fair, but also virtually incomprehensible. Justice must not only be done: it must be also understood to be done.

Council house rents perhaps attract more discussion—and dissension—than any other aspect of local authority housing policy. But it has only been in the last few years that the arena of debate has been widened to include private tenants and owner-occupiers. It is now coming to be appreciated that council house finance cannot be adequately considered in isolation from rent control, taxation and tax reliefs, and the role of the National Assistance Board. An outline of the issues involved is given in the final chapter.

APPENDIX

ILLUSTRATIVE HOUSING REVENUE ACCOUNTS

Examples of Housing Revenue Accounts are given in Tables 27 and 28 for two widely contrasted authorities. Brighton, with 10,500 council houses, makes no rate fund contribution and indeed makes a 'paper profit' on its Housing Revenue Account. This is used partly in repayment of past deficiencies borne by the rates and partly as a balance to be carried forward. (The latter can be used only towards meeting future deficits or for housing purposes.) Gateshead, on the other hand, with 8,300 council houses, make a rate fund contribution of £180,000, equivalent to a rate of 13·8 pence in the £.

The contribution made by these two authorities to the Housing Repairs Account is also markedly different. Brighton contributes £21 15s 0d per dwelling whereas the Gateshead contribution is £16 3s 0d.

As might be expected Brighton rents are very much higher. The average weekly net rent of a three-bedroom pre-war house is 42s 3d compared with 20s 8d in Gateshead. For post-war houses the rents are 45s 3d and 25s 0d respectively.

TABLE 27: County Borough of Gateshead—Housing Revenue Account, 1963–4

Expenditure	£	£	Income	£	£	£
ADMINISTRATION			**RENTS**			
General			Normal		520,750	
Administrative and office expenses		32,898	Additional Earner Charge		5,708	
					526,458	
Special						
Caretakers	13,011		*Less:* Rebates		15,711	
Central heating; lighting corridors, etc.	5,815					510,747
Lifts: Electricity and Maintenance	3,057					
Other expenses	1,404					
		23,287	EXCHEQUER SUBSIDIES			191,537
LOAN CHARGES						
Repayment	134,915					
Interest	475,113					
Management of Loans	3,867	613,895				
CONTRIBUTIONS TO HOUSING						
REPAIRS ACCOUNT		135,924	TOTAL			702,284
REVENUE CONTRIBUTIONS TO						
CAPITAL OUTLAY		76,075	**DEFICIENCY FOR YEAR:**			
OTHER EXPENSES		171	Contribution from General Rate Fund			179,966
		882,250				882,250

TABLE 28: *County Borough of Brighton—Housing Revenue Account, 1963–4*

Expenditure	£	£	Income	£	£
SUPERVISION AND MANAGEMENT			RENTS		
General:			Rent Income	1,185,334	
Administrative and office expenses		66,137	*Less rebates*	63,503	
Special:			Voids and irrecoverables	10,151	
Caretakers	5,570				1,111,680
Central heating, lighting of corridors, etc.	12,586				
Maintenance of gardens and grounds	12,022		Land and way leaves		5,184
Supplementary water charges	1,238				
		31,416			
LOANS					
Repayment	232,009		SALE OF HOUSES AND LAND		
Interest	621,013		Houses—Interest and other charges	99,987	
Management of loans	12,013		Land—Interest	8,614	
		865,035			108,601
CONTRIBUTIONS TO HOUSING REPAIRS ACCOUNT		231,058			
REVENUE CONTRIBUTIONS TO CAPITAL OUTLAY		31,122			
TAXATION		110,638	EXCHEQUER CONTRIBUTION		175,455
ADAPTATION AND RECONDITIONING OF PROPERTIES		6,305			
OTHER EXPENDITURE		16,148			
		1,357,859			
TRANSFER TO GENERAL RATE FUND IN REIMBURSEMENT OF PAST DEFICIENCIES	10,107				
BALANCE CARRIED FORWARD	32,954				
		43,061	NET INCOME FROM HOUSING REVENUE		
		1,400,920			1,400,920

REFERENCES AND FUTURE READING

[1] Central Housing Advisory Committee, *Transfers, Exchanges and Rents* (Part II), HMSO, 1953.

[2] Drummond, J. M., *The Finance of Local Government*, Allen and Unwin, 1952.

[3] Emmott, R. A., *Differential Rents: A Factual Survey*, Institute of Municipal Treasurers and Accountants, 1957.

[4] Hall, P. (editor), *Land Values*, Sweet and Maxwell, 1965.

[5] Hardacre, W. S., and Sage, N. D. B., *Local Authority Capital Finance*, Charles Knight, Second Edition, 1965.

[6] Institute of Municipal Treasurers and Accounts, *Housing Statistics* (Annual), IMTA.

[7] Jarmain, J. R., *Housing Subsidies and Rents*, Stevens, 1948.

[8] Macey, J. P., 'Housing Subsidies', *Housing* (new series), Vol. 1, No. 3, October 1965.

[9] Magnus, S. W., and Tovell, L., *Housing Finance*, Charles Knight, 1960.

[10] Ministry of Housing and Local Government, *Circular No. 1/53*, 'Housing Revenue Account: Housing Repairs Account', HMSO, 1953.

[11] Ministry of Housing and Local Government, *Housing in England and Wales*, Cmnd. 1290, HMSO, 1961.

[12] Ministry of Housing and Local Government, *Circular No. 55/61*, 'Housing Act, 1961', HMSO, 1961.

[13] Ministry of Housing and Local Government, *Report of the Working Party on the Costing of Management and Maintenance of Local Authority Housing*, HMSO, 1964.

[14] Ministry of Housing and Local Government, *Circular No. 62/65*, 'Public Expenditure', HMSO, 1965.

[15] Ministry of Housing and Local Government, *The Housing Programme 1965 to 1970*, Cmnd. 2838, HMSO, 1965.

[16] Ministry of Housing and Local Government, *Local Government Financial Statistics* (Annual), HMSO.

[17] Society of Housing Managers (now the Institute of Housing Managers), *Differential Rents and Rent Rebates*, Revised Edition, 1962.

[18] White Paper, *Local Authority Borrowing*, Cmnd. 2162, HMSO, 1963.

CHAPTER VIII

Slum Clearance

OF THE 15 million houses in England and Wales 6 million date from
before the First World War, and of these more than a million are
over 100 years old. Over 2½ million houses are without baths, 1½ million lack a water-closet, and over 4 million are without an adequate
supply of running hot water. Though many of these old houses can
be—and some are being—modernized (commonly under the improvement schemes discussed in Chapter IX), a significant proportion are so
inadequate or obsolete that demolition is the wisest course. Some of
them—particularly in the large cities—are slums, but, as we shall see,
this term is becoming increasingly inappropriate. The term 'slum'
does not, in fact, appear in the legislation (except in connection with
special compensation provisions): the Acts refer to houses which are
'unfit for human habitation' or which are in areas of 'bad layout' or
'obsolete development'. About 750,000 of these houses are included
in what is usually referred to as the 'slum clearance programme'.

This chapter starts by outlining the powers of local authorities in
relation to the clearance of old houses; it then discusses slum clearance policies, programmes and achievements; finally it highlights the
changing character of the situation—at least outside the major old
industrial areas—as the problem of nineteenth-century slums gives
way to that of mid-twentieth century obsolescence.

THE DEFINITION OF HOUSING 'UNFITNESS'

Local authorities have very wide powers in relation to 'unfit' houses.
They can compel an owner to close or demolish the house, or they
can compulsorily acquire it at site value (i.e. without compensation
for the house itself) and demolish it themselves. Obviously with
powers such as these the definition of unfitness is of crucial importance. In fact, however, it is not easy to define unfitness in a purely
objective manner. The 1957 Housing Act (Section 4) merely provides
a list of factors which have to be taken into account in determining
whether a house is unfit:

M

In determining . . . whether a house is unfit for human habitation, regard shall be had to its condition in respect of the following matters . . .

(a) repair;
(b) stability;
(c) freedom from damp;
(d) natural lighting;
(e) ventilation;
(f) water supply;
(g) drainage and sanitary conveniences;
(h) facilities for storage, preparation and cooking of food and for the disposal of waste water;

and the house shall be deemed to be unfit for human habitation if and only if it is so far defective in one or more of the said matters that it is not reasonably suitable for occupation in that condition.

The real test is thus whether a major defect in one of these matters, or an accumulation of lesser defects in more than one, renders the house 'not reasonably suitable for occupation'.

It is worthwhile commenting on each of the eight points:*

Repair: The state of disrepair must be such that it is impossible for the occupants to live in the houses safely or 'in a reasonable state of comfort'. The standard of 'comfort' is a minimal one and relates more to danger of personal injury than to convenience or attractiveness.

Stability: Again the relevant point is whether the house is safe for occupation. A bulging wall, for instance, may be structurally safe.

Freedom from damp: For a house to be unfit on this ground the dampness needs to be of such a degree or extent that it constitutes a danger to the health of occupants or a real interference with normal comfort. A single patch of dampness is quite a different matter from persistent and extensive rising dampness.

Natural lighting: A house in which the living-rooms have such an insufficiency of natural light as to make it necessary to use artificial light during normal full daylight hours would generally be unfit.

Ventilation: A house is unfit if there is inadequate provision for the circulation of air through the dwelling. Most 'back-to-back' houses would be unfit. (The building of back-to-back houses has been generally prohibited since 1909.) The provision of mechanical means of ventilation can, however, sometimes overcome this particular deficiency.

Water supply: Lack of a sufficient supply of wholesome water can by

* This is based in part on S. Swift and F. Shaw, *Swift's Housing Administration*, Butterworth, fourth edition, 1958, Chapter 5, from which the quotations are taken.

itself render a house unfit. Nevertheless a house which has no piped water supply is not automatically unfit. This is particularly important in rural areas where large numbers of houses have only a well supply: here the test would be whether the supply was wholesome. In urban areas, on the other hand, the absence of an internal piped supply can reasonably be regarded as rending the house unfit.

Drainage and sanitary conveniences: A seriously defective foul drainage system obviously constitutes a danger to health and consequently would be likely to render a house unfit. The same applies if there is an inadequate provision for the drainage of surface and waste water.

It might be thought that a house which had no separate water-closet was thereby unfit, but since there are well over a million such houses it has not been practicable to enforce such a standard. Somewhat paradoxically a house with a water-closet that is so deficient that it cannot be used can be regarded as unfit. As the slum clearance programme progresses it can be expected that the lack of a water-closet will come to be regarded as a sufficient cause of unfitness.

Facilities for storage, preparation and cooking of food and for the disposal of waste water: The requirement that a house shall have a ventilated food cupboard is enshrined in the building regulations, and medical opinion is strongly in support of it. Absence of a ventilated food cupboard is commonly put forward as an item of unfitness. It should be noted however that (in 1960) 4¾ million households were without one, that an increasing proportion of food is packaged, and that increasing numbers of households have refrigerators. These points are frequently made by objectors, but expert opinion still holds that a house is not reasonably suitable for occupation if it does not have a ventilated food store—though a house would not be condemned on this ground alone.

So far as cooking arrangements are concerned the minimum acceptable requirement is simply 'usable cooking facilities', whether these be by way of gas, electricity or solid fuel.

A house which does not have a satisfactory internal sink with a proper waste pipe made to discharge over a trapped drain inlet can be regarded as being unfit.

It will be seen that on every one of the eight matters listed a judgment is necessary on the seriousness of the defects. A house can be unfit either because of a serious deficiency in one of the matters or because of an accumulation of smaller defects in two or more of them. What action is taken in relation to an unfit house depends on several factors, including whether it can be made fit at reasonable expense. Before discussing this, however, it is necessary to outline the provisions relating to *areas* of inadequate housing. The relevant section of the 1957 Housing Act (Section 42) refers to an area in which the houses:

are unfit for human habitation, or are by reason of their bad arrangement, or the narrowness or bad arrangement of the streets, dangerous or injurious to the health of the inhabitants of the area, and that the other buildings, if any, in the area are for a like reason dangerous or injurious to the health of the said inhabitants.

This provision—commonly referred to as the 'bad arrangement' clause—adds another dimension to the concept of unfitness. Here we are concerned with the congestion of buildings, and the narrowness of streets and back alleys. These areas of bad arrangement, however, only come within the scope of the legislation if it can be shown that the health of the inhabitants is likely to be affected. This is virtually impossible to do in a literal sense today, but it has been held that narrow courts, alleys, or back streets which are so narrow that they cannot be properly cleaned, or which seriously interfere with the removal of household refuse, do constitute 'a danger to the health of the inhabitants of the area'.

Inadequate housing can thus be dealt with either because of the unfitness of the individual houses or because of the bad arrangement of houses in an area.

POWERS FOR DEALING WITH INDIVIDUAL UNFIT HOUSES

A local authority has a duty to inspect the houses in their district 'from time to time' in order to ascertain whether any houses are unfit. As is discussed below, periodic returns are required by the Ministry of Housing.[8]

Having determined that an individual house is unfit the local authority have several possible courses of action, one of which they *must* take.* Much will depend on whether the house can be rendered fit 'at reasonable cost'. Unfortunately the legislation contains no definition of this, though 'regard shall be had to the estimated cost of the works necessary to render it so fit and the value which it is estimated that the house will have when the works are completed'. If the local authority consider that a house can be made fit at a

---

* The Housing Act powers outlined in the text overlap to a considerable extent the 'nuisance' clauses of the Public Health Acts. These powers enable a local authority to serve an *abatement notice* on the owner of a house which is 'in such a state as to be prejudicial to health or a nuisance'. The notice requires the owner 'to abate the nuisance and to execute such works and to take such steps as may be necessary for that purpose'. Summary proceedings can be instituted if the nuisance is not abated. It is not always easy to decide under which Act proceedings should be instituted in a particular case, but it seems clear that a local authority should not use Public Health Act powers to require a house to be made fit at unreasonable cost: the authority should select the procedure which is least harmful to the owner. Considerable use is made of these powers for dealing with 'sanitary defects' in old houses.

reasonable cost to the owner they can compel him to carry out the necessary work. For this purpose a formal *repair notice* can be served, though commonly this is resorted to only after informal requests have proved fruitless. There is no legal penalty for non-compliance with a repairs notice but the local authority can undertake the work themselves in default, and recover the expenses incurred from the owner (if necessary through the courts). An owner has the right of appeal to the courts against a repair notice, *inter alia* on the ground that the house is not unfit, that the work required to be done does not relate to matters relevant to unfitness, or that the house cannot be made fit at reasonable expense.

If the local authority consider that an unfit house cannot be made fit at reasonable expense they can make a demolition or a closing order.

DEMOLITION AND CLOSING ORDERS

Before issuing an order requiring an owner to demolish or close a house the local authority must serve a *time and place notice* on the owner. This states the time and place at which the local authority will consider what action to take in connection with the house. The owner has the opportunity to appear before the local authority (who then act in a quasi-judicial capacity) and can, if he so wishes, undertake to make the property fit (i.e. at *unreasonable* expense). If no such offer is made, or if though made it is not accepted or not carried out, the local authority *must* do one of three things. First—and normally—they may make a demolition order, the effect of which is to require the owner to demolish the house at his own expense (there are the usual default powers). Secondly, if it is undesirable to make a demolition order (owing to the effect the demolition would have on adjacent properties or because the house is of architectural or historical interest), they may make a closing order. The effect of this is to prohibit the use of the house for any purpose other than one approved by the authority. (A closing order can be made on part of a house, e.g. an underground room.) Thirdly, if they think that the house could—and should—provide accommodation of a tolerable standard for a temporary period prior to demolition, they can acquire the house (at site value) and patch it for temporary use under the 'deferred demolition' procedure discussed later.

POWERS FOR DEALING WITH AREAS OF UNFIT HOUSING*

Any area containing two or more houses can be dealt with under the

* The powers relating to what are termed *redevelopment areas* are not discussed here, since they have in practice been replaced by the town planning powers discussed below.

clearance area procedure if the houses are unfit or badly arranged, and if the local authority are satisfied 'that the most satisfactory method of dealing with the conditions in the area is the demolition of all the buildings in the area'. Before declaring a clearance area the local authority must also satisfy themselves that the persons to be displaced from residential accommodation can be adequately re-housed. Usually this is interpreted as meaning that the local authority is able to rehouse the displaced families: indeed it is often referred to as an 'obligation to rehouse'. In fact, however, a local authority is statutorily required to provide accommodation only in so far as suitable dwellings do not already exist. There are parts of the country where there is no great shortage of housing and where a significant number of displaced families do rehouse themselves: this applies particularly in the case of those owner-occupiers who receive full market value compensation for their houses. Nevertheless the great majority of displaced families are in fact rehoused by the local authority. (Local authorities have no such statutory obligation in relation to families displaced by demolition or closing orders, but in practice they accept a moral obligation to do so.)

To be included in a clearance area a house must be unfit or danger-ous or injurious to health, but it need not be incapable of being made fit at reasonable cost. Other buildings—factories, schools, shops: indeed, *any* building—can also be included so long as they are so badly arranged as to be 'dangerous or injurious to health'.

Having declared a clearance area the local authority proceeds to secure clearance either by making an order for the demolition of the buildings by the owners—a *clearance order*—or by purchasing the properties and undertaking the demolition themselves. If a clearance order is made, Ministerial approval is required, and all buildings included in the area solely because of 'bad arrangement' must be excluded. In other words the *order* must apply only to unfit houses. In practice clearance orders are usually made only for small groups of houses where the local authority are not intending to redevelop the site. The majority of clearance areas are dealt with by way of a compulsory purchase order on the site as a whole. Even where the local authority are not intending to undertake the redevelopment this procedure has the particular advantage that the whole clearance area —not solely the unfit houses—can be purchased, as well as adjoining land which is needed for the satisfactory development of the area.

It is useful to know the jargon which is used in relation to clearance areas. Maps have to be prepared as part of the formal procedure for submitting proposals to the Ministry. On these, different categories of property have to be identified either by hatching and stippling or by colour. The names of the colours are frequently used as a shorthand description of the different categories of property. Thus, *pink* houses

TABLE 29: *Action Taken on Unfit Houses, England and Wales,* 1961 *to* 1964[14]

	1961	1962	1963	1964
1 Houses in clearance areas (Housing Act 1957):				
Unfit houses demolished	34,668	34,862	37,153	37,629
Other houses demolished	3,273	3,256	3,359	3,524
2 Unfit houses elsewhere:				
Houses demolished*	17,566	18,473	16,137	15,545
Houses closed	8,823	8,250	7,533	7,461
Total*	64,330	64,841	64,182	64,159
Persons moved as result of:				
Demolitions	147,016	151,642	146,879	143,737
Closures	18,822	17,167	15,187	16,153
Total	165,838	168,809	162,066	159,890
3 Unfit houses retained at end of year for temporary occupation under Housing Act 1957:				
Sections 17(2), 46 & 48	35,099	35,005	36,051	34,856
Sections 34 & 53	476	266	221	49
4 Houses which were made fit or in which defects were remedied as result of:				
Formal procedure under Public Health or Housing Acts:				
By owners	68,957	70,263	69,852	53,748
By local authorities (in default of owners)	9,375	11,222	10,246	9,739
Informal action by local authorities	142,866	141,335	149,126	124,619
Total	221,198	222,820	229,224	188,106
5 Houses reconstructed, enlarged or improved (section 24 of Housing Act 1957)	429	399	571	566

* No adjustment has been made for houses demolished which had been previously reported as closed. The figures are:

1961	1962	1963	1964
2,361	2,999	2,754	2,944

are those which are unfit for human habitation; *pink hatched yellow* are buildings included because of their bad arrangement; and *grey* properties are those which, though not in either of the other categories, are needed for the satisfactory redevelopment of the cleared area.

This categorization is important for two reasons. First, the compensation which an owner receives for his property will depend upon whether or not it is 'pink'. If it is he normally receives only cleared site value; if it is not he will receive market value for the site with the house on it. (Qualifications to this are outlined later.) Secondly the matters about which the local authority have to be satisfied vary. With a 'pink' house they must be satisfied that the house is unfit according to the criteria set out in the Housing Act. These in fact make no reference to the effect of the conditions on the health of the occupants—though objectors commonly use the argument that there is no evidence that their houses cause ill-health. With 'pink hatched yellow' properties it is legally necessary to prove that there is danger to health. This is difficult to do, at least in a manner which would be acceptable to a logician. The cynic might legitimately comment that all this is a legal fiction which—though relevant to nineteenth-century conditions—is now quite archaic. We shall return to this point; for the present it is sufficient to note only that it is accepted that severe lack of light and air space; narrow, cramped courts, yards and alleys; and similar overshadowed and congested buildings do fall within the legal definition. In practice these conditions are commonly found in conjunction with internal inadequacies which render the house unfit. So far as 'grey' properties are concerned the only matter at issue is whether their acquisition is reasonably necessary for the satisfactory redevelopment of the area. It is not necessary to prove that it is *impossible* to achieve a layout without them. It is sufficient to show that acquisition is reasonable.

DEFERRED DEMOLITION

The size of the slum problem in some areas, particularly the larger cities, is so large that complete clearance is impossible. Some of the 'best of the worst houses' therefore need 'first-aid' treatment to make living conditions tolerable for the occupants. For this purpose there is a *deferred demolition* procedure. Under this, unfit houses which can be made 'capable of providing accommodation of a standard which is adequate for the time being' can be purchased by the local authority, if necessary by the use of compulsory purchase powers. There is no definition of 'a standard which is adequate for the time being', but it is a bare minimum acceptable only because demolition is impossible. Furthermore, the higher the standard is set the longer it will be before all the houses affected can be brought up to it, and the greater the risk of interference with the rebuilding programme upon which the rate of clearance and replacement depends.

APPEALS AND PUBLIC INQUIRIES *

It will be remembered that where a local authority make a demolition order the owner has a right of appeal to the courts. No such right of appeal exists in relation to clearance orders and compulsory purchase orders made in connection with clearance areas. All such orders, however, are subject to confirmation of the Minister and, if there are any 'objections', a public inquiry is normally held. Where an objection is made on the grounds that a house is not unfit for human habitation the local authority have to serve on the objector a written notice stating the principal grounds on which they allege that the house is unfit. (This is generally known as a 'principal grounds' notice.) Even if they do not contest the unfitness of their houses objectors sometimes argue that they wish to retain and redevelop the sites themselves. In such cases a special procedure can be used for substituting by agreement a clearance order for the whole or part of a compulsory purchase order. This is sometimes done, but more usually the local authority intend to redevelop the site themselves. Nevertheless as in all aspects of the use of these compulsory powers the local authority has to satisfy the Minister that the powers applied for ought to be granted. The Minister here acts in quasi-judicial capacity. It is commonly believed—particularly by objectors—that the whole procedure resembles a litigation between opposing interests. In fact there is an important difference. Though the Minister is concerned with weighing the proposals made by the local authority against the interests and wishes of the individuals to be affected by them, he has to consider the public interest and the general policy issues involved. Thus the view taken by the Minister can be expected to be different according to whether it is Government policy to retain as many houses as possible (as it was in the early post-war years) or to clear unfit housing rapidly (as it is today).

The public inquiry is held by an inspector of the Ministry. He submits recommendations to the Minister but does not himself decide the issue. The Minister normally—but by no means always—accepts his inspector's recommendations. There has been much discussion on the question as to whether or not the inspectors ought to be independent of the Ministry (as they are in Scotland). The main argument for independent inspectors—which was accepted by the Franks Committee on Administrative Tribunals and Enquiries[1]—is that this would increase public confidence in the procedure. The Ministry view is that the inspector needs to be fully conversant with

* For a fuller discussion of appeals and public inquiries see the author's *Town and Country Planning in England and Wales.*

Departmental policy and that it would be difficult for the Minister to accept full responsibility for a decision taken in his name if the report on the inquiry, which is an important part of the advice on which the decision is taken, is not made by someone within the Department. The ideal would be for the Minister himself to hold the inquiry and thus hear the evidence at first hand, but since this is clearly impossible the next best course is for one of his own officials, who can be kept in close touch with the development of policy, to perform this function.

At the public inquiry, after it has been confirmed that the statutory formalities (e.g. serving and posting of notices) have been compiled with, the local authority normally open the proceedings by stating their reasons for seeking the order. When the authority have made their case, their witnesses (the Medical Officer of Health, the Chief Public Health Inspector, the Planning Officer and so on) may be cross-examined. It is then the objectors' turn. (Objectors can be legally represented and may call 'expert' witnesses, e.g. estate agents). They will normally argue that the properties are not unfit, or badly arranged, or reasonably needed for the satisfactory redevelopment of the site. They are likely to stress the hardship that would be involved and may attack the authority's 'extravagance' in seeking to redevelop. Finally the authority will reply.

Following the inquiry the inspector visits the properties involved to form his own opinion of their condition and assesses whether 'added lands' (i.e. the 'grey' areas) are reasonably necessary for satisfactory redevelopment.

A report on the inquiry is submitted to the Minister. (An extract from such a report is reproduced at the end of this chapter.) The Minister may exclude properties from an order and he may reclassify from 'pink' to 'pink hatched yellow' or 'grey', or from 'pink hatched yellow' to 'grey'. (He may, for example, be satisfied that a house is not unfit or badly arranged but that its site is nevertheless needed for the satisfactory redevelopment of the area.) He cannot, however, reclassify a property from 'grey' to 'pink' even if the Inspector thinks that the house is really unfit, nor, of course, can he include any land which was not in the original order.

The Minister's decision is conveyed by letter to the interested parties and gives a summary of the main points made at the inquiry, the Inspector's findings and recommendations, and the reasons for the Minister's decision. If the Minister does not accept the Inspector's recommendations the letter will explain the reasons. (Interested persons can also obtain a copy of the Inspector's full report.)

Six weeks after the notice has been given by the local authority of the Minister's confirmation of an order it becomes operative. During this six weeks the validity of an order can be challenged in the High

Court on the ground that it is not within the powers of the Act (*ultra vires*) or that some requirement of the Act has not been complied with. There have been a number of cases on the issue as to whether or not a property is a 'house' within the meaning of the Housing Acts. It has been ruled for instance that a house and shop can be such a 'house', and that buildings originally designed and used as houses remained houses notwithstanding their later use as stores.

COMPENSATION FOR COMPULSORY ACQUISITION

It has already been pointed out that unfit property is acquired by the local authority at site value. It is now necessary to explain this further and to outline other compensation provisions.

The general principle underlying compensation law is that an owner should get a fair value for his property, with no allowance for the fact that the acquisition is compulsory, or for the increased values which are due to a use which is contrary to the law or detrimental to public health. This is known as *full compulsory purchase value*. But it has been long accepted in legislation that a house which is unfit and incapable of being made fit at reasonable expense has no value at all. An owner of such a house therefore receives compensation only for the site on which the house stands. (This may be reduced if the value of the cleared site is greater than the market value of the site with the house on it: this 'ceiling' is imposed in line with the principle that an owner should not be able to make a profit out of the local authority's action in securing the demolition of unfit property when they are taking the land for a public purpose.)

This severe site-value rule is subject to several modifications—in connection for example with certain owner-occupied houses, houses occupied for business purposes and 'well-maintained' houses.

Unfit houses which were purchased by the occupiers between September 1, 1939, and December 13, 1955, receive special compensation. This provision was introduced because of the special hardship suffered by owner-occupiers who had been forced by the housing shortage to buy unsound and substandard houses. Although they may have paid substantial prices for these houses and kept them in good repair, they were not entitled to anything more than the long-standing owner who would have bought at a considerably lower price. For such owner-occupiers compensation is paid as if the house were fit. This provision (introduced in the Slum Clearance (Compensation) Act, 1956) was due to expire on December 13, 1965—exactly ten years after the Ministerial announcement, but the Housing (Slum Clearance) Compensation Act, 1965, extends it until 1970 for owner-occupiers who have had less than fifteen years' possession when Orders are made on their houses.

Owner-occupiers of houses condemned as unfit can sometimes find that the compensation which they receive is insufficient to pay off an outstanding mortgage. The 1956 Act gave the courts power to 'modify' these outstanding liabilities, but only in the case of those owner-occupiers who bought their houses between 1939 and 1955. The new Act extends this power of the courts to all owner-occupiers of unfit houses. It also provides that, in addition to the matters which the courts already take into account in determining a fair settlement, 'regard shall be had to whether the original purchase price of the house was excessive'.

The 1956 Act also introduced special (and permanent) provision for cases in which a small shop or business forms part of a dwelling-house. Owing to the definition of a house (which can include a house with shop or business) a shopkeeper whose living accommodation was declared to be unfit formerly might have received no compensation for the loss of his premises or his livelihood. Owner-occupiers and tenants who have an interest of more than a year (i.e. in effect a lease) now receive 'full compulsory purchase value' on that part of the house which is used for business purposes. This does not apply, however, to those who have a yearly agreement or (much more usually) a weekly tenancy. Though in such cases businesses may in the free market change hands at quite considerable sums, the tenant has no legal interest in the property sufficient to attract statutory compensation. However, local authorities have discretionary powers to meet the losses incurred by such tenants. Successive Ministers have urged local authorities to make generous use of these discretionary powers.[10, 12, 13]

Finally, in this short account of the law relating to compensation, mention needs to be made of 'well-maintained payments' which are made on houses which, though unfit, have been well-maintained. For houses in clearance areas these are given only on the recommendation of the Ministry's inspector; for individual demolition and closing orders the decision rests with the local authority (subject to appeal to the County Court). These payments can be made not only to owners but also to tenants when they have been responsible for the good maintenance. The calculation of the payments is rather complicated but, in brief, it is based either on actual expenditure over the past five years or a multiplier of the rateable value of the house, whichever is the greater. This additional payment cannot make the total compensation for the house greater than it would be were the house fit, nor can it be made to those owner-occupiers who (under the 1956 and 1965 Acts) receive full compensation.

Certain other rules apply to the amount of compensation payable, but it is not necessary for our purposes to go into the legal complexities. Two further points can, however, be made. First, local authorities have wide powers to give discretionary payments towards the cost of removal and, for businesses, towards losses caused by having to move. Secondly, apart from these discretionary payments which are determined solely by the local authority, the actual amount which the local authority pays in compensation is fixed by the rules laid down in the legislation. Though there may be a little room for negotiation, the local authority could not pay a high above-value price simply, for example, in order to quell opposition. Of course they would seldom wish to do so since they have to hold a reasonable balance between the interests of the individuals affected by compulsory purchases and the general public interest. However, it is not unknown for a local authority to take the view that the level of compensation for unfit housing is unacceptably low. Bristol is perhaps the best example. In this city Clearance Orders and Compulsory Purchase Orders are not made. Irrespective of whether or not a property is unfit the City Valuer acquires at market value.[4]

Criticisms of the site value rule have been mounting in recent years, partly because of the increasing proportion of owner-occupiers to be found in clearance areas—many of whom are not eligible for the special provisions of the 1956 and 1965 Acts. From Ministerial remarks made recently (e.g. in the debates on the Housing (Slum Clearance) Compensation Bill) it seems likely that new legislation is being considered.

In determining compensation local authorities are usually advised by the District Valuer (an officer of the Inland Revenue), though some of the larger authorities have their own Valuer. He advises them of the price which he thinks they can properly offer for the property (or land). If a price which is regarded by both parties as being reasonable cannot be agreed there is a right of appeal to the Lands Tribunal. This body is bound by the same statutory rules of compensation as those on which the District Valuer works. There is no further appeal from a decision of the Tribunal, except on matters of law. A recent case of some interest is worth summarising. The local authority—Leeds Corporation—maintained that the market value of land to be acquired under a compulsory purchase order (for slum clearance) was to be calculated without reference to the fact that they were intending to clear unfit housing on surrounding land. Two objectors argued that the value of their land was increased by this prospect and that this should be taken into account when site value was being calculated. The Lands Tribunal found for the claimants but the Court of Appeal overturned this in favour of the contentions of Leeds Corporation. This view was upheld by the House of Lords (*Davy v. Leeds Corporation* and *Central Freehold Estates (Leeds) v. Leeds Corporation*; Court of Appeal (1964) 1 WLR 1218, *The Times*, June 30, 1964; House of Lords, *The Times*, February 25, 1965).

The issue involved here was a legal one of great importance. The principle is clearly reiterated that a local authority, though having to purchase the land at 'current market value', nevertheless does not have to pay any enhanced value brought about by public improvements (in this case slum clearance) in the neighbourhood.

COMPREHENSIVE DEVELOPMENT AREAS

Before discussing the slum clearance programme note should be taken of the powers of local authorities—under the Planning Acts—to undertake 'comprehensive' redevelopment. These powers are rather wider than those provided in the Housing Acts and are particularly useful where extensive redevelopment for non-housing purposes is intended. An *area of comprehensive redevelopment* is:

> any area which in the opinion of the local authority should be developed or redeveloped as a whole, for any one or more of the following purposes, that is to say for the purpose of dealing satisfactorily with extensive war damage or conditions of bad layout or obsolete development, or for the purpose of providing for the relocation of population or industry or the replacement of open space in the course of development or redevelopment of any other area or for any other purpose specified in the plan.

These planning powers are commonly used in connection with central and inner-area redevelopment schemes, though they can be used in any area where the development is planned on 'comprehensive' lines.*

TABLE 30: *Slum Clearance, England and Wales, 1930 to 1964*[15]

	Total houses demolished or closed†	Persons moved
1930–March 31, 1945	340,961	1,340,293
April 1, 1945–December 31, 1954	96,808	308,737
1955	26,023	79,965
1956	36,336	115,093
1957	47,015	159,223
1958	55,273	159,923
1959	60,205	156,642
1960	56,561	165,607
1961	61,969	165,838
1962	61,842	168,809
1963	61,428	162,066
1964	61,215	159,890
1945–1964	606,275	1,801,793

* For further discussion see the author's *Town and Country Planning in England and Wales*, Allen and Unwin, 1964, pp. 74–6 and 247–50.

† The figures for 1945 onwards exclude houses which were demolished after having been previously recorded as closed.

SLUM CLEARANCE PROGRAMMES

The modern slum clearance programme began in the 1930s, when over a third of a million houses were cleared. Just before the war brought the programme to an abrupt halt, demolitions were running at the rate of 90,000 a year—a figure never since achieved. When the war ended the backlog of housing need involved all resources being devoted to new housing. Even repairs were not undertaken where they made substantial demands on resources which could be used for new building. In effect, therefore, not only was there a postponement of slum clearance, but also an enforced neglect of existing houses for over fourteen years.

It was not until 1954 that slum clearance was resumed in earnest. The Housing Repairs and Rents Act of that year gave local authorities wider powers and required them to submit to the Ministry estimates of the number of unfit houses in their area together with their proposals for dealing with them. The estimates gave a total figure of 853,076 in England and Wales. Of these, local authorities proposed, within five years, to demolish 377,878 and to patch up a further 88,282 under the deferred demolition procedure.

It was generally recognized that these figures were very much an underestimate of the problem. Some authorities, such as Manchester (68,000 unfit houses—33 per cent of all the houses in the City) and Liverpool (88,233 unfit houses—43 per cent of the total), included *all* the unfit houses in their estimate. Others lowered their sights to what could be achieved within, say, twenty years. The note accompanying the published statistics[8] warns that the estimates 'represent the best conclusions which local authorities have been able to reach in the light of their local circumstances. There is a considerable variation in the information on which they are based.' Furthermore it must be remembered that the problem of 'slums', 'unfitness' or 'obsolescence' is a continuing one. The fact that all the houses in a programme (based on an estimate of the situation at a particular date) have been cleared does not mean that the problem is 'solved': in the meantime further houses will have deteriorated into the 'slum' category—or, a point of increasing relevance, the minimum tolerable standard of housing will have been raised.

It is necessary to make these points since an assessment of the problem based on official returns can be of doubtful value—and, indeed, positively misleading.

Added point is given to this by comparing the 1954 returns with the new returns asked for by the Ministry in 1965 and the actual number of demolitions during the intervening period. The 1954 estimate was 853,076; since then 541,525 houses have been demolished. But the 1965 estimate is 770,000. Taking the figures for individual cities at their face value, the four with the largest absolute problem on the basis of the 1954 estimate—Liverpool, Manchester, Birmingham and Leeds—have a smaller problem in 1965 than they had in 1954. But Sheffield and Salford now have larger problems, despite substantial clearance.

TABLE 31 : *Fitness and Future of the Stock of Dwellings, England and Wales,* 1960[5]

	Accommodation Units	
Unfit	622,000 ⎫	
Fit with a life of:	⎬ 1,954,000	
Under 5 years	210,000 ⎭	
5 but under 15 years	1,122,000	
15 but under 30 years	2,956,000	
30 years or over	9,727,000	
Total	14,637,000	

Future		
Not likely to be pulled down for any reason in next		
15 *years*	13,497,000	
Likely to be pulled down within:		
5 years	486,000 ⎫	
5–15 years	654,000 ⎬ 1,140,000	
	14,637,000	

Of course, the figures cannot be taken at their face value. They represent a new assessment of the problem. In the circular asking for the latest returns the Ministry specifically asked local authorities to give an estimate of the total number of unfit houses 'regardless of the time which would be needed to clear them'.

TABLE 32: *Slum Clearance—Estimates and Programmes, England and Wales and Selected Cities, 1954 to 1965*

	1954 Estimate	Unfit Houses Demolished 1955–64	1965 Estimate*
England and Wales	853,076	541,525	770,000
Liverpool	88,233	12,206	73,733
Manchester	68,000	18,545	54,700
Birmingham	50,250	16,005	40,915
Leeds	22,500	16,802	17,220
Sheffield	13,500	9,665	28,500
Salford	12,026	5,792	18,000

* The national figure was given in the Second Reading Debates on the Housing (Slum Clearance Compensation) Bill, *House of Commons Debates*, Vol. 720, Col. 856, November 16, 1965. The figures for individual towns were kindly provided by the local authorities.

INADEQUATE HOUSING—UNFIT OR OBSOLETE?

All these estimates of the slum problem are supposedly based on the statutory standard of unfitness. The adequacy of this standard in contemporary conditions is at present under review by a Sub-Committee of the Central Housing Advisory Committee. Since the present writer is a member of this Sub-Committee it would not be appropriate to attempt a forecast of what recommendations are likely to emerge. Nevertheless it is clear that the concept of 'unfitness' is becoming increasingly out-moded—at least outside the large older industrial cities which have such a large back-log of nineteenth-century housing.

The study of housing conditions in Lancaster shows how the situation is changing:

> The problem of old housing in Lancaster is not one of slums. The majority of the remaining old houses in the city are basically sound, and with adequate maintenance and improvement could usefully provide for local needs for at least another generation. Two-thirds of these houses were owner-occupied in 1960 and the proportion has undoubtedly increased since then. In this situation the ninteeenth-century concept of slum clearance is becoming increasingly outmoded. The problem is no longer one of old insanitary courts, of back-to-back houses, of dangers to the public health, or of abject poverty. Rather it is one of sound old houses needing improvement and continued maintenance. The political problem is also changing: in the phraseology of stereotypes, the unpitying and unpitied landlord tis being replaced by the up-standing owner-occupier. Dispossession of owner-occupiers for the sake of redevelopment is quite a different matter from the dispossession of landlords in the interests of public health. . . . The problem is now one of raising the quality of housing in the city. This calls for a policy of improvement, rehabilitation and conservation—of the neighbourhood as well as of individual houses.[2]

Increasingly, therefore, attention will be focused on new standards of 'satisfactory' housing and of adequate environment. This forms the subject of the next chapter. It should not be forgotten, however, that even though 'slums' may become a thing of the past, 'obsolete' housing will always be with us—unless it should prove possible (and economic) to design and build a permanent house of infinite flexibility in an environment which can be moulded to meet ever-changing needs. It is more likely that increasing affluence will demand housing with a shorter life than is currently thought practicable. But even an average life of a century implies a demolition rate of 1 per cent of the total housing stock each year. With a stock of 15 million houses this means demolition at the rate of 150,000 a year. It follows

N

that though the term 'slum clearance' may be superseded the problems of physical clearance will remain.*

Appendix: Extract from an Inspector's Report on a Clearance Area Compulsory Purchase Order†

To The Minister of Housing and Local Government

Sir,

I have the honour to report that on . . . 1964, I held a public local inquiry at the Town Hall, . . . in connection with an application for confirmation of the . . . Area Compulsory Purchase Order, 1963, made under Part III of the Housing Act 1957 by the . . . Borough Council.

The order relates to 10 clearance areas totalling about 7·63 acres and comprising 260 houses (including 5 with shops and 1 with a garage) and to about 6·32 acres of added lands comprising 96 houses (including 6 with shops, 1 with a shop and bakehouse, 1 with a veterinary hospital and 1 with a school), 4 public houses, builders' and coal merchants' yards and buildings, garages, a former school building, stores, warehouses, workshops and 18 cleared sites.

The Council seek to clear the unfit houses and to redevelop the land, together with the 'added lands', for housing and ancillary purposes and to effect road improvements.

Objections
167 objections, relating to 264 properties, were outstanding when the inquiry was opened. During the inquiry 10 more objections were lodged, relating to 11 properties (2 of which were already the subject of other objections), 2 objections were extended to include 3 more properties; 13 objections and part of 7 others (relating in all to 32 properties) were withdrawn.

The outstanding objections were on the grounds that properties included in Part I of the order schedule were fit, or could be made fit at reasonable expense or that they were business premises and not houses, and that the acquisition of properties in Part II of the order schedule was not reasonably necessary for the satisfactory development of the cleared areas. Objections were also on the grounds that the Council's action was premature, having regard to its other commitments, extravagant and over-ambitious and that other land should be redeveloped first; and on grounds of hardship.

---

* A short discussion of social aspects of slum clearance is to be found in Chapter XII.
† Published by permission of the Ministry of Housing and Local Government. Several minor changes have been made to preserve anonymity.

Claims for Well-Maintained Payments
Claims had been submitted in respect of sixty-nine properties. During the inquiry two of these were withdrawn and claims were made in respect of another sixteen properties.

THE GENERAL CASE FOR THE COUNCIL

Two-hundred-and-sixty houses in ten clearance areas were included in Part I of the order schedule. These were unfit for human habitation on the basis set out in Section 4 of the Housing Act 1957. Main defects were disrepair, dampness, poor natural lighting, external water-closets and inadequate arrangements for food storage. The most satisfactory method of dealing with conditions in the areas was the demolition of all the buildings in the areas.

The Council proposed to acquire the properties in order to demolish them and redevelop the land. It was the Council's policy to redevelop decayed central areas with a proper balance of residential and commercial users. This could be achieved only by comprehensive development.

The order lands comprised a decaying area, generally obsolete and depressing, lacking modern residential amenities and without trees, open areas, or play spaces for small children. The amenities considered necessary to modern living could only be provided by comprehensive development.

Acquisition of the added lands was reasonably necessary for the satisfactory development of the cleared areas. It would give a site of 13·954 acres gross, of regular shape, suitable for high density residential development (130 persons an acre was the average density proposed in the town centre).

The order land could be developed with 500 dwellings (in eight-storey flats and maisonettes, four-storey flats and maisonettes and three-storey houses), seventeen shops (including licensed premises) and car parking space for 432 vehicles. A layout was submitted showing the way in which this might be done.

There would be about the same number of dwellings as were on the site at present, but the accommodation would be vastly improved.

The order land was expected to be redeveloped in about three to four years and the road improvements to be carried out at about the same time.

Rehousing
Other housing accommodation would be offered to occupiers of residential accommodation and removal expenses would be paid where necessary. The Council tried to rehouse people in the most suitable accommodation available; sometimes this involved moving

a Council tenant into other accommodation so that older accommodation at a comparatively low rent could be made available for a person being displaced.

Business occupiers
There were comparatively few business premises on the site. Although the Council could not guarantee to offer suitable alternative accommodation, the proposed development provided for shops and commercial premises, and applications for this accommodation from owners or occupiers of existing premises in the area would be sympathetically considered. Shops similar to those proposed had been let by the Council at £250 per annum exclusive.

The Council was trying to buy land allocated in the Development Plan for industrial purposes, specifically for the purpose of relocating businesses displaced from the central area. If they were successful, they would be prepared to allocate space there for builders' yards and coal storage.

THE GENERAL CASE FOR THE OBJECTORS

The Council's proposals were over ambitious, extravagant and premature, and had been formulated without due care.

It was generally agreed that there were some unfit properties in the order (although they were fewer than the Council said), and that they should be dealt with. The Council should have determined which they were and then added the minimum lands necessary to secure satisfactory development.

Instead they appeared to have decided upon the area which they wished to redevelop and had then put a large number of the properties into Part I of the order so as to buy them more cheaply. Many of the principal grounds of unfitness were trivial or related to defects which could be remedied at reasonable expense, some had already been remedied.

Some properties in Part I of the order had been included in the 1966–70 slum clearance programme submitted to the Minister under Section 1 of the Housing Repairs and Rents Act 1954; others were not included in any slum clearance programme. Some properties which had been listed in the programme had been included in the order as added lands.

Classification of properties into Part I and Part II of the order had been inconsistent. Adjoining properties, apparently similar, had been put in different categories. The Council had failed to distinguish properly between slums, twilight houses (which it was not economic to put into good order), those with a useful life of fifteen years, and fit houses; they had simply divided them into fit and unfit.

Some objectors had bought properties from 1959 onwards after local land charges searches which had not revealed the Council's proposals, and now found their houses were classed as 'unfit'. The resultant hardship should be taken into account.

In deciding whether or not the properties were unfit the opinion of the occupiers was relevant. If they were happy, and content to remain there, this should go a long way towards defeating the Council's contention that the properties were unfit. An element of sympathy should be present, particularly in the case of elderly owner-occupiers who had invested their savings in a house, in deciding whether a borderline property should be included as unfit or as 'added lands'.

Inclusion of much of the added lands was extravagant and unnecessary. The Council was proposing to take 138 properties, many of which were fit houses, in order to redevelop the site of 260 houses which they claimed were unfit; the added lands totalled 6·32 acres compared with 7·63 acres in the clearance areas. This was an unreasonably high proportion of added lands.

The cost of buying the fit properties alone might be of the order of £250,000. If 138 families had to be rehoused from them, at a cost of about £2,000 a family for other accommodation, this would add another £250,000. For this sum of £500,000 (an estimate which was on the low side) the Council would not have demolished a single unfit house. It was quite unreasonable and would throw an unjustified burden on the ratepayers.

The substantial road improvements indicated on the layout submitted by the Council were of doubtful value and might not take place for twenty-five years. The usefulness of such a layout was, in any event, questionable.

Whilst no one expected such a layout to be adhered to exactly, it was misleading to produce one at an inquiry unless the development which ensued was substantially in accordance with it. At the inquiry into a previous order a layout had been submitted and a phased redevelopment had been proposed. It now seemed unlikely that the development would be on the lines of the layout; as for phasing, it seemed that the Council were proposing to clear the whole of the site before carrying out any development. There had been other cases also where layouts produced at public inquiries bore little relation to the development which had subsequently taken place.

It seemed likely that the Council would have to charge more than £250 per annum exclusive for the proposed new shops. Even that rent, however, would be quite out of proportion to the existing rents of traders in the area, or to the capital value which they might receive from their properties, and also out of relation to their present or anticipated future trade. Many businesses would probably be extinguished.

The order needed so many amendments that it should be quashed altogether.

The Council's earlier slum clearance operations had dealt with small groups of unfit properties and had resulted in a number of small cleared sites unsuitable for redevelopment, some of which had been used for car parking. It has now been decided that clearance and re-development should proceed together, and to this extent there had been co-operation between the Public Health Department and the Borough Engineer and Surveyor's Department.

The Council was satisfied that their resources were adequate to deal with both [a previous area order and their present order].

The cost of housing in the Borough did not fall on the rates, it was borne by the Housing Revenue Account, and was met by the rents charged. The estimated cost of development (excluding acquisition and demolition) was 500 units at £3,000 a unit, i.e. £1,500,000. The Council had considerable experience of development on this scale.

The list of properties submitted to the Minister under Section 1 of the Housing Repairs and Rents Act 1954 was primarily to enable the Council to plan ahead. It was not intended to be conclusive as regards individual properties, which might improve or deteriorate. It did not, of course, deal with properties which might be included as added lands. Although the Council endeavoured to give as much help as possible to prospective purchasers, when an inquiry was limited to a local land charges search the reply was strictly in accor-dance with the questions asked. Professional people in the town, how-ever, aware of properties in the list, would be expected to be on guard in dealing with other properties in the vicinity. Only twenty-eight of the 260 properties in Part I of the order had been included in the 1966–70 slum clearance programme.

There had been adequate opportunity for owners to bring proper-ties up to standard if this had been possible. The Council's action was not premature, having regard to the condition of the properties.

Acquisition of all the added lands was reasonably necessary for the satisfactory development of the cleared areas.

There had been no unreasonable delay in dealing with the previous order lands. In about twelve months people had been rehoused from about 150 properties.

THE OBJECTIONS*

Lands within the Clearance Area (Part I of the Schedule)

Reference No. 7—was in good repair, apart from the rooms which

* Only a small number of illustrative objections have been reproduced.

were called basements and some minor defects which could be remedied at small expense. The pointing was perfect except for about 6 inches round the window, etc. Floors were bound to be shaky in property of this age but they were satisfactory. Bulging to the wall was imperceptible. The so-called basement rooms comprised a cellar used only for storage and a wash-house with access only from the back garden; they had not been inhabited for twenty years. The tenant did not wish to move.

Reference No. 9—was similar to Reference No. 7. Most of the roof had been renewed about ten years ago. Both properties were owned by a widow of extremely limited means who would suffer great hardship if she did not get market value for the property.

Reference No. 118—Defects were exaggerated. The property was capable of being brought up to standard at reasonable cost. It should be included as 'added lands'. The owner was a widow of small income.

Reference No. 102—This property could be made fit at reasonable expense. The mortgagee was likely to be in possession soon. The mortgagor, owing to financial troubles, had not kept the house up to the standard it had been in, two-and-a-half years before, when he bought it.

Reference No. 130—Although old, the house was not unfit. In 1957, £170 had been spent on it, including rebuilding the back-addition kitchen which was wrongly stated to be bulging and buckled. The property was owned by a widow of limited means.

Reference Nos. 119–25 (consec.) and 127—Reference Nos. 119, 123, 124 and 125 were not included in any slum clearance programme. The others had been included in the 1966–70 programme. The whole block of properties should be excluded from the order or, alternatively, included as 'added lands'.

Each house had four rooms, scullery and a contiguous outside WC. They were suitable for improvement with the aid of grants and the owners would be prepared to have such work carried out. An extension could be built to each back-addition to provide a lobby and a bathroom with WC.

The tenants wished to remain; all were protected under the Rent Acts. Seven of the properties were let at rents not exceeding £1 a week inclusive. It would be better for the Council to build for young married couples who could afford the higher rents charged by the local authority and to allow tenants to remain in existing houses at low rents.

Reply for the Council

The general reply applied. It was accepted that the houses were let at low rents, but they were sub-standard. Although Council tenants had not the legal protection of the Rent Acts, provided they paid their rent and observed the conditions of tenancy they had similar security in practice.

The owners had had plenty of opportunity of improving properties if this had been possible and they had wished to do so. It was doubtful whether References Nos. 119–25 (consec.) and 127, even if they had fifteen years of life, could be satisfactorily improved as suggested; the length of the proposed back-addition would probably not be permitted under the by-laws.

Findings of Fact

Reference Nos. 7, 9, 118, 102, 130, 119–25 (consec.) and 127 comprise two-storey houses, some also having basements or cellars, built mainly of brick with slated roofs, probably about 80–100 years old.

Accommodation varies from four rooms and a kitchen to six rooms. Each has an outside WC. Reference Nos. 122 and 125 each have a bath in the kitchen.

All the properties suffer from rising and/or penetrating damp, severe in most cases, lack of natural light, and have unsatisfactory sanitary conveniences; some also suffer from disrepair, some lack facilities for the storage of food. All are unfit on the basis of Section 4 of the Housing Act, 1957.

Although they have some defects of repair, the general condition of Reference Nos. 119, 124, 125 and 127 justifies well-maintained payments.

Each of the others has three or more of the following defects of repair: slipped slates, perished brickwork, defective pointing, rusty or missing ironwork, rotted woodwork, broken rendering, defective yard paving, perished wall plaster, fallen ceiling plaster, defective floor, badly worn stair treads, broken glazing. They have not been well-maintained.

Reference No. 15—Objection on behalf of the owner-occupier.
Reference No. 73—Objection on behalf of the owner-occupier.
Reference No. 79—Objection on behalf of the owner-occupier.
    These objectors had the same representative.

Case for the Objectors

There was no evidence that the health of the occupants had suffered, nor was there any reason for them to be ousted from the properties for reasons of public health or safety.

The houses were not in perfect repair, but defects were minor. The properties were said to lack light, but they had been in the same condition for years and had not previously been found unfit. The Council were trying to buy these houses cheaply. There were probably houses in similar condition elsewhere which had not been included in clearance areas. The houses had been bought for owner-occupation. Mr . . . had just bought out his partner's share in Reference No. 79; if he were allowed to keep the property repairs would be done.

Reply for the Council

The general reply applied. Reference No. 15 had been in the slum clearance programme since 1960. The Council was not seeking to buy land cheaply; it would not, in fact, be cheap land, but the Council considered acquisition worthwhile as they were the only people able to achieve redevelopment in the town on this scale. They were not seeking to acquire land capriciously.

Findings of Fact

Reference No. 15 has two storeys and basement with six rooms, kitchen and an outside WC. Reference No. 73 has three storeys and basement with eight rooms and an outside WC. Reference No. 79 has three storeys with three rooms, a back-addition kitchen and an outside WC.

All the properties suffer from disrepair, rising and/or penetrating damp and unsatisfactory sanitary conveniences. Reference Nos. 15 and 73 also lack natural light. Reference No. 15 lacks facilities for the storage of food. All are unfit on the basis of Section 4 of the Housing Act 1957.

Each has four or more of the following items of disrepair: broken slates, defective pointing, rusty ironwork, rotted woodwork, defective yard paving, perished wall plaster, defective ceiling plaster (fallen in Reference No. 15), defective floor, badly worn stair treads and broken glazing. They have not been well-maintained.

Reference No. 80—Objection on behalf of the owner-occupier.

Case for the Council

The general case applied.

Case for the Objector

The owner carried on business as an electrician from the premises. One room had been turned into a garage, with the Council's permission, a few years ago. Lots of improvements had been made to the property and it was in good condition.

Findings of Fact

This comprises a two-storey building, probably about 100 years old and designed as a coach-house with a coach-man's quarters over. Part of the ground floor is used as a plumber's store and part as a garage. A flat over has two rooms and a kitchen. There is an outside WC.

The first floor flat, said to be the subject of an undertaking not to relet, is apparently occupied for residential purposes.

Although the property has defects it is not so far defective in the matters set out in Section 4 as to be unfit.

Opinion

The position of this property is such that its acquisition is essential for the satisfactory development of the cleared area. I shall therefore recommend that it be transferred to Part II of the schedule and coloured grey on the order map.

Lands outside the Clearance Area (Part II of the Schedule)

Case for the Objectors

Reference No. 100—comprised a builder's yard, office, workshop, paint stores, machine shop and garage. Part was let to a signwriter. It has been owned and occupied by the objector and his father before him as a builder's yard for forty years. They were the only premises he had for business purposes.

Considerable goodwill attached to the premises, and business would be lost if the objector had to move. It would be difficult to find suitable alternative premises.

The objector expected to have about another ten years working life. If he had to move in five years time he would have to face disturbance for probably only about another five years' business.

Reply for the Council

Reference No. 100—comprises a builder's yard, offices, workshops, stores, etc., and a building used by a signwriter. All the buildings are either old or temporary and are generally in poor condition.

Opinion

Reference No. 100—The position, type, condition and use of this property is such that the clearance areas to the north, east and south of it could not be developed satisfactorily if it were omitted. Its acquisition is justified under Section 43(2).

REFERENCES AND FURTHER READING

[1] Committee on Administrative Tribunals and Enquiries: *Report* (Franks Report), Cmnd. 218, HMSO, 1957; *Memoranda Submitted by Government Departments*, Vol. 2, HMSO, 1956.

[2] Cullingworth, J. B., *Housing in Transition*, Heinemann, 1963.

[3] Donnison, D. V., Chapman, V., and others, *Social Policy and Administration*, Allen and Unwin, 1965, Chapter 5: 'Slum Clearance Begins Again in Bethnal Green'.

[4] Fleming, J., 'The Housing Department—City and County of Bristol', *Housing* (new series), Vol. 1, No. 2, July 1965, p. 47.

[5] Gray, P. G., and Russell, R., *The Housing Situation in 1960*, The Social Survey, Central Office of Information, 1962.

[6] Ministry of Housing and Local Government, *Houses—The Next Step*, Cmd. 8996, HMSO, 1953.

[7] Ministry of Housing and Local Government, *Circular No. 55/54*, 'Housing Repairs and Rents Act, 1954 (Part I)', HMSO, 1954.

[8] Ministry of Housing and Local Government, *Slum Clearance: Summary of Returns by Local Authorities*, Cmnd. 9593, HMSO, 1955.

[9] Ministry of Housing and Local Government, *Moving from the Slums*, HMSO, 1956.

[10] Ministry of Housing and Local Government, *Circular No. 43/56*, 'Slum Clearance (Compensation) Act, 1956', HMSO, 1956.

[11] Ministry of Housing and Local Government, *Circular No. 9/58*, 'Report of the Committee on Administrative Tribunals and Enquiries', HMSO, 1958.

[12] Ministry of Housing and Local Government, *Circular No. 48/59*, 'Town and Country Planning Act, 1959', HMSO, 1959.

[13] Ministry of Housing and Local Government, *Circular No. 36/63*, 'Discretionary Payments to Occupiers Displaced by Acquisition of Land or Slum Clearance', HMSO, 1963.

[14] Ministry of Housing and Local Government, *Annual Reports*, HMSO.

[15] Ministry of Housing and Local Government, *Housing Returns* (Quarterly), HMSO.

[16] Swift, S., and Shaw, F., *Swift's Housing Administration*, Butterworth, Fourth Edition, 1958.

CHAPTER IX

Improvement of Older Houses

DURING THE LATE nineteenth and early twentieth centuries a formidable-looking body of powers was built up to secure the adequate upkeep of private property. These not only made it the clear duty of owners to maintain their houses in a 'fit' condition, but also armed local authorities with default powers. The principle was also established that an owner of an 'unfit house' could be compelled to demolish it or be bought out at site value only. The start of a major slum-clearance programme in the early 1930s raised hopes that the worst of the old houses would be speedily dealt with. But there still remained the much bigger problem of 'below-standard' and deteriorating property. Despite the powers which existed, little inroad was made into this problem. According to the Moyne Report of 1933, one of the major factors was believed to be 'the existence of a large number of small owners with limited resources who neither can nor will repair satisfactorily and whose management is limited to the collection of their rents. Many local authorities . . . hesitate to exercise compulsion on owners whose whole capital is in such properties and whose interest in them is in fact the equity of a mortgage'.[10]

Similar views had been expressed before numerous committees of inquiry into 'the problem of housing the working classes' in the previous half-century. In 1906, for example, 'a good deal of evidence [was] submitted showing that there are in villages many owners of cottage property, of a class little removed from the station in life of their tenants, to whom cottage property appeals as a safe investment, and who are indisposed to curtail their profits'.[18]

Many of these smaller owners thus could not afford any major outlay on repairs, let alone improvements. Furthermore, the evidence, such as it is, suggests that some owners did not allow for the fact that their properties needed a greater expenditure on repairs as they became older. As the second Ridley Committee observed:

> There is evidence of a tendency among some owners to look upon house property as an investment to give a perpetual income without much expenditure on repairs or replacement, and it is per-

haps more difficult for the owner of a small number of houses to accumulate from taxable income the relatively large sum needed for periodical major repairs or for replacement when the house becomes obsolete.[11]

The Moyne Committee, though at pains to stress that they believed in the principle of private property and private ownership, felt that the time had come when owners who did not fully discharge 'the modern obligations of ownership', should be replaced by a public or quasi-public authority. They recommended that local authorities should be given compulsory powers and encouraged to acquire for reconditioning any working-class houses which were 'not in all respects fit for human habitation but can be made fit and to which a probable life of at least twenty years can be given'.[10]

The 1935 Housing Act provided local authorities with wide powers for acquiring 'houses which are, or may be made, suitable as dwell-houses for the working classes' and for 'altering, enlarging, repairing or improving', but there is no record of any such reconditioning being undertaken in urban areas. Local authorities were apparently fully occupied with slum clearance and the relief of overcrowding. Probably the fact that reconditioning did not rank for subsidies acted as a deterrent.

There is, however, record of some activity in the field of rural housing. Housing conditions in rural areas were generally accepted to be worse than in the towns. The lack of sanitary arrangements was greater, the average age of houses was older, and the rent-paying capacity of agricultural workers was lower. Special housing subsidies for houses built for 'members of the agricultural population' were paid from 1924 onwards, and an attempt to encourage reconditioning by private owners was made in 1926 by providing loans and grants. The loans amounted at a maximum to 90 per cent of the value of the dwelling after improvement; the grant was two-thirds of the approved cost of improvement, subject to a maximum grant of £100. The improved dwelling had to be let for twenty years to an agricultural worker 'or employee of substantially the same economic condition employed by the person who is rated in respect of the dwelling', and the rent could be raised by a maximum amounting to a 3 per cent return on the owner's share of the cost of improvement. The provisions were intended to be temporary, but were extended several times and remained in operation (with amendments) throughout the inter-war years. Progress, however, was very slow, mainly, it was thought, because of the reluctance of rural councils to give grants to 'persons of substantial means', but also because of the lack of co-operation from owners. Indeed, by 1937 it was being suggested by the Hobhouse Committee that where owners were unwilling to carry out reconditioning, local authorities should use their powers of compulsory acquisition and undertake the reconditioning themselves.[3] A report from the same Committee in 1947 went further.[5] They then maintained that the scheme had failed in the inter-war years largely because no one had been given the duty 'of ensuring that every house which was in need of it was, in fact, brought up to a proper standard'. In their view the only way of securing that all cottages in need of reconditioning were dealt with was to introduce a measure of compulsion. Where property needed reconditioning, the owner should have a duty to bring it up to modern standards; and if he failed to do so the local authority should have a duty to buy the property and carry out the work. Furthermore, they argued that it was undesirable to restrict grant-aid dwellings occupied by agricultural workers. The 'vital necessity' for reconditioning rested upon the fact that rural housing as a whole was of a low standard. The scheme should, therefore, be extended in such a way as to ensure that the greatest number of suitable houses were eligible to benefit by the grant.

Befogging the whole issue, however, was the question of whether grants benefited the tenant or the owner. Throughout the 'thirties the Ministry of Health repeatedly stressed that the benefit did in fact accrue to the tenant. The Acts had been specifically designed to ensure this. With a strange logic the Committee argued that since this was the case 'the qualification for grant should depend upon the financial position of the occupier of the house'. But the general opposition was against paying grants to landlords who did not 'need' them. Indeed one member of the Committee, Miss Jennie Lee, felt so strongly on this that she submitted a minority report. She agreed that a duty should be placed upon owners, or in default upon the local authority, to recondition property in such need, but she strongly dissented from the view that grants for reconditioning should be given to private persons—whatever their financial circumstances.

This question was also relevant to another problem under consideration at this time—that of the conversion and adaption of socially obsolete large houses. The Silkin Committee, reporting on this in 1945, stressed the fact that 'from the point of view of the community, the benefit of conversion is to replace obsolete and worn-out accommodation by sound habitable dwellings'.[4] They recommended low-interest loans and a subsidy of a percentage (unspecified) of the approved cost of actual conversion up to a maximum (again unspecified) per dwelling provided.

The concentration of resources on war-damage repairs and on new housing involved a postponement of these questions. Not until 1949 was any action taken on any of these reports. The Housing Act of that year made improvement grants available for urban as well as rural housing, on condition that the improved houses had an expected life of thirty years or more. The intention was, in the words of Mr Bevan, not to 'rescue slums' or 'to permit landlords to make good the arrears of repairs that they should themselves have carried out long ago'. The grants were not for repairs, but for 'improvements'— the installation of a bath, a water-closet, a piped water supply, and so forth.

THE 1949 ACT

The grants available under the 1949 Act were for improvements costing between £100 and £600 (raised to £800 in 1952), and were at a maximum of a half of the approved cost. The rent could be increased by an amount not exceeding 6 per cent of the owner's share of the cost. Certain other conditions were laid down, including a requirement that the dwelling was either kept available for letting (at a controlled rent) or occupied only by the applicant for the grant or by a member of his family. All the conditions were to be observed for a period of twenty years.

Little use was made of these grants, partly because of lack of publicity and the fact that local authorities did not wish to promote any activity which might draw resources of men and materials away from their building programmes, and partly because the conditions were restrictive. Between 1949 and 1953 only 6,000 grants were given in the whole of the country.

The easier economic climate of 1954 (and the resulting abolition of building licensing), together with a change in Government policy (announced in the White Paper, *Houses—The Next Step*),[12] brought about a liberalization of the conditions on which grants were given. The 1954 Housing Repairs and Rents Act reduced the minimum life of a house on which a grant could be made to fifteen years (but with the added condition 'that it is expedient in all the circumstances that the application should be approved'); raised the landlord's return to 8 per cent; and abolished the upper cost limit and provided instead for a maximum grant of £400 or half the cost of the works, which ever was the less.

The rate of improvements shot up to over 30,000 a year and by the end of 1958 had totalled about 160,000. The following year saw a further easing of the conditions on which grants were given and, to encourage a faster rate of improvement in privately-owned *rented* property, the landlord's return was increased to 12½ per cent. At the same time a new simplified scheme of 'standard grants' was introduced. The effect was dramatic: in the single year of 1960 over 130,000 grants were made. By the end of 1964 the number of houses improved under the various schemes had exceeded 800,000. Attention was increasingly now being directed (at least on the part of the Ministry and the more progressive authorities) to *areas* of houses needing improvement, and in 1964 extended powers were introduced to enable local authorities to achieve this.

The gradual easing of the conditions accompanying the giving of improvement grants, the simplification of procedures, and the growing emphasis on the improvement of whole streets or areas rather than individual houses all reflect the increasing concern of housing policy with the problem of obsolete housing.

The problem at which this policy is directed is an enormous one. It was estimated that in 1960 some 4·3 million houses in England and Wales were fit and had a 'life' of fifteen years but were deficient in amenities such as a fixed bath or an adequate hot water supply. The figures, which are taken from the Government Social Survey Report on *The Housing Situation in 1960*,[8] are summarized in Table 33. These figures are, of course, now over five years old. More up-to-date figures will be available when the Social Survey report on the 1964 housing survey is published. Since 1960 nearly 700,000 dwellings have been improved with grant. Allowing for improvements without grant and some demolitions (of 'fit' property adjacent to slums or for other redevelopment) which were not allowed for in the 1960 estimates, the total for 1965 would probably be of the order of 3 million. Not all of these dwellings will be 'improvable'. A significant number may be too small or otherwise physically unsuitable. Furthermore, owing to the considerable amount of sharing of amenities, an allowance has to be made for double counting. A reasonable guess at the number of improvable houses might be around 2 million.

The objective of the improvement grants schemes is to encourage owners to provide services and amenities in basically sound houses which are lacking the amenities which modern standards and aspirations demand. The justification for the spending of public funds on this is not only that living conditions are thereby improved, but also that unless old houses are modernized they will deteriorate into slums which then need to be cleared and replaced at public expense. The responsibility for awarding these grants lies with local authorities, though three-quarters of the cost is borne by the Exchequer.

The grants are given on the basis of one half of the approved cost of the works, subject to a maximum limit. They cover only improvements—not ordinary repairs and replacements. This often presents some difficulties. In ordinary language 'improvement' might be taken to include works of both repair and replacement: at the least, one would expect the condition of a house to be 'improved' after such works had been undertaken. But it is not the object of the schemes to give financial assistance for work which merely prevents a property from deteriorating (i.e. maintenance) or which simply involves the replacement of an item by its modern equivalent. The aim is to assist 'improvements' which involve something more than holding one's own—works which are a positive increase in housing standards. For instance the replacement of a worn-out bath is not regarded as a proper call on public funds, but the installation of a bath in a house which does not have one is. The line is obviously a difficult one to draw, but it must be drawn somewhere if every house-owner is not to have a statutory right to public assistance for normal maintenance and replacement.

TABLE 33: *Deficiencies in Basically Sound Houses, England and Wales, 1960*[8]

Whether households are with (+) or without (−) the sole use of:

Fixed bath	Wash bath	Hot water at 3 points*	WC in or attached to dwelling	Households in Fit Rateable Units with life of 15 years or more
−	−	−	−	1,570,000
−	−	−	+	995,000
+	−	−	+	925,000
+	+	−	+	323,000
Other combinations of above				499,000
Total				4,312,000
Lacking none of above for sole use				8,195,000
Total				12,507,000
Households in Rateable Units reported unfit or with a life of less than 15 years				1,915,000
All households				14,422,000

The two types of scheme—discretionary and standard—are complementary to each other rather than alternatives. Discretionary grants are given for dwellings which can be brought up to a defined standard comparable with that of a modern house—given due allowance for age and limitations in design, layout and construction. The amount of the grant can be substantial, with a maximum of £400 on an owner's total expenditure of £800 or more. Expenditure of this order—equivalent to one-third of the construction cost of a new three-bedroom local authority house—can be justified only if the dwelling after improvement has a reasonably long life. The normal rule is that these grants are given only when the dwelling will have a life of at least thirty years, though in exceptional circumstances

* Bath, wash-basin and sink.

O

improvement of a shorter life dwelling (minimum fifteen years) may be justified.

Standard grants are intended in the main for houses which cannot be brought up to such a high standard but which nevertheless warrant some expenditure to make them more comfortable for the remainder of their life. The only requirements are that the improved dwelling must be fit for human habitation and have a life of at least fifteen years. If a dwelling is likely to warrant formal clearance action (e.g. because of structural defects) or be affected by redevelopment proposals within fifteen years it is not suitable for an improvement grant. In these circumstances, however, the deferred demolition procedure referred to in the previous chapter, may be appropriate. This involves the acquisition of the dwelling by the local authority and then a minimum of expenditure to make it wind and weather proof.

The grants are available to all owners, irrespective of their means. Local authorities are not supposed to take into account an applicant's financial resources when considering whether to award a grant. This applies equally to discretionary grants (which, by definition, are given at the discretion of the local authority) and standard grants (which local authorities are bound to approve in all cases where the statutory requirements are met). The only test is the suitability of the property for the type of improvement which is proposed.

DISCRETIONARY GRANTS—THE TWELVE-POINT STANDARD

For houses to be improved with a discretionary grant a number of requirements have to be complied with. This is known as the Twelve-Point Standard. This standard requires that after improvement a dwelling must:

(i) be in a good state of repair and substantially free from damp;

(ii) have each room properly lighted and ventilated;

(iii) have an adequate supply of wholesome water laid on inside the dwelling;

(iv) be provided with efficient and adequate means of supplying hot water for domestic purposes;

(v) have an internal water-closet if practicable; otherwise a readily accessible outside water-closet;

(vi) have a fixed bath or shower in a bathroom;

(vii) be provided with a sink or sinks and with suitable arrangements for the disposal of waste water;

(viii) have a proper drainage system;

(ix) be provided in each room with adequate points for gas or electric lighting (where reasonably available);

(x) be provided with adequate facilities for heating;

(xi) have satisfactory facilities for storing, preparing and cooking food;

(xii) have proper provision for the storage of fuel (where required).

These requirements have been drawn up in such a way as to strike a reasonable balance between the need for a definite standard of adequate housing conditions and an equal need for flexibility in the face of an almost infinite variety of houses and of 'satisfactory' housing conditions. For instance some requirements which, it might be thought, should be included in all adequate houses—electricity, for example—may be quite impracticable to provide because of the unavailability of main services. Again, an internal water-closet is surely a desirable 'minimum' requirement, but many old houses which have a substantial life left in them cannot be provided with one because of their design and layout. It would be wrong to deny the occupiers of such houses other improvements which are equally desirable. This is a clear case where the best should not become the enemy of the good. A reasonable approach to these issues is usually taken by local authorities and where a normal requirement cannot be met they can seek the Ministry's consent to waive it.

However the argument must not be carried too far. After all, public money is being spent on these improvements and it is important to ensure that it is money well spent. It is for this reason that the condition is normally laid down that all requirements should be met: an owner is not allowed to receive a subsidy to 'half-improve' his house. This would be to abandon the main object, namely the improvement of a house to a defined standard. Should an owner be unable to afford his part of the cost of total improvement, the local authority can advance him a loan. The more progressive authorities have a special loan scheme for improvements which can be dealt with at the same time as an application for an improvement grant. Loans may similarly be given for the cost of repairs which are not eligible for grant.

Discretionary grants are also given for the conversion into separate self-contained dwellings of houses which are too large for a single family under present-day conditions. The same rules apply as in the case of grants for improvements. Here, of course, much more work of structural alterations, changes and improvements to existing services and installations is often necessary. All these works are eligible for grant, as well as the costs of fire precautions and of sound and thermal insulation. The grants payable for conversion are related to the number of dwellings provided: thus a conversion into three dwellings would attract a maximum grant of three times £400, i.e. £1,200. Where the house being converted has three or more storeys the maximum grant is increased from £400 to £500 per dwelling. This is to enable the extra structural and other costs involved in this type of conversion to be met.

STANDARD GRANTS

Standard grants are available towards the cost of providing a house with certain basic amenities. This scheme has been amended twice since it was introduced in 1959 so as to make it more attractive.

Normally dwellings to be improved with the aid of a standard grant must meet a Five-Point Standard The maximum grant is normally £155 or half the cost of the works, whichever is the lower. The grant is calculated on the following basis:

Amenity	*Maximum Grant* Half the approved cost of the work, subject to a maximum of:
(i) A fixed bath or shower in a bathroom	£25
(ii) A wash-hand basin	£5
(iii) (a) A hot and cold water supply at a fixed bath or shower	£35
(b) A hot and cold water supply at a wash-hand basin	£15
(c) A hot and cold water supply at a sink	£25
(iv) A water-closet	£40
(v) A satisfactory food store	£10

A higher grant, up to a maximum of £350, can be given in three cases—first, where it is not reasonably practicable to provide a fixed bath or shower in a bathroom except by building on to the house, or converting outbuildings attached to it; secondly, where, owing to the impracticability of connecting a new water-closet to main drainage, septic tank drainage has to be installed; and, thirdly, where piped water is being brought into the dwelling for the first time.

The purpose of the standard grants is to encourage the improvement up to a basic condition of houses which are not suitable for improvement to the higher Twelve-Point Standard. But even the Five-Point Standard cannot always be met; it was for this reason that the 1964 Housing Act introduced an even lower Three-Point Standard. Standard grants are now available, under these new provisions, for houses which after improvement will be provided at least with a hot and cold water supply at a sink, a water-closet and a satisfactory food store.

The range of methods for dealing with different types and conditions of houses is thus now a wide one. The very worst houses can be demolished or closed, or, where this is not practicable, patched under the deferred demolition procedure; the next houses in the hierarchy of condition can be improved to the Three-Point Standard or the Five-Point Standard; and the best of the inadequate houses can be improved up to the full Twelve-Point Standard.

The grants are available to private owners—landlords or owner-occupiers—and to local authorities themselves. In all cases three-eighths of the cost of the approved works (i.e. three-quarters of the grant) is borne by the Exchequer.

THE ADMINISTRATION OF IMPROVEMENT GRANT SCHEMES

Responsibility for awarding grants rests with local authorities. Naturally with over 1,400 separate local authorities it is to be expected that there will be differences in attitude to these schemes. Indeed, prior to the introduction of standard grants some local authorities refused to give grants on grounds that it was wrong to give public money in aid of improvement of private property. Other authorities have insisted on the carrying out of an excessive number of repairs (which are not grant-aided). This tendency to be over-zealous about repairs was one of the reasons which led to the introduction of standard grants. With these local authorities have no discretion, but they have to be satisfied that when the work is complete the dwelling will not be unfit for human habitation and that it is likely to remain fit for at least fifteen years. This must often be a matter of judgment, and complaints are still heard that some local authorities take a too strict definition of unfitness and insist on relatively minor repairs being carried out. The Ministry can do little about this formally since a judgment would require a special inspection of the properties concerned. Nevertheless it is noteworthy, not only that the statutory conditions have been continually relaxed, but also that more recent Ministry circulars have become more critical of reluctant authorities. Circular 29/62, for instance, urges local authorities to take a 'common-sense' approach, and not to be 'pernickety'.[13]

On the other hand, some local authorities have taken a very progressive line. Manchester has even taken local Act powers to give standard grants (from the rate fund) for *unfit* houses which have a probable life of less than fifteen years and which, by definition, do not come within the scope of the normal scheme. This power is to be used only where it is thought that a dwelling has a life of at least eight years in its improved state. This is an exceptional provision—

which the Ministry were none too keen to accept—but it was recognized that Manchester had a particularly difficult slum problem which could not be dealt with at a desirable rate. The scheme in effect lies somewhere between 'patching' (under the deferred demolition procedure) and full 'standard' improvement. It is intended generally to apply to individual terraced houses, rather than areas.

Other local authorities have operated an 'improvement area' policy—which (as will be shown later) now has received some legislative backing. Foremost is Leeds which has been able, by good administration, publicity and public relations to secure more success with the improvement grants schemes than any other authority. Emphasis has been placed on the discretionary rather than standard grants. Early experience, however, showed that since they were discretionary on the owner as well as on the local authority, the rate of improvement was undesirably low. Since 1955, therefore, the Housing Committee has aimed to secure the improvement of all the houses in particular areas. This is being carried out without the use of any legislation other than that generally available for improvement grants and the power to purchase houses compulsorily under Section 96 of the Housing Act, 1957. In areas judged suitable for improvement, contact is made with all the owners drawing their attention to the grants and (100 per cent) loans available and offering, as an alternative, to negotiate for the purchase of the houses by the Council to enable them to carry out the improvements themselves. General experience in Leeds—which is not shared by all authorities who have tried this—is that where an owner has raised an objection this has usually been because he was not fully acquainted with the improvement grant scheme, or did not realize that he could obtain a loan from the Council to cover the balance of the cost. In the majority of cases the work of improvement is carried out with the tenants remaining in the house. If improvement reduces living accommodation (e.g. by converting a bedroom into a bathroom) and results in overcrowding, the Council rehouse the tenants on the understanding that the owner will accept new tenants in the improved houses from the Council's waiting list. Sometimes the tenant does not wish to accept the improvement, but is willing to be rehoused by the Council; in these cases also the Council rehouses, subject to their nominating the new tenant for the improved house. After explanation and discussion it has been found that most of the initial objections have been withdrawn.

As a last resort—and in order to prevent deterioration both of the individual houses and the area generally—the Council seek compulsory powers to purchase. But this is not done where the owner undertakes to improve the house within a reasonable time or where houses are occupied by old and infirm people whom it is considered undesirable to disturb.

Twenty-two improvement areas had been approved by March 31, 1964, comprising 4,286 houses. At this date 2,690 houses had been improved or were being improved or acquired; fifty-two houses were being left because of the age or infirmity of the occupants, and 266 houses were the subject of compulsory purchase.

The great advantage of this policy is that by improving a whole area—rather than isolated houses—all the houses in the area can be expected to enjoy a lengthened life. It avoids the difficulties which arise when some houses are allowed to decay close to or adjoining improved houses.

In spite of the success achieved in Leeds the programme in that city has been held up by the lengthy negotiations which are necessary with reluctant owners and by the cumbersome and time-consuming nature of the compulsory purchase procedure. Elsewhere results have been generally much more disappointing; so much so, in fact, that suggestions have been afoot for some time that local authorities should be given powers to compel private owners to undertake improvements—in the same way in which they may be compelled under the Clean Air Act to 'improve' open fire-places. There has been great reluctance to do this but a certain element of compulsion has now been provided in the 1964 Housing Act.

IMPROVEMENTS BY ORDER

About four-fifths of all the improvements and conversions carried out over the last five years have been by owner-occupiers and local authorities. The rate of improvement by private landlords has been only some 30,000 a year (and this figure includes housing associations). In the early stages of the scheme it was thought that the deterrent was the rate of return allowed to private landlords—6 per cent per year of their part of the cost (excluding expenditure on repairs). Accordingly the return was increased first to 8 per cent and then to 12½ per cent. Experience since that date suggests that the cause is more deep-seated. The evidence is not clear cut: we know too little about the characteristics of private landlords to be dogmatic. In some areas a high proportion of property is owned by elderly poor widows (commonly with only one house each),[7] whereas in London a considerable proportion is owned by companies—though even here 78 per cent of landlords own only one building.[16] However, though some believe that size of holding is an important factor in house management and attitude towards improvements, others hold that this is irrelevant and that what is important is the low level of con-

trolled rents which make the financing of adequate repairs (which are
not grant-aided) impossible.

Perhaps the most important factor, however, is the tax position.
Landlords have to pay tax on funds used to amortize loans or set
aside for depreciation. As a result the apparent return of 12½ per cent
on an investment in improvements is greatly reduced. The Milner
Holland Report convincingly argued that the tax position formed a
serious disincentive to the improvement of privately-rented property.[15]

This is particularly unfortunate since it is the privately-rented
sector which is most in need of improvement. (Nearly all the houses
lacking a sink are privately rented.) But it also needs to be noted that,
according to the Social Survey Report on *The Housing Situation in
1960*,[6] rather less than a half of private tenants say that they would be
prepared to pay more rent if missing amenities were provided. The
question of compulsion may therefore be of importance in relation to
tenants as well as owners.

The new powers enable local authorities to compel owners to
improve tenanted dwellings in 'improvement areas', tenement blocks
and, at the request of the tenant, elsewhere.

TABLE 34: *Grant-aided Improvements and Conversions, England and Wales,
1949 to 1964*[16]

	Improvements			Conversions
	Standard	Discretionary	Total	
1949–59	33,061	187,595	220,656	18,209
1960	82,819	42,988	125,807	5,025
1961	79,831	42,808	122,639	5,137
1962	68,738	36,835	105,573	4,933
1963	77,278	37,563	114,841	5,138
1964	76,635	40,072	116,707	4,978
	418,362	387,861	806,223	43,420

Improvements 1960–64 by Type of Owner

	Standard	Discretionary	Total	%
Local Authorities	126,558	53,496	180,054	30
Private Landlords and Housing Associations	62,200	55,055	117,255	20
Owner-occupiers	196,543	98,731	295,274	50
Total 1960–64	388,301	207,282	592,583	100

TABLE 35: *Analysis of Standard Amenities Provided with Grant-Aid 1959–64*[16]

	By Local Authorities	By Private Owners	Total No.	%
Dwellings concerned	137,693	217,541	355,234	100
Baths or Showers	9,994	163,768	173,762	49
Wash-Basins	124,320	178,520	302,840	85
Hot Water Supplies	90,677	179,306	269,983	76
Water-Closets	12,524	160,194	172,718	49
Food Stores	3,631	115,775	119,406	34

IMPROVEMENT AREAS

Local authorities now have a duty to arrange for the inspection of their areas with a view to identifying areas suitable for comprehensive improvement. The intention, however, is not only to secure the provision of amenities in individual houses and to ensure that the good effect of this is not negatived by deterioration of adjacent properties: it is also intended to be part of a process of urban renewal —or what in Newcastle-upon-Tyne (which has been experimenting with such a policy) is called 'revitalization'. This involves such measures as providing trees, parking facilities, better open spaces, new street furniture: indeed, any action (including smoke control) which will improve the quality of the environment. The Ministry advise that the need to carry through all the processes of consultation, persuasion and—only as a last resort—the full statutory procedure of compulsion, within a limited period suggests that a total of about 300 houses may be as many as it would be prudent to include in one area, at least until decisions can be based on practical experience.[14]

Compulsory improvement applies only to tenanted houses—not those owned by their occupiers. Before a local authority can declare an *improvement area* they must be satisfied that the area contains some dwellings which lack one or more of the standard amenities and that at least half of these are capable of improvement up to what is called the *full standard*—namely the Five-Point Standard. After advertising the declaration of an improvement area, the next step is for the local authority to select those tenanted dwellings which could be improved *at reasonable expense* to the full standard. A *preliminary notice* is then served on the owner and the tenant specifying the works required and their estimated cost, together with the time and place at which the future of the dwelling will be discussed. (The notice is thus similar to the time and place notice served in respect of individual unfit dwellings.) If the dwelling can only be brought up to the reduced standard (i.e. the Three-Point Standard) at reasonable expense, the

TABLE 36: *Loans by Local Authorities for Conversions, Alterations, etc., 1959–64*

	For Conversions		For Improvements with the aid of Standard Grants		For Other Alterations	
	No.	£	No.	£	No.	£
1959–62	1,418	714,000	16,307	2,108,000	18,178	5,064,000
1963	255	133,000	5,307	791,000	5,245	1,650,000
1964	347	199,000	6,114	938,000	8,147	2,380,000
1959–64	2,020	1,046,000	27,728	3,837,000	31,570	9,094,000

notice will specify accordingly. There is no statutory time limit for the service of a preliminary notice, but after it has been served, follow-up action must be taken within two years of the declaration of the area. This is intended to allow sufficient time before taking any formal action for the council to make a final effort to persuade the owner to carry out the needed improvements voluntarily. At the 'discussion' the local authority can accept a formal undertaking by the owner (with the consent of the tenant) to carry out the necessary works. If such an undertaking is not given—with the consent of the tenant—or is not fulfilled, the local authority may serve an *improvement notice*. There are two types of such notice. If the tenant agrees to the improvements being made an *immediate improvement notice* is served, requiring completion of the works within twelve months. If the consent of the tenant has not been received, the authority can serve a *suspended improvement notice*; this can be converted into a *final improvement notice* (having the same effect as an immediate improvement notice) if the tenant's consent is obtained or if there is a change of occupier. The local authority can serve a final improvement notice without having obtained the tenant's consent subject to certain conditions including offering the tenant a council house, but only after five years have elapsed since the declaration of the improvement area. There are certain rights of appeal to the county court.

Outside improvement areas the compulsory improvement procedure can be used on the application of a tenant. In other words, if the tenant wants the improvements, compulsion can be used against the landlord.

Special provisions apply to tenement blocks. These present particular problems, in particular it may not be reasonable or practicable to improve some of the dwellings without improving all of them, for example because of interference with common services. Furthermore since a requirement that all tenants should consent to improvements might mean that one individual tenant could hold up the improvement of the whole block, a degree of compulsion on tenants is needed—at least as a reserve. It was accepted that it was right to provide for compulsory improvement, e.g. where a majority of the tenants are agreeable. Though the legislation does not in fact impose any such rule, local authorities have been advised to follow it.

This short outline of the procedure illustrates the complexities which have resulted from attempting to provide the maximum safeguards for owners and tenants and the maximum opportunity for voluntary improvements. The powers were given with reluctance and only because of the urgent need to speed up the rate of improvements and the widespread feeling that some element of compulsion was now required. The justification can be seen in the figures of the annual number of improvements and the number of houses capable of being improved—in round figures 115,000 and probably 2 million. The necessity for an expanded rate of improvements is further underlined by the forecasts of future slum clearance needs. Given no improvements and repairs it is estimated that the annual rate of clearance will need to rise first to 130,000 and later, in the nineteen-eighties, to nearly 200,000 a year (See Table 31). Whether the degree of compulsion and the new procedures will prove adequate remains to be seen.

REFERENCES AND FUTURE READING

[1] Armes, A., 'Improvement Grants—Past, Present and Future', *The Sanitarian*, Vol. 71, May 1963.

[2] Budden, A., 'Conversions and Modernization in Birmingham', *Chartered Surveyor*, Vol. 98, No. 3, September 1965.

[3] Central Housing Advisory Committee, *Rural Housing* (Hobhouse Report), HMSO, 1937.

[4] Central Housing Advisory Committee, *Conversion of Existing Houses* (Silkin Report), HMSO, 1945.

[5] Central Housing Advisory Committee, *Reconditioning in Rural Areas* (Second Hobhouse Report), HMSO, 1947.

[6] Cohen, K. C., 'Improvements and Conversions', *Housing Review*, November–December 1961.

[7] Cullingworth, J. B., *Housing in Transition*, Heinemann, 1963.

[8] Gray, P. G., and Russell, R., *The Housing Situation in 1960*, The Social Survey, Central Office of Information, 1962.

[9] Housing Centre, 'Conference Report: New Life for Old Houses', *Housing Review*, September–October 1962.

[10] Ministry of Health, *Report of the Departmental Committee on Housing* (Moyne Report), Cmd. 4397, HMSO, 1933.

[11] Ministry of Health, *Report of the Inter-Departmental Committee on Rent Control* (Second Ridley Report), Cmd. 6621, HMSO, 1945.

[12] Ministry of Housing and Local Government, *Houses—The Next Step*, Cmd. 8996, HMSO, 1953.

[13] Ministry of Housing and Local Government, *Circular No. 29/62*, 'Improvement and Conversion Grants—Practice Notes', HMSO, 1962.

[14] Ministry of Housing and Local Government, *Circular No. 53/64*, 'Housing Act 1964—Compulsory Improvement of Dwellings to provide Standard Amenities; Assistance for Improvement of Dwellings', HMSO, 1964.

[15] Ministry of Housing and Local Government, *Report of the Committee on Housing in Greater London* (Milner Holland Report), Cmnd. 2605, HMSO, 1965.

[16] Ministry of Housing and Local Government, *Housing Returns*, HMSO, Quarterly.

[17] Nash, W. W., *Residential Rehabilitation: Private Profits and Public Purposes*, McGraw-Hill, 1959.

[18] *Special Report of the Select Committee on Housing of the Working Classes Acts Amendment Bill, 1906*, HMSO, 1906.

CHAPTER X

Overcrowding and Multiple Occupation

MEASURES TO DEAL with the problem of overcrowding have a long history in England. The nineteenth century Public Health Acts gave local authorities powers to deal with houses which were so overcrowded as to be 'dangerous or injurious to the health of the inmates'. It was not, however, until 1935 that overcrowding was defined. The standard—which has never been revised—is a penal one. It has two parts: one dealing with sex separation, the other being a standard of capacity. Under the first part a house is overcrowded if any two persons aged ten or over of opposite sexes and 'not being persons living together as husband and wife' must sleep in the same room. This part of the standard obviously can apply only to one-room houses since if there is more than one room it is always possible to separate the sexes at night. The second part of the standard is more complicated. It provides for a 'permitted number' of persons per house. This number is determined by reference to the number of rooms in the house and their size. Where all the rooms are 110 sq ft or more the permitted number is as shown in the first part of Table 37. For smaller rooms the number is reduced in accordance with the second half of the Table. Children under the age of one are not counted, and children aged between one and ten are counted as half a person.

Any landlord who permits a higher rate of occupancy than this is liable to prosecution. In fact, overcrowding (except in cases of 'multiple occupation') is now dealt with by local authorities rehousing the overcrowded tenants and not by penal sanctions. Furthermore the standard is so low that it has ceased to have relevance to existing conditions over the major part of England and Wales, if not in Scotland. Only 81,000 households (0·6 per cent) were overcrowded on this standard in 1960,[2] and the standards used by local authorities in selecting tenants on the basis of their overcrowding, though of immense variety, are considerably higher. Indeed many local authorities find themselves more concerned with 'under-occupation' than overcrowding.

TABLE 37: *Statutory Overcrowding Standard*

Number of Rooms in the House	Permitted Number of Persons
1	2
2	3
3	5
4	7½
5 or more	10, with an additional two in respect of each room in excess of five

Floor Area of Room	Permitted Number of Persons
110 sq. ft. or more	2
90 sq. ft. or more, but less than 110 sq. ft.	1½
70 sq. ft. or more, but less than 90 sq. ft.	1
50 sq. ft. or more, but less than 70 sq. ft.	½
Under 50 sq. ft.	Nil

The way in which the situation has changed since the 1931 Census is illustrated in Table 38. In 1931, 3·9 per cent of households lived at a density of over two persons per room—a density very roughly similar to the Housing Act overcrowding measure. By 1951 the proportion had been reduced to 1·2 per cent and the absolute number was more than halved. The 1961 Census dropped this statistic entirely —a striking commentary on its irrelevance to modern conditions— but it can be calculated that the number was about 90,000 or 0·6 per cent. Taking the 1961 Census highest measure of overcrowding— more than 1½ persons per room—this has fallen from 2·7 million or 26·1 per cent in 1931 to 1·5 million or 10·3 per cent in 1961.

In short, 'statutory overcrowding' has ceased to be a significant problem, at least in national terms. It does, however, still exist in a particularly acute form in the central areas of large cities where it forms part of the larger problem of 'multiple occupation'. In some of the London Metropolitan Boroughs over a tenth of households in 1961 were living at more than 1½ persons per room.

THE 'BEDROOM STANDARD'

Recent social surveys have made use of a higher and more refined 'bedroom standard'.[1,2] This allocates bedrooms on the following basis:
  (i) Each married couple and each unmarried person aged 21 or more in the household is given one bedroom;
  (ii) Persons aged 10–20 of the same sex are paired off and a bedroom given to each pair;

(iii) Any person aged 10–20 not so paired off is then paired with a child under 10 years of age of the same sex, and given a separate bedroom. If no pairing with a child under ten years is possible such a person is still given a separate bedroom;

(iv) Any remaining children under 10 years of age are then paired irrespective of sex and a bedroom given to each pair;

(v) Any remaining child is given a separate bedroom.

In operating this standard any room described by the person interviewed as a 'bedroom' is counted as one.

About a third of all households in 1962 had bedrooms equal to this standard.[1] Only 12 per cent were below it, but over a half were above: 35 per cent with one 'extra' bedroom and 17 per cent with two or more 'extra' bedrooms. Differences between tenure groups were striking. Owner-occupiers had the highest proportion above the standard while council tenants had the highest proportion equal to the standard. Private unfurnished tenants occupied an intermediate position.

TABLE 38: *Density of Occupation of Dwellings, England and Wales, 1931–61*

	1931		1951		1961	
	No.	%	No.	%	No.	%
Total houlsholds at all densities	10,233,000	100·0	13,118,000	100·0	14,641,000	100·0
Over 2 persons per room	397,000	3·9	155,000	1·2	(90,185)	(0·6)
Over 1½ perosns per room	1,174,000	11·5	664,299	5·1	415,292	2·8
Over 1 person per room	2,672,000	26·1	2,098,923	16·0	1,510,291	10·3

This standard, of course, has no statutory basis. It is, nevertheless, a more appropriate standard to take than the statutory one—at least so far as the majority of areas in the country are concerned.

MULTIPLE OCCUPATION

'Multiple occupation' is the modern equivalent of 'houses-let-in-lodgings'. These have for long met the needs of groups of people—from the otherwise homeless poor family to the grant-aided student—for whom neither public authorities nor the private market have been able to make adequate provision. Commonly the houses which today are in multiple occupation are the socially obsolete Victorian piles designed for an age when the distribution of wealth allowed rich families to live in large houses which could be serviced by a plentiful

TABLE 39: *Position of Households in Relation to the 'Bedroom Standard', by Tenure, England, 1962*[1]

		Household's Tenure of Accommodation				
	Owns/is buying	*Rents from Council*	*Rents privately unfurnished*	*Rents furnished*	*Has rent-free etc.*	*All households*
Number of households in sample	1,398	673	1,018	73	69	3,231
	%	%	%	%	%	%
Households having:						
2 or more bedrooms below standard	1	4	3	3	–	2
1 bedroom below standard	5	16	12	16	4	10
Equal to standard	27	47	38	63	41	36
1 bedroom above standard	43	26	33	14	38	35
2 or more bedrooms above standard	24	8	15	4	17	17

supply of cheap domestic labour. Properly converted and managed they can provide reasonable accommodation particularly for smaller households—of which there are great numbers in the centres of large cities. These, of course, are the areas of acute housing shortage in which the housing demand far exceeds the supply. This demand, particularly from newly-formed households, migrant newcomers (British and foreign), single and childless people and the aged can—and does—result in abuses which have been forced on public attention in recent years. Unlike the nineteenth-century situation, the problem is not simply one of poverty: though the households in the worst conditions are those with the lowest incomes and those with average incomes but large families, the situation is made more difficult because of 'competition' from newcomers and from those with higher incomes. Indeed the demand for better quality accommodation 'in multiple occupation' and the increasing trend in some areas (at least in London) for areas of working-class housing to be invaded by middle-class families has tended to reduce both the total supply of accommodation in general and cheaper accommodation in particular. The problems are complex, as can be seen from the Milner Holland Report published in 1965.[7] In the areas of greatest stress very high rents are charged for appalling housing. The Milner Holland Report even quotes cases of a landlord dividing a room into separate lettings by chalking marks on the floor, and of a single room letting divided into space for two households by blankets hung up across the room.

TABLE 40: *Sharing of Dwellings, England and Wales, Conurbations and Selected Areas,* 1961

	Percentage of households sharing a dwelling 1961
England and Wales	6·1
Tyneside Conurbation	2·3
West Yorkshire Conurbation	1·3
South East Lancashire Conurbation	2·3
Merseyside Conurbation	7·4
West Midlands Conurbation	5·0
Greater London Conurbation	19·6
London County	29·9
Paddington Metropolitan Borough	47·5
Islington Metropolitan Borough	58·9
Liverpool County Borough	9·0
Birmingham County Borough	7·6

Strictly speaking, 'multiple occupation' has a similar meaning to 'sharing', but the term is used more commonly to refer to the use of large houses by several families or lodgers. In its pejorative sense—and frequently in practice—it implies badly run-down houses where there has been no proper conversion and where cooking and sanitary facilities are quite inadequate for the number of families living in the house. Overcrowding further increases the squalor in which these families are living.

Up to 1961 the powers of local authorities for dealing with conditions such as these was limited. Improvements generally could be made only if some of the families were rehoused, but almost by definition it was the shortage of alternative accommodation which gave rise to the bad conditions in the first place. Furthermore, the houses which were in the worst condition were frequently owned by landlords of a peculiar astuteness: their skill in managing property might be of a low order but their skill in evading the provisions of the law could not be questioned. The position was made worse by the staff shortages of local authorities in the pressure areas. There is no easy answer to this: indeed, new powers may increase the staffing problem!

The 1961 Act provided the first instalment of a new set of powers.[5] Multiple occupation was defined as 'a house which, or any part of which, is let in lodgings or which is occupied by members of more than one family'. Local authorities were enabled to apply a 'code of good management' to houses in multiple occupation, to require certain services to be provided and to fix the maximum number of inhabitants who should live in a house. After further press publicity in 1963 to questions of exploitation of tenants in this type of property, and consultations between the Ministry and the officials of a selection of local authorities (thirteen in number) who had considerable experience of the problems of multiple occupation, further provisions were incorporated in the 1964 Housing Act.

REGISTRATION OF MULTI-OCCUPIED HOUSES

Local authorities have a power—not a duty—to register houses in multiple occupation, subject to the approval of the Ministry. There has been considerable discussion on this issue. On the one hand it is argued that registration would enable authorities to have a detailed knowledge of multi-occupied houses in their area, enable them to step in before conditions became too bad, and avoid the problems created (e.g. by threats of eviction) when tenants themselves sought official action. On the other hand it was held by the Government that registration was quite unnecessary in most areas and that where it was possibly desirable for the reasons mentioned above there were two decisive objections. First, multiple occupation covered such a wide range of conditions that registration would cover a large number of houses over which control was quite unnecessary and for which the powers in the legislation were not designed. Secondly, the areas with the biggest problems of multi-occupancy are the very areas where local authorities are particularly short of staff. To divert staff to registration would involve a reduction in the more substantive and fruitful work of actually bringing about an improvement of conditions.* In the event the choice has been left to local authorities themselves, subject to Ministerial approval. Compulsory registration can be brought in for the whole of a local authority area or for particular parts of it. The Ministry recommend that the latter may sometimes be preferable— covering the 'black spots'.⁶

Birmingham have taken special Local Act powers to control multiple occupation. Under the Birmingham Corporation Act, 1965, the local authority can compel existing and proposed new lodging houses and houses containing more than one family to be registered. Permission can be refused if the house or the owner is unsuitable, or if the house is in 'a locality the amenity or character of which would be injured'. Landlords of overcrowded or unfit houses can be given notice to evict their 'surplus' tenants, and to carry out improvements. Heavy fines can be imposed for non-registration, and second offenders can face a prison sentence.

This particular Act has been the subject of considerable criticism. Opponents have argued that, since a large proportion of the families living in multi-occupied houses are coloured immigrants, the effect of the Act will be to prevent them moving into other areas and will thus create 'black ghettoes'. The intention, of course, is the opposite: to encourage the dispersal of immigrant families so that certain parts of the City do not become concentrations of lodging-houses. As *The Observer* recently commented, it will be the *results* of the scheme which will be carefully watched.†

MANAGEMENT ORDERS

Where a house in multiple occupation is in an unsatisfactory state and manifestly is in need of improvement, a local authority can make a *management order*. This covers such matters as repairs, cleanliness and good order of the communal parts of the house; the proper main- tenance of installations for water supply, drainage, gas and electricity;

---

* An inquiry undertaken by the Public Health Inspectors Education Board showed that in December 1963, about 12 per cent of public health inspectors' posts in England and Wales were unfilled. The shortage was said to be due particularly to the extension of the scope of their duties under recent legislation. (*House of Commons Debates*, Written Answers, November 16, 1965.)

† *The Observer*, October 31, 1965.

the repair and good order of means of ventilation and escape from fire; and the provision of refuse bins. Notice must be given of intention to make an order and the landlord (or to use the legal terminology, the 'manager', i.e. the person responsible for managing the house—the owner, agent or whoever can be traced as being responsible) can make 'representations'; for example he can give an undertaking to carry out the necessary repairs and improvements. There is also the normal right of appeal to the courts. As an example of the battle of wits which goes on between bad landlords and local authorities, the Act specifically states that the court shall disregard any improvement made in the condition of the house between the time when notice of intention to make an order is served and the time when the order is made, unless they are satisfied that effective steps have been taken to ensure that the house will, in future, be kept in a satisfactory condition. This is aimed at landlords who rapidly carry out superficial works to forestall a court ruling against them. One of the Ministry Circulars is couched in terms which is suggestive of a battle: 'So as to be able to meet challenge, the local authority will need to ensure that an adequate report on the original condition of the house is available.'[5]

A copy of the management order has to be displayed in the house, and the local authority has certain powers of enforcement. The landlord can be required (both when the order is first made and later in the case of subsequent failure to comply with the order) to make good an 'accumulated neglect of management'. The landlord has the right of appeal to the court, and the local authority have power to carry out works in default and recover the cost from the landlord.

Landlords of this type of property often have little idea of the standards which are required of them, and local authorities have found that they need to spend considerable time and patience on what is, in effect, an educational process.

OTHER POWERS FOR DEALING WITH MULTI-OCCUPIED HOUSES

Multi-occupied houses are frequently deficient in such matters as lighting, ventilation, water supply, personal washing facilities, sanitary conveniences, means of escape from fire, and the like. Local authorities now have power to require the provision of such essential services. Again there are default powers and the right of appeal to the courts.

As has already been pointed out, merely to prohibit overcrowding is to deal only with symptoms. Evicted families would in effect be compelled either to obtain other unsatisfactory accommodation or to become actually homeless—in which case they would become the responsibility of the local authority in another guise. (Under the National Assistance Act counties and county boroughs have the duty to provide 'temporary accommodation' for homeless families.) In an attempt to reduce overcrowding in a painless way the local authority can set a limit on the number of people who can live in a house; the effect is not to cause the eviction of existing families, but to oblige the owner to ensure that the number of occupants does not exceed the limit, or where the limit is already exceeded, to ensure that any vacancies which arise are not refilled.

The 1964 Act provides new and very drastic powers for dealing with the worst cases of mismanagement of multi-occupied houses. If the situation is so bad that immediate action is required (rather than the more protracted processes outlined above) a local authority can issue a *control order* and summarily take over the control and management of the property. This constitutes a complete abrogation of the landlord's rights. He is entitled to compensation, but only at the rate of one half of the gross value of the house.

The procedure is peremptory and is designed to meet the special situation where tenants fear eviction (or worse) if they seek to invoke action by the local authority. No prior notice is given and any appeal to the courts comes after a *fait accompli*. This drastic power is intended to be used only judiciously and sparingly, but it is hoped that its occasional use will bring beneficial results extending far beyond the properties directly concerned.

All these powers are, of course, in addition to the more traditional housing powers of local authorities. Unfit houses in multi-occupation can be condemned or purchased for 'deferred demolition', or for the purpose of securing improvement. Local authority practice has varied considerably here: some authorities have effectively used these powers, but others have been frankly reluctant to accept the responsibilities involved.

The truth of the matter is that in some areas where there is an acute housing shortage it is not easy to see any real 'solution' to the problem. All that can be done is to attempt to prevent exploitation and abuse.

It is likely that we shall see further legislation for dealing with this problem. Already the Milner Holland Committee have recommended the idea of *areas of special control* where some special executive body should be established 'with responsibility for the whole area and armed with wide powers to control sales and lettings, to acquire property by agreement or compulsorily over the whole area or large parts of it, to demolish and rebuild as necessary, to require improvements to be carried out or undertake such improvements themselves, and to make grants on a more generous and flexible basis than under the existing law. Many of the necessary powers are already available to local authorities, but they need substantial extensions'.

This, it should be noted, was written after the 1964 Act, not before it. The Ministry is now carrying out an investigation of multiple occupation in different parts of the country, of the use being made of the existing powers, and of the possible need for new powers.

RENT ACT 1965

Houses in multiple occupation, like most other lettings, are affected by the 1965 Rent Act. Briefly, this provides protection for tenants against harassment and eviction, and also establishes a system for the registration and determination of 'fair' rents. This should go some way towards meeting the problem of excessive rents and abuses in multi-occupied houses, but it is not designed to deal directly with questions relating to the improvement of squalid or inadequate housing conditions.

REFERENCES AND FURTHER READING

[1] Cullingworth, J. B., *English Housing Trends*, Occasional Papers on Social Administration, No. 13, Bell, 1965.

[2] Gray, P. G., and Russell, R., *The Housing Situation in 1960*, The Social Survey, Central Office of Information, 1962.

[3] Harvey, A., *Tenants in Danger*, Penguin Books, 1964.

[4] Jephcott, P., *A Troubled Area: Notes on Notting Hill*, Faber, 1964.

[5] Ministry of Housing and Local Government, *Circular No. 16/62*, 'Housing Act 1961: Part II, Houses in Multiple Occupation', HMSO, 1962.

[6] Ministry of Housing and Local Government, *Circular No. 51/64*, 'Housing Act 1964: Part IV, Houses in Multiple Occupation', HMSO, 1964.

[7] Ministry of Housing and Local Government, *Report of the Committee on Housing in Greater London* (Milner Holland Report), Cmnd. 2605, HMSO, 1965.

CHAPTER XI

Aid to Owner-Occupiers and Housing Associations

BEFORE THE WAR less than a quarter of households were owner-occupiers; today the proportion is well over two-fifths and is increasing year by year. Most house purchasers obtain their mortgage from a building society or insurance company, but about a tenth obtain them from local authorities.[2]

Local authorities have had powers to lend money for house purchase since 1899 when the Small Dwellings Acquisition Act was passed—an Act which Joseph Chamberlain argued would not only enable working-class families to secure healthy and comfortable homes but would also 'have a tendency to make them better citizens, to give them a larger stake in the country, and to provide for them a popular and favourite form of thrift'. Since then the powers have been greatly extended. Actually there are two quite separate legislative codes—one under the Small Dwellings Acquisition Acts 1899–1923 and the other under the Housing (Financial Provisions) Act, 1958. However, the provisions of the latter are so much wider and more flexible that, in practice, they have largely superseded the earlier legislation.

In brief, local authorities (including county councils) can lend up to 100 per cent of the value of a house whether or not it is within their administrative area. This is part of their wider power to lend money for acquiring, constructing, converting, altering, enlarging, repairing or improving houses. There used to be a limit of £5,000 on the value of houses on which loans could be made but this was abolished in 1959.

Over 80 per cent of local authorities operate mortgage loan schemes. The normal loan period is twenty to twenty-five years. There is a wide range of variation in the terms on which loans are made. Some lend up to 100 per cent of valuation, particularly on properties with a value of up to, e.g. £3,500; others have a normal maximum of 90 per cent or even lower. (The normal building society loan is 80–85 per cent.)

The granting of 100 per cent loans is, as might be expected, popular among house purchasers, but many local authorities regard the practice as risky. Nevertheless the experience of the Greater London Council which has made over 25,000 loans since a 100 per cent loan scheme was introduced a few years ago is encouraging. Legal action has been necessary in only 1 per cent of cases; foreclosure has been resorted to in only thirteen cases, and in only one of these did the Council suffer any loss.

Local authorities do not usually lend on higher value houses, and a limit of £5,000 or thereabouts is common. Many authorities will lend only on houses situated within their administrative area, though commonly loans are also given to people who work within the area. The Greater London Council gives 100 per cent loans to anyone living or working in the area or who move from London under the overspill scheme to a new or expanding town.

It should be noted that the percentage loan is given on the basis of the valuation, not the purchase price. Given the present situation of excess demand the difference between the valuation and purchase price finally agreed can be significant. The Greater London Council find that in only about a third of their cases is the valuation and the purchase price the same; and in about 4 per cent of cases the difference is 'substantial'. Many authorities (including the GLC) refuse to give loans in such cases particularly where it is considered that the applicant's ability to repay the loan is limited by the necessity of having to borrow further money elsewhere.

Most—but not all—authorities take into account the income of the would-be purchaser. Here the normal building society rule-of-thumb is commonly used, i.e. that the loan should not exceed two-and-a-half to three times the annual gross income. Some authorities, however, do not have fixed income conditions but judge each case 'on its merits'; so long as the purchaser is 'capable of making repayments without undue hardship being caused' a loan is made. A wife's income might be taken into account, particularly if she is over child-bearing age. Some local authorities appear to be more concerned with the value of the property than the income of the would-be purchaser. Where this is so it represents a difference from building society practice and is based on the argument that if the borrower defaults the house can be taken over and let by the council. Building societies do not manage property, and therefore are more concerned to ensure that a purchaser will be able to meet the repayments. The same argument applies to the principle of giving 90 or even 100 per cent loans. The risk of 'loss' to the local authority on a high mortgage has to be weighed against the financial burden which would fall on them if they had to house the applicant in a normal council house.

Local authorities are generally more willing to lend on older property than building societies. This is due partly to the considerations just outlined and the fact that local authorities do not have the same degree of concern over the effects of falling values in this type of property (whereas a building society has to insure itself against a danger that the current market value of an old house would be considerably lower than the value at the time the loan was made, and indeed even lower than the outstanding mortgage). There is, however, another factor, namely the interest of the local authority in ensuring that old property does not deteriorate into a slum. With the higher standards of maintenance in owner-occupied property local authority loans for old houses can constitute a sound social policy.

Most local authorities lend at a rate of interest of $\frac{1}{4}$ or (more rarely) $\frac{1}{2}$ per cent above the rate at which they can borrow money. The Ministry advise that the rate should be sufficient to cover the administrative overheads. In fact, however, this can be very difficult to estimate, particularly if there is only a small number of loans each year. If the local authority department's staff spend 5 per cent of their time dealing with loans then this proportion of their salaries is charged. But what proportionate charge should be made for office space? Practice differs but unless the amount of work grows to such a scale that extra staff and office space is needed, the total administrative costs tend to be lower than those of building societies (which are generally $\frac{1}{2}$ to $\frac{3}{4}$ per cent).

Another difference between a local authority loan and one from a building society is that the latter always has a variable rate of interest: the actual rate is determined by current market conditions. (When interest rates are increased, the mortgagor can either pay bigger instalments or extend the period of repayment.) Local authorities' loans, on the other hand, are commonly at a rate of interest which is fixed for the total period of the loan. Until 1957 this was a statutory requirement: since then increasing numbers of local authorities are changing over (on new loans) to variable rates of interest. Some even give borrowers the choice of a fixed or variable interest rate.

In a tight money market rates of interest rise. During the early 'sixties actual rates charged by building societies and local authorities averaged 6 and $6\frac{1}{2}$ per cent respectively, but during 1965 they rose above this level. In such conditions building societies tend to restrict lending on older property, but the reaction of local authorities is generally to suspend mortgages, or to reduce the percentage loan granted to borrowers.

Local authorities generally regard their house loans schemes as a social service rather than as a business to be advertised and expanded. It has been a distinguishing characteristic of British social services that the client is assumed to know what is available and will seek the requisite service when he needs it. A few authorities, however, have pursued a more active line. The Greater London Council, for instance, gave a great deal of publicity to their scheme. By mid-1965 applications were being made at the rate of 1,000 a week, and financial limitations forced the Council to restrict the scheme somewhat.

The powers of local authorities to make loans extends to private builders and developers. Some authorities use these powers to encourage a higher rate of private building, but generally loans are in practice restricted to individual purchasers. Assistance can also be given to private developers by making land available. The 1965 White Paper[7] specifically refers to this power and states that local authorities 'will be asked to work out the housing needs of their areas in terms of houses for owner-occupation as well as houses to rent; and where necessary to use their powers (i.e. of planning and compulsory acquisition) so that private builders can acquire in good time the land they must have if they are to carry out their part of the programme'.

Total (net) lending by local authorities for house purchase tends to fluctuate greatly. Figures for the last fifteen years are given in Table 41.

TABLE 41: *Net Lending by Local Authorities for House Purchase, 1949/50 to 1963/4*

	£m		£m
1949/50	4	1957/58	30
1950/51	12	1958/59	27
1951/52	19	1959/60	25
1952/53	17	1960/61	48
1953/54	22	1961/62	68
1954/55	38	1962/63	45
1955/56	56	1963/64	69
1956/57	49		

LOCAL AUTHORITY GUARANTEES

Building societies are not, by their very nature, risk-venturing bodies. Indeed some critics strongly maintain that they are far too cautious and conservative. It is perhaps fairer to say that they are not adequately geared to meet the scale of the demand for the finance of owner-occupation which has developed since the war. Be that as it may, attempts have been made from time to time to provide means for enabling building societies to operate more widely than their available funds or their financial conventions allow. The 1959 House Purchase and Housing Act, for instance, provided £100 million of Exchequer loans to approved societies willing to lend on pre-1919 houses. (£92 million was earmarked before the scheme was brought to an end in the economy drive of 1961.) Of considerably longer standing is the power of local authorities to give guarantees to building societies—intended to enable people of 'small means' to buy their own homes. The guarantee allows a society to advance a larger proportion (up to 95 per cent) of the cost of a house than its rules would normally permit. Any loss incurred (in excess of that which would have arisen had there been no guarantee) is shared equally by the building society, the local authority and the Exchequer. The risk involved is apparently a very small one. In the five years 1954 to 1959, for example, something over 50,000 guarantees were given; Exchequer payments amounted to less than £2,000 and total losses were in the region of £5,000.

Little use is made of this provision, mainly because a would-be purchaser can more easily obtain a loan direct from a local authority, and because it is restricted to houses with a valuation limit of £2,500.

REPAIRS INSURANCE

One of the problems facing an owner-occupier is the risk which he bears of irregular and sometimes embarrassing repair costs. An interesting but little-known provision introduced by the Housing Repairs and Rent Act of 1954 goes some way towards meeting this problem. It enables a mortgagor to make regular (or irregular) interest-bearing payments to the local authority from whom he obtained his mortgage to cover the cost of maintenance and repair. Little use appears to be made of this despite the fact that it put on a statutory basis a practice already adopted by a few authorities.

The Labour Party 1956 policy statement, *Homes of the Future*,[3] proposed making it a condition of a local authority loan that the purchaser should contribute to a repairs fund which would be designed to provide enough money to cover the cost of exterior decorations and a reserve for structural repairs. This proposal now seems to be forgotten.

SALE OF COUNCIL HOUSES

Local authorities do not necessarily have to let the houses which they provide. Though most do in fact prefer to retain them in their own management some do, on occasion, sell them to owner-occupiers. Sometimes this is done as a matter of policy, sometimes to avoid swelling the total housing accounts, sometimes to shed an embarrassingly expensive development, sometimes to get a 'balance' between public and private housing.

Political arguments on this policy have tended to be heated—and even more so in relation to the sale of houses which have been previously let. Between 1945 and 1951 it was Government policy to refuse consent for the sale (or long leasing) of council houses, but the change in Government in 1951 brought about a change in policy. Briefly, the statutory provisions are that local authorities have a general power to sell or lease their houses, but subject to the consent of the Minister where a house has been provided with the aid of an Exchequer subsidy. A general Ministerial consent has been given for the sale of houses providing that the sale price is not less than twenty times the annual net rent for pre-war houses and not less than the total all-in cost for post-war houses. Additionally for pre-war houses certain conditions must be laid down relating to the right of pre-emption, the price of resale, and the maximum rent at which the house can be let by the new owner.

As the Ministry have stressed[6] the crucial issue for local authorities who wish to sell council houses is the price which they should ask. Pre-war rents vary enormously and often can be no guide at all. Various formulae have been suggested, but clearly there is a wide area for argument as to what would be a fair price.

So far as demand is concerned the experience of local authorities varies—depending to some extent at least on their rent policies. One authority which warrants special mention is Brighton where certain council estates have been designated as 'private estates' in which the aim is to sell all the houses. Between 1954 and 1962 over 740 houses were sold.

About a half of all local authorities have sold some of their houses since the war, but the total number of houses involved is small, amounting to only 33,402 by the end of 1964.

HOUSING ASSOCIATIONS

A large number of the housing powers of local authorities can be operated through housing associations. These do not have the same position in Britain as on the continent but it has been official policy in recent years to stimulate and develop their field of activity. In part this has been because of the concern over the decreasing range of housing choices. With the steady decline in the private rented sector more and more families have to choose between owner-occupation and a local authority tenancy. Where there are long waiting lists for council houses there is virtually no choice: a family has to buy, or if that is beyond their means, has to take furnished rooms. Housing associations form a 'third arm'.

There are several types of housing association. Two of these—the 'cost-rent' housing society and the housing co-operative—are now being officially stimulated and assisted by the Housing Corporation set up under the Housing Act of 1964. This has £100 million of

TABLE 42: *Advances and Guarantees for House Purchase made by Local Authorities, 1960, 1963 and 1964*

	1960		1963		1964	
	No. of dwellings	Amount £000	No. of dwellings	Amount £000	No. of dwellings	Amount £000
Advances						
For acquisition of existing houses	38,852	49,403	45,879	74,566	59,810	123,592
For construction of new houses	8,839	17,071	10,529	25,013	18,953	47,678
For conversion	318	146	255	133	347	200
For alterations, etc.	4,588	1,212	5,245	1,650	8,147	2,380
For improvement with aid of standard grants	4,897	595	5,307	791	6,114	938
To housing associations	1,125	1,340	1,304	1,928	3,278	3,261
Total	58,619	67,766	68,519	104,081	96,649	178,049
Guarantees	9,185		3,816		3,084	

Exchequer money at its disposal with which it can advance loans on second mortgage to housing societies. The intention is that the societies will raise two-thirds of their capital from building societies and one third from the Housing Corporations. No subsidies are available, so in effect, these 'cost rent' societies are non-profit making organizations which have to cover their costs entirely by rent income. Housing co-operatives are societies which provide dwellings to be occupied solely by their own members. These members collectively own their dwellings. A pilot scheme established under the 1961 Housing Act showed that there was a significant demand for dwellings of these two types. The whole of a £25 million Exchequer fund had been lent or committed by 1964. At the end of this year eighty-nine schemes were in hand, providing for 5,709 dwellings.

Though local authorities can assist such societies by making loans or sites available, their assistance is largely confined to subsidized schemes. Local authorities have wide powers to make grants and loans to housing associations. The provisions are complex, but briefly local authorities can assist housing associations by helping in the acquisition of suitable land, by lending money towards capital expenditure on the security of a mortgage, by passing on certain Exchequer grants and subsidies, and by giving grants. All these powers can be used either for new building or for the acquisition and conversion of existing buildings.

Since the war housing associations have provided over 50,000 new dwellings in 440 local authority areas. The number has been increasing in recent years—1,561 in 1962, 1,925 in 1963, and 2,852 in 1964. At the end of 1964 well over 7,000 housing association dwellings were under construction. (The figures do not distinguish between subsidized and unsubsidized houses.)

The attitude of local authorities to housing associations varies. Some are very willing to give them assistance—including 100 per cent loans and rate-fund grants. Others regard them as an unnecessary competitor for scarce land or as an out-of-date and redundant form of housing provision. Some give assistance only in return for rights of nomination of a certain proportion of (or, indeed, all) tenants; others impose no such conditions. Some may be prepared to use compulsory powers of land acquisition; others will give no assistance at all unless an association has obtained a site. As with many aspects of local government, generalization is difficult.

Housing associations devote a considerable part of their effort to providing for old people. This is a field in which there is a great shortage of suitable dwellings. It is also one to which people are willing to contribute time and money. Dwellings provided by housing associations can benefit not only by the normal Exchequer subsidy but also from local authority 'welfare grants'. These can be given for 'grouped dwellings' where there is a resident warden and certain community facilities such as a common room or a guest room. These grants are given by the local welfare authority (county boroughs and county councils) and commonly amount to £30 per dwelling annually —though again there is wide variation in practice.

REFERENCES AND FURTHER READING

Aid to Owner-Occupiers

[1] Consumers' Association, 'Loans for Houses', *Which?*, April 1961.
[2] Cullingworth, J. B., *English Housing Trends*, Occasional Papers on Social Administration, No. 13, Bell, 1965.
[3] Labour Party, *Homes of the Future*, 1956.
[4] Merrett, A. J., and Sykes, A., *Housing Finance and Development*, Longmans, 1965.
[5] Ministry of Housing and Local Government, *Circular No. 37/59*, 'House Purchase and Housing Act, 1959', HMSO, 1959.
[6] Ministry of Housing and Local Government, *Circular No. 5/60*, 'Sale and Leasing of Council Houses', HMSO, 1960.
[7] Ministry of Housing and Local Government, *The Housing Programme 1965 to 1970*, Cmnd. 2838, HMSO, 1965.
[8] Sage, N. D. B., 'Housing Advances—The Alternative Codes', *Local Government Chronicle*, May 22, 1965.
[9] Stevens, G., 'Home Loans in London', *New Society*, July 15, 1965.
[10] White Paper, *House Purchase: Proposed Government Scheme*, Cmnd. 571, HMSO, 1958.

Housing Associations

[11] Housing Centre, Report on the Conference on 'Housing's Third Arm', *Housing Review*, Vol. XI, May–June 1962, pp. 77–93.
[12] Housing Centre, Report on the Conference on 'Housing to Let and for Co-ownership', *Housing Review*, Vol. XIV, July–August 1965, pp. 105–23.
[13] Housing Corporation, *Report of the Housing Corporation for the Period September 1, 1964, to March 31, 1965*, House of Commons Paper No. 349, (Session 1964–5), HMSO, 1965.
[14] Ministry of Housing and Local Government, *Circular No. 12/62*, 'Housing Associations in England and Wales', HMSO, 1962.
[15] Ministry of Housing and Local Government, *Circular No. 41/64*, 'Housing Act, 1964', HMSO, 1964.
[16] National Federation of Housing Societies, *Housing Associations and Societies*, 1964.
[17] Waddilove, L. E., *Housing Associations*, PEP Planning, Vol. 27, No. 462, May 1962.

CHAPTER XII

Some Social Aspects of Housing

A WIDE RANGE of issues could be discussed under the heading of this chapter. Indeed a separate book would be needed to deal with all the 'social aspects' of housing. But irrespective of the length of treatment possible it is not an easy matter to decide how the subject should be delineated. The 'social' is not just a category that can be added to a list of housing problems: rather it is a particular way of approaching these problems. Social aspects cannot be separated into a compartment distinct from, for example, financial, design and management aspects. Furthermore a consideration of the social aspects of housing brings one into the wider fields of social policy and applied sociology.

It follows that the discussion in this chapter must be highly selective and illustrative, rather than comprehensive.

'SOCIAL BALANCE'

One of the key concepts in planning is that of 'balance'. Thus it is held that there should be a balanced distribution of employment, of social classes and age and income groups, of land uses, and of housing provision. In some ways the concept resembles that of the economists' 'equilibrium' which similarly is rarely found in the real world. So far as the balanced provision of housing is concerned what often happens in practice is that, by the process of tenant selection, families with children move to the suburbs, leaving the elderly and the unmarried—who are not overcrowded—in the more central areas. This raises a range of problems: there has to be a rapid (and possibly temporary) expansion of family and educational services in the suburbs, while the problems of old people become concentrated in the centre (and are actually increased by the absence of younger relatives). Furthermore, as time passes, the pressures on the newer estates mount and there arises the curious situation of 'overspill from overspill': the newer estates have no room to house the next generation of families—the married children of the original tenants—and so they have to move to seek housing elsewhere.

This problem can be acute in the big cities, particularly London. For example the London County Council built a large (100,000 population) overspill estate in the inter-war years at Becontree— some 8 miles out. The younger families on this estate are now having to be housed at places such as Canvey Island, a further 20 miles to the east. (One family interviewed by Peter Wilmott in his study of this estate summed up the problem with humour: 'where they go from Canvey Island in the next generation, God knows; we can only assume they'll put them on rafts and set them adrift'.[21]) At the same time a half of the 27,000 houses on the Becontree estate are, on the Council's standards, underoccupied. This results from the concentration on family type houses: only 4 per cent of the houses are of one or two rooms; and there is no space left for building the small houses which are now needed.

Here then there is clearly a need for a more balanced provision of house types. But since the heavy demand, at least from those who wish to move to outlying estates, is for family type houses, this is not easy to achieve. The solution adopted by some local authorities is to reserve some land for later development. Unfortunately this raises a further problem of finding a temporary use for the land in the inter-vening years—and a 'temporary' use, as any planner knows, may be difficult to change when the appropriate time comes. Furthermore, few of the larger local authorities have sufficient land for housing to enable them to leave part of it undeveloped for any considerable length of time.

A less frequently adopted approach to the problems created by changes in family size (which is nevertheless now receiving more attention) is to design a flexible house. This is an old idea which took on a new form with the Duplex house of the early post-war years. Basically this was a normal two-storey house designed for temporary use as two flats. More recently the Ministry of Housing's Development Group have designed an 'adaptable' house. The adaptability stems from the fact that the internal walls are not load bearing: they can thus take the form of light movable partitions. There is also more living space on the ground floor than on the upper floor. Thus at the time of maximum occupation, when the children are still at home but growing up, a downstairs room can be used as a bedroom or bed-sitting room. When the children leave home this room can be used to provide more living space on the ground floor. On the same principle the first floor is designed so that it can be divided into three or two bedrooms.

A later design, using industrialized building methods (a steel frame instead of brick walls), has been built at Sheffield, Hull and various other places. This is the '5M Flexible House', so-called because it is substantially based on dimensions of five times a 4 in. module.

This problem of balance in the provision of house types received a good deal of attention in the study carried out by the London County Council in connection with their proposal to build a new town at Hook in Hampshire.[9] Unfortunately the proposal was rejected by the Government, so it is not possible to assess how far their proposals aimed at achieving a greater degree of balance than is usual in such developments would work out in practice. It is nevertheless instructive to examine the assumptions which were made.

Architecturally, the Hook planners wished to create a modern town that would look urban and exciting. It would be 'living architecture'—in contrast to what the critics have called the 'prairie planning' of the early new towns. Socially, they wanted to cater for the demand of young families with children for houses with gardens. These two objectives work in opposite directions. To attain an urban atmosphere it is necessary to develop with at least a moderately high density: this is difficult to achieve if a large proportion of the dwellings have gardens. The Hook planners saw an answer to this apparent conflict in another problem—that of providing for the needs of households at different stages of their lives. A new town takes a long time to build and by, say, the fifteenth year, the first families will be contracting—the children will be getting married and establishing their own separate households. The theoretical needs of both the contracting households and the newly-weds is for small dwellings. Therefore, so long as people change houses at various stages in the family cycle, it is possible to provide quite a high proportion of small dwellings in flats. And by this means it is also possible to achieve a high density and thus a truly urban environment.

This happy result, however, can only be obtained if there are 'policies on rents, management and planning which enable and assist the easy movement of housholds into a home of the size and type appropriate to their needs at different times of life'. The major social assumption here is that families not only can be persuaded to move around like this, but that this is what they would wish to do given the opportunity. But all the evidence strongly supports the view that this is not so.[5] The housholds which move for housing reasons are predominantly of the young family type with children. The least mobile are the middle-aged and the elderly. They become settled and attached to their houses, and there is no compelling reason for them to move. Though they may have too much space on some arbitrary planning standard, this does not (until very old age) constitute much of an incentive to move. And it is difficult to devise an equitable rent scheme which would encourage them to do so. It would be possible to charge low rents for small flatted dwellings, but quite apart from the fact that these are expensive to build, the corollary is that high rents are charged for large dwellings—and this would penalise the families with children who are the least able to afford high rents. Indeed the capacity to pay high rents tends to vary inversely with the need for large dwellings. Finally, and most important, sociological inquiries have shown that rent differentials have to be very large before people will move in order to cut their housing costs.

Some critics have complained that the social arguments and assumptions of the Hook plan (which are unusually explicit) have merely been dragged in to support the case of the architects to design a 'truly urban' environment. This is somewhat unfair, but clearly the 'social aspects' are more complex than was assumed.

The relative immobility of old people has wider implications. A large number of houses are 'underoccupied' (though the amount of underoccupation in council houses is far smaller than in privately rented and owner-occupied houses). Indeed, if rooms and people could be shuffled around at will every person in England and Wales could have one-and-a-half rooms. Yet, despite its moral overtone, 'underoccupation' is simply a measurement of the use of housing space. It does not follow that household needs and aspirations accord with the conclusions which may be drawn from statistical manipulations of persons and rooms. Nevertheless two points remain valid. First, there is a shortage of small dwellings for those small (and predominantly elderly) households who occupy houses which are too large for their needs and who may wish to move to more conveniently sized dwellings. The immobility of old age is relative, not absolute: though old people move at only half the average rate for all agegroups the proportion who do move in any one year is nevertheless over 3 per cent. An increase in small dwellings could bring about an increase in this rate.

Secondly, if a range of dwelling types is provided *in the same area*, elderly households will be more disposed towards moving. A move within the same small area does not involve a break with the kinship and friendship network which will have been built up over the years. Local authorities have found it much easier to encourage elderly people to move into small dwellings which have been built on small sites within existing developments. In a curious way the sometimes wasteful layout of pre-war estates has proved particularly useful in assisting this. Open corner sites and odd pieces of undeveloped land which so often disfigured an estate are now at a premium. Some of the bigger cities have even demolished groups of pre-war threebedroom houses to allow development at a higher density with small dwellings.

The question of a balance of family and house types is not the same thing as a balance of social classes. A previous Minister of Town and Country Planning maintained that he was 'very concerned indeed not merely to get different classes living together in a community, but to get them actually mixing together'.[17] In the early post-war years this ideal was shared by many. This was a period of intense optimism and enthusiasm for social as well as physical reconstruction. The catalyst was, of course, the war itself. At one and the same time war occasions a mass support for the way of life which is being fought for, and a critical appraisal of the inadequacies of that way of life. Modern total warfare demands a unification of national effort and a breakdown of social barriers and differences. On no occasion was this more true than in the Second World War. The new and better Britain was to provide equality of opportunity for all. Within this social climate it was easy to assume that the social cohesion of the war years would continue after the war was finished—particularly since the major tasks of reconstruction were to be tackled as a 'military operation' (a phrase commonly used at this time). Furthermore local authorities were, in any case, now to be the main providers of housing for all classes: no one could easily accept the idea that a publicly accountable body should build different estates for different social classes.

It is important to remember this background now that experience has brought about disillusionment. Both the practical experience of those local authorities and new town development corporations who have attempted 'mixed' developments, and the studies of academic sociologists[21] demonstrate the strength of the desire for people to live in what used to be designated as 'one-class communities'. It is this which, in part at least, explains the lack of success of schemes for the sale of council houses. Only where a whole estate or a recognizably separate part of an estate is marked out for sale to owner-occupiers has a significant number of sales been effected. Similarly authorities who have wished to provide 'better-type' housing for letting at economic rents have found that an essential ingredient of success has been a definite separation from 'ordinary' council houses.

COMMUNITY FACILITIES ON NEW ESTATES

Small housing developments can often be carried out by local authorities without any major expansion of community facilities. A few shops and an extended bus service may be all that is required. But the larger the development the greater is the need for the full range of services—schools, a library, community centre, youth clubs, a health centre and perhaps even a hospital and a public hall or theatre. On the large estates the speed of development and the abnormal age structure of the population may present really difficult problems of matching the provision of these services with the house-building programme. And the families moving to the new area may be much more critical of their environment and the local services than an established community. Furthermore in assessing the provision which has to be made in a new area the local authority may be faced with an acute political problem of weighing its clamant needs with those of older areas. The latter may not be so obvious, but the local councillor will (quite legitimately) not be hesitant in pointing out the unfairness of concentrating the expansion of services in the new area. This is particularly the case with schools where the Ministry of Education policy has been to give priority to the provision of schools in areas where there is a major quantitative shortage, rather than to the upgrading, modernization and replacement of old and inadequate schools.

Local authorities have varied greatly in their success in ensuring a balanced provision of services along with houses. They have also differed markedly in the importance which they have attached to these services. But even the best authorities face difficulties not only of finance but also of persuading other public bodies of the urgency of the situation. The majority of the services required by a new community are the responsibility of a local authority committee other than the housing committee. Some fall completely outside local government—hospitals and family practitioner services for example. In areas outside county boroughs the most important local authority social services are the responsibility not of the local housing authority (i.e. the district council) but of the county council. Thus the provision of new schools and local health and welfare services is a county function; and even where there are delegated powers to the district the county holds the purse strings.

Generally speaking public utility services such as water, gas and electricity are, like drainage and sewerage, provided in advance of or at least *pari passu* with housing development. Indeed, the Ministry of Housing would not allow a housing scheme to proceed unless they were satisfied that these services could be provided for the first tenants. The same does not apply, however, to major roads, particularly those linking the development with the existing town: here priority may be given to other more urgent road schemes needed to alleviate congestion. Indeed the further one gets away from the essential physical services needed to make a house habitable, the more there is an inevitable competition with other demands. A house cannot be inhabited if it has no water supply, but a family can live in it even if the children have to travel by public transport to school and the housewife into the town to do her shopping. Schools in fact have had a high priority, but other services such as libraries, swimming baths, community centres and the like, have generally lagged far behind. After all—to quote the usual and not entirely unjustifiable argument—why should New Estate have a new youth centre when Old Town has been in need of one for decades?

It should not be thought that the determination of priorities is solely a matter for local authorities. National priorities are laid down by Parliament and are subject to Ministry and Treasury control. A local authority may be keen to go ahead with the provision of community services but if loan sanction is not forthcoming their hands may be tied. (At the time of writing severe restrictions are being imposed on 'non-essential' public expenditure.) Nevertheless the fact remains that, whether by good management or good luck, some authorities have been noticeably more successful than others. In the last resort this depends on the quality of local administration and the scale and character of competing claims on the local authority.

MOVING FROM THE SLUMS

Over two million people have been rehoused from slum houses since the end of the war, and the rate is continuing at about 160,000 a year. Families living in these houses tend to be poorer and to include more than average numbers of small households of elderly people. A large proportion are keen to obtain better housing: indeed, some are rehoused in advance of slum clearance because of their high position on the housing waiting list. But though the two groups overlap, there is an important difference between rehousing for slum clearance and providing houses for famlies on the ordinary waiting list. This stems from the fact that with slum clearance there is an element of compulsion: families are forced to move, irrespective of whether or not they wish to do so. And though their housing conditions may be socially unacceptable, some of the residents may not share either the higher aspirations of the planners or the view that their housing conditions warrant compulsory eviction. The houses may be inadequate by modern standards but some of the families may find the low rents particularly attractive and, in any case, may have become conditioned to the poor living standards. (As the Ministry's study of an obsolete area in Rochdale[12] pointed out, this conditioning 'is understandable, because if they allowed themselves to become seriously discontented they would only make themselves miserable. Most do not enjoy a reasonable hope of bettering their housing conditions substantially and have decided to "make do" with what they have got'.) Furthermore some of the dwellings will be owner-occupied (and recent experience shows that the proportion of owner-occupied houses in clearance areas is increasing.) These owner-occupiers may have spent considerable sums on improving their property and will object strongly to the proposed clearance scheme—and the amount of compensation to which they are entitled. Some of these houses will not even be unfit, but have to be cleared because they are surrounded by bad property.

Generally speaking the main opposition comes from elderly people who may find the prospect of a move profoundly disturbing. The problem is even greater if the clearance scheme entails a movement of a proportion of the families into a different area—as it often does. Particularly for old people such a move requires not only acclimatization to a new house but also to a new area, which may be a distance away from their friends and relatives upon whom they are socially dependent.

Again, though these older areas may be grossly inadequate in many ways, they do have their own advantages. Frequently they are close to the centre of the town; there are plenty of shops (often open till late in the evening); the rents are low; and there may be a high degree of social interaction and an intricate and close network of family and kinship ties—though it should not be forgotten that change is continually taking place, and that these areas have lost, and are continuing to lose, large numbers of families to both local authority and private suburban estates.

Though some of these problems of enforced movement can be mitigated by thoughtful and sympathetic housing management and good public relations, earlier social studies argued that the social cost involved in clearance and redevelopment was so high that policy ought to be reviewed. (In essence this was a plea for either a greater degree of improvement rather than clearance or for redevelopment at a sufficiently high density to obviate the need for 'overspill'.) Brennan, for example, argued that the population in the two worst parts of Gorbals had adapted themselves very well to their conditions; 60 per cent of the households interviewed said definitely that they did not want to leave the area.[1] Young and Willmott in their fascinating and now famous study of Bethnal Green and the 'Greenleigh' overspill estate came to the conclusion that 'very few people wish to leave the East End. They are attached to Mum and Dad, to the market, to the pubs and settlements, to Club Row and the London Hospital'.[20]

The shortcomings of this type of argument—as Peter Willmott has pointed out in his later study of the Becontree housing estate[21]—is that the vital element of time is left out. The intense social life of the *older* inner areas of towns is to a large extent the product of sheer length of residence. To compare a new estate with a long established community is not to compare like with like. Any move is bound to be disturbing and an area into which all the families have recently moved cannot be expected to exhibit the same range of social activities or the same character of social life as one which has become 'settled'.

This, however, is not to deny the importance of the earlier sociological studies. They should be regarded as a welcome swing of the pendulum of thought and a reaction against a preoccupation with physical problems.

Nor is it to deny the fact that however sympathetic and socially conscious housing management may be, slum clearance involves some difficult social problems. Two groups in particular need special assistance—elderly households and 'unsatisfactory families'. These two groups are discussed in a wider context in the following two sections of this chapter.

One final point needs to be made here. In documenting some of the social aspects of housing policy it is natural to dwell on 'problems'. This can give a distorted picture. Obviously there must be some very real problems in moving 160,000 people a year out of slum houses, but it is perhaps more significant that the great majority of these moves are made smoothly and to the satisfaction of the families concerned. Slum clearance is not an official policy forced by an unfeeling Government on reluctant local authorities; nor is it a means by which local authorities merely rid themselves of the less beautiful parts of their towns and villages. As anyone with experience of bad housing conditions will know, there is a clamant popular demand for a high and sustained rate of slum clearance. The social problems to which slum clearance gives rise are by no means insignificant, but they need to be viewed in this wider context.

UNSATISFACTORY TENANTS AND PROBLEM FAMILIES

A great deal has been written about 'unsatisfactory tenants' and 'problem families'. Indeed one can sometimes get the impression that they constitute one of the most formidable problems facing local authorities. This, of course, is a gross distortion of the situation. The number of such tenants is very small, even in slum clearance areas where it can be expected that the cheapest housing will be found and where the bad condition of the housing may exacerbate family problems. The reason for the extensive writing on the subject is simply that a small number of families create management and administrative problems out of all proportion to their numbers. And this may be due as much to the administrative structure of the social services as to the character of the social problems involved.

So far as the housing manager is concerned an 'unsatisfactory tenant' is one who does not pay his rent regularly, or who neglects or damages his house, or who makes himself a nuisance to his neighbours. At one time it was fashionable to use the term 'problem family' for those who proved difficult to deal with through the normal administrative channels. This term, however, seems to have dropped out of favour, partly because it indiscriminately lumped together all 'difficult' families—irrespective of the nature of *their* problems—in a single category. It also highlighted rather too neatly the fact that the only common denominator was the administrative one of organizing the social support which these families needed.

There seem to be a remarkable number of definitions of a problem family and an equal if not greater number of suggested explanations for their unconventional behaviour. Philp and Timms have provided a thoughtful and thought-provoking analysis in their monograph on *The Problem of The Problem Family*.[15] One commonly held view is that a problem family is one which has multiple problems and therefore is known to several agencies at one time, but Philp and Timms point out that much depends on the administrative organization of the social services. 'Multiple visitation does not necessarily mean multiple problems or even a problem family. The problem family may be, in some respects, what public administrators say it is, but we must first learn what public administration is like.'

Thus a family which is well known to the local authority housing department for rent-arrears, to the children's department for child neglect, to the education department for absence of the children from school, and perhaps to the Courts and the probation service and a host of voluntary agencies as well, does not necessarily have a multiplicity of problems. The root trouble may be mental illness, or inability to cope, or simply an inadequate income. But clearly the family presents a multiplicity of administrative problems.

A local authority is in a different position in relation to such families than is a private landlord, if only for the reason that eviction merely results in the problem being passed on to another department either of the same local authority (in county boroughs) or of another (in counties). Furthermore, while a private landlord may refuse to accept tenants who appear likely to present him with problems, the very principles of selection which are operated by local authorities are such that unsatisfactory tenants are likely to be specifically included. There is, of course, a great deal of difference between tenants who are 'simply' unsatisfactory in that they are bad rent-payers and those which have major social, economic or health problems. The former can be dealt with by good housing management —by such measures as transfer to a cheaper house, a rent rebate scheme or by the normally effective shock procedure of issuing a distress warrant for the recovery of arrears, a 'default summons' or a notice of eviction. But where there are some basic underlying problems the housing authority will need to have the assistance of other agencies. In recent years great stress has been laid on the co-ordination of the various agencies involved—thus recognizing the problems which flow from administrative separatism. The object of such co-ordination is partly to ensure that the family has the benefit of the services which they need and partly to avoid the administrative waste of visiting by too many different officials. Many local authorities have established Co-ordinating Committees consisting of representatives of the various agencies concerned—medical officer of health, children's officer, housing manager, health visitor, probation officer, NAB officer and officers of the voluntary organizations. The effectiveness of these Committees varies; at the least they keep the various agencies in touch; the more successful have been able to provide really effective help to families with problems.

But however successful these efforts may be, local housing authorities are forced to evict some tenants from their houses. The 1955 Report of the Central Housing Advisory Committee on *Unsatisfactory Tenants*[3] thought that the number was probably of the order of 0·1 per cent: this now would represent over 3,500 families a year. The question arises as to who is responsible for such families—the housing authority or the welfare authority. Under Part III of the National Assistance Act 1948 the welfare authority (i.e. the county borough or county council) has a duty to provide 'temporary accommodation for persons who are in urgent need thereof, being need arising in circumstances which could not reasonably have been foreseen, or in such other circumstances as the authority may in any particular case determine'. This 'Part III' accommodation (as it is often termed) was not intended to provide shelter of a permanent kind or for any long period for families whose real needs could be met only by the provision of a house. And evictions (at least from council houses) can hardly be regarded as 'unforeseen'. Nevertheless most local welfare authorities are prepared to accommodate families who are homeless as a result of eviction although some will only do this for the mother and the younger children. Some authorities carry out rehabilitative work in their Part III accommodation, while others have established centres for families evicted as unsatisfactory. The aim is to fit the families to return to normal life in the community. It has on occasion been suggested that specially built houses of tough construction should be provided for these families or that they should be segregated in groups of houses specially put aside for them. Neither of these ideas has found much support, largely because any type of segregation hinders rehabilitation. Though the distinction may appear to be a fine one, it is generally held that what is required is some type of 'intermediate accommodation'—i.e. intermediate in standard between new houses and those which are unfit for human habitation. Older houses, suitably converted or improved, provide the easiest and cheapest form of intermediate accommodation. The cost of providing such houses is very much lower than the cost of institutional accommodation, but it falls on the housing authority rather than the welfare authority. Where—in county boroughs—this is the same authority this should not constitute a real problem but in counties it can be source of considerable friction. Some county councils, in fact, do provide financial assistance to district councils providing intermediate accommodation, either by way of a capital grant or, more usually, by a contribution towards the losses incurred on the scheme. (A few counties are prepared to give similar contributions to housing authorities towards losses of rent which they may incur if they allow unsatisfactory tenants to remain in normal council houses after rent arrears have begun to accumulate.)

In a short account it is not possible to describe in any detail the various measures which can be used to assist unsatisfactory tenants. It is, however, worth summarising the main conclusions of the 1955 CHAC Report.[3]

(a) The aim of the housing authority should be to enable every family who cannot provide accommodation for themselves to live together as a unit, in conditions in which a decent standard of family life can be achieved.

(b) Those families whose standards make them unacceptable to other landlords must be regarded as the responsibility of the community, and, so far as their housing is concerned, of the housing authority. For this purpose housing authorities will need some houses of a standard intermediate between new houses and the poorest dwellings.

(c) In helping families of this kind the mere provision of a house is usually not enough. Many of them may need skilled and persistent help for a considerable time if they are to make the best use of the accommodation provided, and if standards are to be maintained at a level high enough to avoid eviction in the future. In the case of council tenants the first help will come from the housing manager but this may need to be supplemented by other statutory and voluntary services.

(d) To prevent the break up of families through eviction and to lead to their re-establishment in the community if evicted, services of a rehabilitative nature are required. These are available from various sources but can most effectively be employed only in the surroundings of an individual home. Thus successful action presupposes collaboration between the housing authority and those responsible for the provision of other services.

One final point needs to be made. It is often held that a characteristic of 'problem families' and 'unsatisfactory tenants' alike is that they are inept in managing the family budget. This view stems in part from the belief that primary poverty (i.e. an income below the 'minimum' level required) has been abolished by 'the welfare state'.

Even if the highly subjective categorization of expenditure into essential and non-essential is acepted, it must not be assumed that primary poverty has been abolished. It may be rare, but it still exists, even though it may be difficult to distinguish from the lack of skill in managing on a low income.[8, 15]

HOUSING AND THE WELFARE OF OLD PEOPLE

Over a fifth of households in England and Wales are elderly small households—consisting of one or two persons at least one of whom is aged 60 or over. The housing conditions and needs of these elderly people differ in some significant ways from younger households. Generally they are well housed in terms of space: indeed, they often have an embarrassing abundance of it. Some can, and do, let off part of their accommodation to younger households, or to other elderly people, but the great value which is attached to independence and privacy prevents this from becoming significant. Despite their plentiful space elderly people commonly have inferior housing. For these are the people whose crucial housing decisions were made thirty or forty years ago, when the housing shortage was considerably more acute than it is today, when owner-occupation was less widespread, and when council housing was in its infancy. As a result a large proportion of them now live in privately rented property: a third do not have the use of a fixed bath, and a sixth are entirely without or have to share a toilet.

Their inclinations to move to better accommodation are tempered by a wish to retain the stability and familiarity afforded by the house and district which they have known for so long, and restrained by falling income and incapacity to borrow. And as they get older they need increasing support from their families and friends and from the social services.

The post-war development of social policy has paid increasing attention to the needs of elderly people. The social security system together with national assistance provide an income-maintenance service. So far as housing is concerned the national assistance scheme is of great importance. At the end of 1964, over 1,330,000 elderly people were receiving national assistance. Over 1,150,000 of these were living in separate households and had their full housing costs met by the National Assistance Board.

By this means the financial problem facing old people moving into better and more expensive housing can usually be solved. Local authorities are now providing over 30,000 dwellings a year of the one bedroom type, many of which are suitable for old people. In part this has been a direct result of encouragement from the central government, but it has also been due to the increasing number of elderly people on the housing waiting lists, in areas scheduled for slum clearance, and living in family-type council houses.

Traditionally local authorities have built one-bedroom dwellings for old people. Any domiciliary services needed are then provided by the health and welfare services. But in recent years increasing attention has been paid to specially designed *flatlets* served by a resident warden. A flatlet is a type of accommodation mid-way between a self-contained dwelling and a residential home which provides care. Basically flatlets consist of bed-sitting rooms with kitchenettes or kitchen units but with shared bathrooms and often with shared toilets. These are not intended to be a substitute for normal one-bedroom dwellings but as an additional and different form designed especially for elderly people who are less active and less able to live completely independently. Their purpose is to provide old people with a specially designed, comfortable and labour-saving home in which, though they have a large degree of independence, they can benefit from the additional services which can be provided in a grouped scheme.

Not all local authorities have taken well to the idea of shared bathrooms and toilets: some regard this as an undesirable lowering of housing standards. The official view is that this is a misconception of the purpose of flatlets, which is to provide accommodation which combines some of the advantages of a communal living (as in a home) with those of completely independent housing.

A resident warden is a common feature of flatlet schemes. He—or more usually she—is not (necessarily) a trained medical or social worker: the job is to visit the tenants regularly, to make arrangement for a meals service and medical attention when required, to contact relatives and to organize social functions. The flatlets are usually centrally heated and fitted with some kind of alarm system so that the tenants can call the warden at any time when they need help. A visitor's bedroom, a communal lounge or TV room and a laundry room may also be provided.

By their very nature flatlet schemes are partly a responsibility of the housing authority and partly of the welfare authority, which outside county boroughs, are different local authorities. The same applies where a warden service is provided in a scheme of normal aged persons' bungalows. A variety of financial arrangements exist for dealing with this, the most usual of which is for the welfare authority to pay an annual grant to the housing authority for the cost of the 'welfare service'.

It is likely that the provision of 'sheltered housing' will increase markedly in the future. There are thought to be a large number of elderly people living in institutions who could live in the community if properly designed houses could be provided in sufficient numbers together with the necessary supportive services. Peter Townsend has even argued that in the long run such housing could largely replace residential houses as understood and administered today.[20]

As has already been noted, it is frequently found that slum clearance areas contain a relatively high proportion of elderly people. This is partly because the elderly have been given lower priority for rehousing than families with children. But the elderly are generally less mobile than younger people. Many have lived in their houses for a long period of years and, whatever the shortcomings of the house and the district, are loth to leave a familiar district, their friends and neighbours, the convenient shops, and all the intangibles of a settled way of life. But change is continually taking place even in 'settled' areas and there comes a time when the physical deterioration is such that the area has to be redeveloped. Local authorities differ greatly in the way in which they approach the problems of rehousing elderly families from clearance areas. The best go to great lengths to meet the wishes of old people. Frequently old people are only too glad of the chance to obtain a better house if they can remain in the same area. This is one of the reasons why some local authorities are now providing a high proportion of one-bedroom dwellings in redevelopment areas.

Slum clearance often brings to light social problems which were previously hidden. This is as true for old people as it is for the 'problem families'. A good local housing department will be on the watch for these and will organize welfare and health services to meet the needs. Voluntary Old People's Welfare Committees can also provide useful personal services. But perhaps the most important feature of the rehousing operation is close contact with the families concerned. This is particularly important in relation to old people. As the CHAC Report on *Moving From The Slums*[4] pointed out, in addition to a dread of change, some old people may find the whole process is beyond them. 'Going to see the new house, giving up furniture which is no longer suitable, buying more, taking up lino and taking down curtains—these are some of the physical difficulties even when the move is to a new house quite close at hand. With greater distances there are further worries—separation from relatives and friends on whom they depend for help, loss of social contacts, the transfer to another doctor's list and getting a new home help, finding another coal merchant or having the pension book transferred to a different post office.'

It is here that the staff of the housing department can render much assistance, either directly or in conjunction with other departments and social agencies.

R

REFERENCES AND FURTHER READING

[1] Brennan, T., 'Gorbals—A Study in Redevelopment', *Scottish Journal of Political Economy*, Vol. IV, No. 2, June 1957.

[2] Central Housing Advisory Committee, *Living in Flats*, HMSO, 1952.

[3] Central Housing Advisory Committee, *Unsatisfactory Tenants*, HMSO, 1955.

[4] Central Housing Advisory Committee, *Moving from the Slums*, HMSO, 1956.

[5] Cullingworth, J. B., *English Housing Trends*, Occasional Papers on Social Administration, No. 13, Bell, 1965.

[6] Greve, J., *London's Homeless*, Occasional Papers on Social Administration, No. 10, Codicote Press, 1964.

[7] Hall, M. P., *The Social Services of Modern England*, Routledge, Seventh Edition, 1965.

[8] Herbert, W. B., 'Who Owes Rent?', *Sociological Review*, Vol. 13, No. 2, July 1965.

[9] London County Council, *The Planning of a New Town*, LCC, 1961.

[10] Ministry of Housing and Local Government and Ministry of Health, Joint Circular on *Homeless Families*, March 1959, HMSO.

[11] Ministry of Housing and Local Government, *Living in a Slum: A Study of People in a Central Slum Clearance Area in Oldham*, MHLG, 1963.

[12] Ministry of Housing and Local Government, *A Social Survey of Deeplish, Rochdale*, MHLG, 1965.

[13] Ministry of Housing and Local Government, *The First Hundred Families: Community Facilities for First Arrivals in Expanding Towns*, HMSO, 1965.

[14] Nicholson, J. H., *New Communities in Britain*, National Council of Social Service, 1961.

[15] Philp, A. F., and Timms, N., *The Problem of 'The Problem Family'*, Family Service Units, 1957.

[16] Schorr, A. L., *Slums and Social Insecurity*, Nelson, 1964.

[17] Silkin, L., 'Housing Layout in Theory and Practice', *Architects' Journal*, July 8, 1948.

[18] Stacey, M., *Tradition and Change*, Oxford University Press, 1960.

[19] Taylor, Lord, and Chave, S., *Mental Health and Environment*, Longmans, 1964.

[20] Townsend, P., *The Last Refuge*, Routledge, 1963. (Also published as a paper-back by Penguin Books.)

[21] Willmott, P., *The Evolution of a Community*, Routledge, 1963.

[22] Young, M., and Willmott, P., *Family and Kinship in East London*, Routledge, 1957. (Also available in a paper-back edition published by Penguin Books.)

CHAPTER XIII

Council Housing—A Wider View

THE MAIN BODY of this book has been devoted to explaining the housing policies and practices of local authorities, and the legal and administrative framework within which they operate. In this chapter a different approach is adopted. The aim is to raise questions not only of 'how', but also of 'why'. Why is the State involved in housing policy? What are—and what should be—the objectives of policy? Are present policies adequate to the needs of the contemporary situation? The answers to such questions will, of course, vary in accordance with social and political beliefs. No attempt is made to provide 'full' answers. The purpose is the more limited one of attempting to look at council housing in a wider (and sometimes international) context and to raise a series of questions to which the reader must supply his own answers.

THE ROLE OF THE STATE*

Houses have a very high capital cost and are extremely durable. As a consequence, government action is commonly required to ensure an adequate supply of housing, to provide financial assistance to families unable to pay market prices, and to maintain socially acceptable standards. At the same time, the importance of housing in relation to national investment and national and regional economic development programmes is such that 'housing policy' cannot be regarded merely as a social policy having little impact on, or connection with, economic growth. Furthermore, the interest which a government has in both the social and economic objectives of housing policy involves a concern for a wide range of related issues such as the building industry and the supply and price of land. Indeed, policies in relation to the building industry and to land might even be the major features of a 'housing policy'.

---

* This account is based partly on the author's paper to the 1965 meeting of the International Economic Association, 'Housing and the State: The Responsibilities of Government'.

R*

The importance of these various aspects differs in different countries, and it is instructive to lift one's sights beyond national boundaries. At the least this enables a more critical view to be taken of housing policy in an individual country.

THE HIGH CAPITAL COST OF HOUSING

Housing is different from other economic goods in many ways. A house is (compared with other household purchases) extremely costly. The capital cost of a new social dwelling in many European countries is about four times the annual earnings of an adult male industrial worker. In the least industrialized countries of Europe the relative cost of a dwelling is even greater, rising in some cases to over ten times the annual average earnings.[11] Furthermore, though there is no uniform pattern of building costs in the more economically advanced countries, it seems that the cost of a dwelling in terms of wages is higher now than at the beginning of the century. These higher (real) costs are partly due to higher standards imposed by the State. Both the high capital cost and the pressure for higher standards are related to another peculiarity of housing—its extreme durability. Though the life of houses may differ according to standards of construction, design, maintenance, the tempo of social and economic change, and a host of other factors,[12] they are generally regarded, in Europe at least, as items of capital investment destined to last for several generations. Attempts to design short-life houses at a low cost have not yet proved successful. The situation in the United States, however, is significantly different: the average one-family house in that country is typically of light construction designed to last for a considerably shorter period than is usual in Europe. At the same time the American social attitude towards housing (as illustrated, for example, by the very high rate of residential mobility—which is nearly three times the English rate) is markedly different from that in Europe: rather than being regarded as a long-term capital asset, a house is commonly viewed more as a consumption article of limited life. This attitude, which is but one aspect of the highly mobile character of the American way of life,* is facilitated by the high real incomes of American families. Despite the fact that American houses are typically of a much higher standard than European houses, and that

* There is, of course, a large amount of literature on this subject. For a recent sociological comparison of Britain and the United States see H. E. Bracey, *Neighbours on New Estates and Subdivisions in England and the USA*, Routledge and Kegan Paul, London, 1964, particularly Chapter 2. A more general comparison of British and American housing is given in D. D. Newman, 'Housing in Britain and America', *Monthly Labour Review*, US Department of Labour, May and June, 1960.

building costs in the United States are higher than in Europe, the cost of an American dwelling is less than three times the average annual income of its purchasers.[11]

Nevertheless, even at this favourable average cost-wages ratio, annual charges (including maintenance) must not be higher than 7 per cent of the capital cost if the proportion of income to be devoted to rent is not to exceed 20 per cent. In countries where the cost-wages ratio is 4, the annual charges have to be 5 per cent or less of the capital cost if housing is to account for no more than a fifth of income. In most European countries, for this requirement to be met, interest rates would have to be about 2 to 3 per cent. In fact, interest rates are generally very much higher than this. Alternative calculations based on different assumptions do not significantly affect the general proposition that the high capital cost of new housing in terms of average wages, necessitating long-term credit, involves annual costs that may be regarded as being undesirably high for those on average incomes and *a fortiori* insuperably high for those with low incomes. This is a major field within which governments have operated a housing policy.

HOUSING STANDARDS

The long life of housing has another aspect which is inter-related with these financial issues. Since houses last for such long periods of time it follows that the standard of new housing (and the standard of upkeep of old housing) is of concern to future generations as well as the one for which the houses are initially provided. What is regarded currently as a socially acceptable housing standard may well be considered inadequate for future needs. This line of thought should not be pressed too far: the future can be under- as well as over-discounted. But it is here that one peculiar feature of housing assumes particular importance: the fact that houses are located in a (generally) fixed position on land. In other words a house cannot be considered in the same way as most economic goods since it is (generally) im-mobile in itself and (until it is demolished) determines the physical use of the land on which it is situated. Thus when assessing future needs the question is not merely whether new houses are of an ade-quate construction (which can be decided on the basis of a broad estimate of life), but also whether they provide sufficient space both within and outside for future demands. Future space needs within a house are difficult to predict in spite of the common assumption that houses will need to be bigger to accommodate the increasing number of possessions future households may be expected to have. (Rele-vant factors here are the future size distribution of housholds, the rate at which the very young and the elderly form separate households, the amount of residential mobility, the growth of secondary dwellings, and so forth.) Future space needs outside a house can (on current indications) be expected to increase as private car owner-ship increases. Thus a significant aspect of policy (even if termed 'planning' rather than 'housing policy') which can affect the supply and cost of housing is the insistence on a level of density or a type of layout which will accommodate an expected future increase in the ownership and use of cars. Some English local planning authorities are currently insisting that all new dwellings shall have at least one car space: since these authorities are generally situated in the more affluent areas of the country, where car-ownership is comparatively high but where land costs are likewise high, the effect can be a significant increase in the cost of new housing.

This question of future needs and standards is complex, but clearly it is one which, *given the long life of houses*, falls within the scope of government responsibility. Politically it may be difficult to impose standards based on future needs if these are very markedly different from the standard of existing housing. Added point is given to this when the new standards involve financial costs which have the effect of further increasing the proportion of households who are unable to meet the full economic cost of housing. A balance has to be struck between the standards required for future needs and those which can currently be afforded. If the standards are set only slightly above the existing level the houses will become obsolete rapidly, but if the standard is set too high the gap between costs and rent-paying capacity may be unbridgeable. Basically, however, the issue is the same as that which was raised when minimum standards of sanitation were introduced in the nineteenth century. If the State imposes standards which involve costs greater than can be borne by lower-income groups it forces upon itself the further responsibility for ensuring that these costs are met in some other way.

Similar issues arise where, for 'non-housing' reasons, a particular costly type of housing development is required, for example in national parks, in remote areas, or on sites of high land cost. Again a policy of restraining the growth of large cities will, in the absence of an equally effective policy restraining demand, have the effect of increasing housing costs possibly to the level where lower income groups are forced to occupy—and over-occupy—houses at a standard well below that which is socially acceptable, or even be driven into institutional accommodation for the homeless.

As these illustrations show, Government policies aimed at particular problems can create further problems thus involving an extension of the area over which State responsibility is necessary. But State responsibility does not necessarily involve direct State provision. Indeed, even a cursory study of policies in Western Europe and the

United States is sufficient to demonstrate that the techniques of direction, control, persuasion and encouragement are multitudinous.[11, 14, 19]

THE SUPPLY OF CAPITAL FOR HOUSING

So far attention has been concentrated on questions of housing costs and standards. These are crucial, but there are many other issues which are inter-related and which warrant discussion. Though the increased real cost of housing, due to State-imposed minimum standards, does not necessarily involve State intervention in the supply, capital financing or subsidizing of housing, in most countries other factors have combined to make some action essential. In particular, the high capital cost of housing and the necessity for long-term credit has meant that capital for housebuilding has had to be obtained in competition with other investments. These other avenues have increased markedly during this century. There are now many demands for short-term credit which provide better returns for the investor. Indeed, with the exception of Switzerland, where special conditions apply, State intervention in the capital market for housing has been necessary in all West European countries. The character of this intervention, however, has ranged widely from direct public provision of housing, to tax concessions for lenders and special taxes on employers.

The role of Governments in supplying or influencing the capital market for housing in the post-war period has coincided with an increased concern with national investment programmes. Indeed, in practice, this aspect of housing policy cannot be divorced from general economic policies. Even where, as in East Europe, the State *directs* the national economy, the scale of the housing programme must be determined in the light not only of housing considerations, but also of the availability of resources and other claims on them. Furthermore since a major objective of Government policy throughout Europe has been a rapid rate of economic growth, this has involved a large scale programme of industrial development, movement of workers (particularly from agriculture to manufacturing industries) and a parallel growth in towns. Quite apart from other factors such as population growth, household formation and rising standards of living, economic policy has involved a commitment to major housebuilding programmes.[14] (This is another aspect of the immobility of housing—migrant workers cannot take their houses with them. Indeed, migration tends to increase the total number of houses required since it breaks up larger households.) Planning policies to restrain urban growth and regional migration, to develop new and expanding towns and to promote regional development, have likewise committed Governments to economic planning and related housing programmes.

THE BUILDING INDUSTRY

Even when national economic considerations have forced Governments to restrain investment programmes, housing has often received special consideration, either nationally or regionally. In this connection it is interesting to note that restraints imposed on housing programmes in order to combat problems of inflation and the balance of payments have led to increasing concern about the impact on the development of the building industry. Furthermore, the commitment of Governments to long-term housing and other programmes has necessitated an appraisal of the overall demand on the building industry and its capacity to meet this demand. In Britain the indications are that the demand cannot be met without 'drastic changes'. The National Economic Development Council has stressed that 'steps already taken by Government, by public authorities, and by the industry to introduce new techniques must be pressed forward. What is clear is that there is no certainty, in present conditions, that the industry will be able to meet the demands upon it. And the possibility cannot be ruled out that by falling short it may hold back the expansion of the economy as a whole.'[23]

Government has thus become deeply concerned with the promotion of efficiency in the building industry, the expansion of the supply of skilled manpower, the forward planning of construction programmes, and the promotion of industrialized building.

Industrialized building methods can achieve significant increases in construction output only if the number of systems is kept low, since their effectiveness is dependent upon large-scale demand for a limited number of components. With a large number of competing systems the danger is that no one system can attract sufficient orders to maximize the benefits of large-scale production. In countries where there is direct control over (or public ownership of) the construction industry this problem does not arise, but where the construction industry is privately organized there may be a particularly difficult organizational and political problem. This is so at the present time in Britain where there appear to be over 400 different industrialized building systems. State encouraged oligopoly is not easy to achieve in political terms, particularly since it does not seem clear which system should be selected. The solution which appears to have found acceptance is the establishment of a National Building Agency responsible for research, evaluation and co-ordination of local authority and private building programmes.

A review of problems such as these underlines the importance of political factors. Public control of the building industry or the capital market may seem a logical theoretical answer to particular problems, but where this is not politically acceptable some other *modus operandi* has to be sought. In West European countries planning is of a pragmatic and predictive character, and though such terms as 'national plan' are used, the meaning is different from that in East European countries. The relevant techniques are designed to *influence* rather than to direct. Indeed, it is a declared long-term aim in some countries to recreate a 'free market' in housing. More generally, policy is directed towards supplementing or influencing the market in order to achieve socially desirable objectives.

RENT CONTROL

The distinction between short-term and long-term aims, however, is often an elusive one. Thus rent control, though commonly devised as a short-term measure 'pending the return to normal conditions', has, in some countries, a history of forty years. Debates on rent control have been—and still are—heated, not only because of differing views on the character and timing of decontrol proposals but also because of basic disagreement on the adequacy of a free market in privately-rented housing. Though one school of thought regards rent control as a necessary temporary expedient in conditions of acute shortage, others look upon it as a desirable permanent technique for maintaining rents at a socially desirable level.

Within the compass of a short discussion it is not possible to analyse all the relevant issues, but it is worth noting that rent control is frequently blamed for problems which have much deeper causes—underoccupation, and the decline of private investment in rented housing, for example. In several countries where rent control has taken the form of frozen rents the argument that this has led to inadequate maintenance seems to be well justified, though the extreme old age of many of the houses in this sector makes it debatable whether free-market rents would result in a wholesale improvement. This is a field in which evidence is often scanty and arguments are put forward with an intensity in inverse ratio to the amount of evidence. It is clear, however, that Governments have been more concerned to accept responsibilities for the supply of new housing than they have for the fate of existing housing. Furthermore, measures designed to encourage the improvement of privately-rented old houses may take insufficient account of the changes which have taken place in the pattern of property ownership, in the relative attraction of other investments, in the comparative cost of improving old and building new houses, and so forth. It is these changed circumstances which have considerably enlarged the role of Governments in housing. As an early ECE Report noted (in relation to the frequent assertion that rent control has had the effect of limiting the total output of housing): 'In some countries, the true explanation of the low level of new building appears to be in the failure of the State to recognize its responsibilities in conditions quite different from those which ruled in the heyday of the speculative builder, rather than in its failure to create conditions for successful enterprise in building.'[10]

'FILTERING'

Nevertheless in some countries it has been argued that by a process of 'filtering' the needs of successively lower-income groups are automatically met. This seems an eminently reasonable proposition until it is examined in detail. It then appears that the concept of filtering is by no means a clear one,[17] and that even when it is precisely defined the process is limited in operation by several factors. Among these is the size distribution of the different income groups. The higher-income groups constitute a relatively small group, whereas the houses they vacate in preference to new buildings will (at a lower price) be demanded by the much larger groups in the next income tier. The resultant reduction in price will therefore tend to be small. The lower in the price scale at which it is possible to inject new houses, the greater will be the benefit to lower-income families. But to the extent that the filtering process is successful the result may tend to be 'self-corrective'. Lower rents and lower purchase prices for owner-buyers will reduce the profitability of the provision and tend to dry up the new supply. Institutional arrangements for lending, and tax reliefs for borrowing, may increase the effective demand and thus benefit further groups. Yet, unless there is direct aid to the lowest-income groups the supply will cease before prices fall to the level which they can afford.

The dynamics of the situation are, of course, much more complex than this highly capsulated summary may suggest. But it is clear that so far as the lower-income groups are concerned direct aid is likely to be more effective in improving housing conditions than reliance on processes of filtering.[17, 29] This is now generally accepted, and public policies in many countries are increasingly directed to providing housing assistance to defined needy groups. The improvement in the general housing supply, the desire to reappraise policies in the light of this, and the need to devote more resources to improving the quality of older housing and to redevelop obsolete areas, have all contributed to this. Rehabilitation and redevelopment in particular bring to the fore the problems of the lowest income groups which are not so obvious when attention is concentrated on increasing the total stock of housing. The necessity for Government assistance with redevelopment is further underlined by the difficulties of site assembly, and by the high cost of clearance and redevelopment. Without Government aid, policies designed to achieve physical urban renewal may actually exacerbate the housing conditions of the poor, since the effect will be a reduction in the availability of low-cost dwellings.

HOUSING FINANCE—THE BRITISH MUDDLE

In Britain the growth of direct financial assistance for council housing and indirect, but nonetheless very real, assistance to owner-occupiers (by way of tax reliefs on mortgage interest), has placed the private provider of rented housing in an extremely unfavourable position. Table 43, taken from the Milner Holland Report on London Housing, illustrates this.

At the same time various other policies have operated to the benefit of particular groups. Thus the abolition of Schedule A tax (on the imputed income of one's own house) confers very considerable financial benefits on the owner-occupier compared with the renter. A person who invests money in buying his own house now pays no tax on the imputed income, but if he rents a house and invests his money in shares he gets no tax allowance for his rent payments and pays tax on the dividends he receives on the shares. Mrs Hemming has estimated this benefit to owner-occupiers at around £190 million a year[18]—considerably more than the total cost of council house subsidies.

The role of the National Assistance Board should also not be overlooked. One and a half million households have their total costs met by the Board.[22] In 1964, 216,000 owner-occupiers received an average housing allowance of 17s 6d; 649,000 council tenants an average of 31s 5d; and 697,000 private tenants an average of 26s 3d. The total cost of this assistance amounts to over £100 million.

Finally, there is the financial 'assistance' received by rent-controlled tenants. Kaim-Caudle has estimated this at roughly £40 to £50 a year.[20] The direct 'cost' here is not, of course, borne by public funds but by private landlords (though some of the real cost has been passed on to the houses themselves by way of neglect).

State financial assistance for housing has developed in a piecemeal way with little or no thought as to how the 'pieces' ought to fit together. The total amount of financial aid assumes very large proportions—£137 million for council house subsidies, £100 million direct aid by the National Assistance Board to all who are 'eligible', £190 million tax-saving on 'Schedule A' for owner-occupiers and a further £125 million in tax relief for mortgage interest, and finally something of the order of £40 million 'subsidy' to rent-controlled tenants. These aids have helped to establish higher aspirations for

TABLE 43: *Illustration of the Weekly Cost of Accommodation under Various Types of Owner*[57]

Area	Average Total Cost of Dwelling including land £	Local Authority[a] £ s d	Landlord (rent per week) Housing[b] Association £ s d	Private[c] Landlord £ s d	Owner-Occupier (per week)[d] Before Tax Relief £ s d	After Tax Relief £ s d
A	5,500	3 3 8	7 14 1	10 1 8	8 13 1	6 7 6
B	3,750	2 7 0	5 9 0	7 1 6	5 18 4	4 7 0

(a) Local authority rent set by LA owning the dwellings used in the two examples.

(b) Housing association rents calculated on 60 year loan at 6¼ per cent. The new housing societies borrowing from the Housing Corporation are only obtaining 40 year loans so that their rents would be higher than those shown. £30 a year has been allowed for repairs and management.

(c) Private landlords' rent has been calculated on a 9 per cent gross return. No allowance has been made for the cost of repairs.

(d) Owner-occupiers' weekly costs have been calculated on a 25 year mortgage at 6¼ per cent. No allowance has been made for the cost of repairs.

housing in all social classes. Yet they are distributed between different tenure, age and income groups in a very odd manner, and they have the effect of channelling the demand from those who are either unable or unwilling to buy houses almost entirely into the council house sector.

This is not the place to outline a comprehensive recasting of housing finance, but clearly if the two objectives are to be the raising of housing standards and the channelling of direct assistance to families who need it, then the recasting must be comprehensive. The marked separatism which has characterized British housing policy must be broken down. At present the assistance which a family obtains depends to a large extent on the housing sector in which it finds itself, and total housing costs often depend more on history than current ability to pay. A comprehensive system of housing assistance could encompass not only the groups who are already benefiting, but also those who are now excluded, such as the owner-occupier who, because of his small income or large family size, has no tax liability and therefore is not eligible for tax relief.*

THE FUTURE OF COUNCIL HOUSING

Popular descriptions of the council house tenant range from that of an opulent TV and car-owner openly flaunting his subsidized affluence in front of the righteous and independent owner-occupiers who pay a major part of his rent through their rates and taxes, to a poor and large problem family fettered by innumerable petty restrictions of the local housing manager. These gross distortions flow from a widespread feeling that council housing is not adequately geared to contemporary needs. The subsidy question has already been discussed. (The wider view of the situation shows how inadequate are proposals such as the eviction of affluent council tenants.) It is more difficult to comment on the management of council housing since so little research has been carried out. But such surveys as have been undertaken show a generally lower level of satisfaction on the part of council house tenants than for owner-occupiers (though private tenants are considerably less satisfied than both—which is not surprising in view of their generally inferior housing conditions).[5]

Owner-occupation is satisfying because it provides security, freedom and pride of possession, and at the same time represents a con-

* A. J. Merrett and A. Sykes have recently proposed a scheme by which all housebuyers would be able to claim the full tax relief on their mortgage interest payments, irrespective of their taxable income. This would considerably help lower income families and would make housing assistance to owner-occupiers more rational. But it would, of course, do nothing for the other sectors. Indeed it would increase the 'penalties' suffered by the private renter. See *Housing Finance and Development: An Analysis and a Programme for Reform*, Longmans, 1965.

siderable investment. At first sight the tenancy of a council house has few such advantages to offer. Tenants have no legal security (except the statutory one month's notice); they may be subject to a lengthy list of rules; and they are perpetual rent-payers (even after the house has been 'fully paid for'). This, however, does not represent the whole picture. In the first place, council tenants have a *de facto* security of tenure which is equivalent to that of an owner-occupier: evictions are rare and are only resorted to when tenants perpetually have large arrears of rent. Secondly, though the list of 'conditions of tenancy' may look formidable they are generally accepted as being reasonable and in the general public interest. (The occasional tenant may be considerably annoyed at a rule which prohibits the keeping of cockerels, but his neighbours are unlikely to be in sympathy with him.) Thirdly, council tenants have some considerable advantages over owner-occupiers. They have no direct responsibility for external painting or major repairs: they pay for these, of course, but in a relatively painless way by what amounts to a weekly premium. They can move to other houses as their family size grows or declines—or even (in some local authority areas) when they merely wish for a change, and a transfer involves none of the legal or capital costs borne by the owner-occupier. On the other hand they are much less 'free' to move beyond the administrative boundaries of their local authority than an owner-occupier.

These are very considerable advantages, but might not it be possible to combine these with some of the advantages of owner-occupation? Could not tenants be given a greater degree of responsibility for the upkeep of their houses and, probably more important, for the general appearance and amenities of housing estates? There is a growing discussion of the value of 'citizen-participation' in urban renewal and in the rehabilitation of 'twilight areas'. Is not a similar line possible with council housing estates? Surely it is not only owner-occupiers who are hit by the 'do-it-yourself revolution' and who have a real concern for the houses and the environment in which they live? But if it is, are we right in continuing to extend municipal housing? More fundamentally, why do we need council housing? If it is a question of ensuring that low-income families can obtain good housing at a price which they can afford, could not this be achieved by a system of family housing allowances? If it is a question of ensuring that sufficient houses are actually built, could not local authorities simply confine their attention to house-building and hand over the completed houses to associations of tenants, housing co-operatives, housing societies, or even (with the aid of generous mortgage facilities) to individual families? A 'reserve' of houses could be kept for special needs, but it need not be on the vast scale of today.

In a sense these are, of course, academic questions. But the fact that they are rarely raised does not mean that they are unimportant or irrelevant. Council housing has developed in response to the particular needs of post-war shortages, of overcrowding and slum clearance, of large families and old people, of industrial development and regional planning. It is not the only answer. Donnison, raising similar questions, has suggested (in the same spirit of stimulating thought as is employed here) that 'we need a system that will provide adequate housing of varied types with complete security of tenure. Down payments should be negligible but subsequent payments may well be higher than council rents. The occupier should be given responsibility and incentives for maintaining and improving his own home, but should be insured against the costs of major repairs. Some body responsible to the occupiers themselves should retain a continuing interest in the character and development of the immediate neighbourhood and might provide open space and other shared amenities for its residents. In fact, a way must be found to combine the advantages of owner-occupation and tenancy, both in new housing and in existing property.'[7]

Though no answer is attempted to these questions here it is surely a point worth noting that Britain has a higher proportion of publicly-owned dwellings than any other Western country.

Less academic are questions relating to the adequacy of the British systems of providing capital for housing, of the structure and character of the building industry, and the organization of local government. These questions go far beyond the scope of even the 'wider view' attempted in this chapter. But if 500,000 houses (or more) are to be built annually[26] at least it must be asked whether our legacy of institutions is adequate to the task. The issue is seen in even more acute form when consideration is given to the size of the problems of slum clearance, urban renewal and the development of new and expanding towns within the context of national and regional planning. It is encouraging to note that the latest White Paper on Housing[26] makes a start at asking some of these questions.

REFERENCES AND FURTHER READING

[1] Broady, M., 'A New Trend in Residential Change: Some Southampton Data', *Housing*, Vol. 22, No. 4, March 1961.

[2] Carmichael, J., *Vacant Possession*, Hobart Paper, No. 28, Institute of Economic Affairs, 1964.

[3] Cullingworth, J. B., *Housing Needs and Planning Policy*, Routledge, 1960.

[4] Cullingworth, J. B., *Housing in Transition*, Heinemann, 1963.

[5] Cullingworth, J. B., *English Housing Trends*, Bell, 1965.

[6] Dickens, H., *Whose Home?* The E. D. O'Brien Organization, 1958.

[7] Donnison, D. V., 'Housing Policy—What of the Future?, *Housing*, Vol. 23, No. 3, December 1961.

[8] Donnison, D. V., 'The Next Step in Housing Policy', *Housing Review*, Vol. 14, No. 6, November–December 1965.

[9] Donnison, D. V., *et al*, *Essays on Housing*, Occasional Papers on Social Administration, No. 9, Codicote Press, Welwyn, 1964.

[10] Economic Commission for Europe, *European Rent Policies*, United Nations, 1953.

[11] Economic Commission for Europe, *Financing of Housing in Europe*, United Nations, 1958.

[12] Economic Commission for Europe, *Cost, Repetition and Maintenance: Related Aspects of Building Prices*, United Nations, 1963.

[13] Economic Commission for Europe, *A Statistical Survey of the Housing Situation in European Countries Around 1960*, United Nations, 1965.

[14] Economic Commission for Europe, *Major Long-Term Problems of Government Housing and Related Policies*, United Nations, 1966.

[15] Grebler, L., *Housing Issues in Economic Stabilization Policy*, National Bureau of Economic Research, New York, 1960.

[16] Greve, J., *London's Homeless*, Occasional Papers on Social Administration, No. 10, Codicote Press, Welwyn, 1964.

[17] Grigsby, W. G., *Housing Markets and Public Policy*, University of Pennsylvania Press, 1963.

[18] Hemming, M. W. F., 'The Price of Accommodation', *National Institute Economic Review*, No. 29, August 1964.

[19] Howes, E. G., *Housing in Britain, France and Western Germany*, Planning Broadsheet, No. 490, PEP, 1965.

[20] Kaim-Caudle, P., 'A New Look at Housing Subsidies', *Local Government Finance*, March 1964.

[21] Local Government Chronicle, 'The Future of Rented Homes', *Local Government Chronicle*, October 4 and 11, 1958.

[22] National Assistance Board, *Annual Reports*, HMSO.

[23] National Economic Development Council, *The Construction Industry*, HMSO, 1964.

[24] Macrae, N., *A Nation of Council Tenantry*, Rented Homes Campaign, 1958.

[25] Merrett, A. J., and Sykes, A., *Housing Finance and Development: An Analysis and a Programme for Reform*, Longmans, 1965.

[26] Ministry of Housing and Local Government, *The Housing Programme 1965 to 1970*, Cmnd. 2838, HMSO, 1965.

[27] Ministry of Housing and Local Government, *Report of the Committee on Housing in Greater London* (Milner Holland Report), Cmnd. 2605, HMSO, 1965.

[28] Nevitt, D. A., *Housing Taxation and Subsidies*, Nelson (forthcoming).

[29] Schorr, A. L., *Slums and Social Insecurity*, Nelson, 1964.

[30] Waddilove, L. E., *Housing Associations*, Planning Broadsheet, No. 462, PEP, 1962.

Index

www.ingramcontent.com/pod-product-compliance
Lightning Source LLC
Chambersburg PA
CBHW070353270326
41926CB00014B/2523